H/O 455

More Than 50 Years of High Performance

HURST EQUIPPED

Factory-Special Muscle Cars, Speed Parts & Legendary Race Cars

Foreword by Tomi Fay (Campbell) Forbes

Mark Fletcher & Richard Truesdell

CarTech®

CarTech®, Inc.
838 Lake Street South
Forest Lake, MN 55025
Phone: 651-277-1200 or 800-551-4754
Fax: 651-277-1203
www.cartechbooks.com

1st Edition Published 2012

Edit by Paul Johnson
Layout by Monica Seiberlich

ISBN 978-1-61325-593-3
Item No. CT676

Library of Congress Cataloging-in-Publication Data

Fletcher, Mark
Hurst equipped : More Than 50 years of high performance / by Mark Fletcher & Richard Truesdell.
p. cm.
ISBN 978-1-934709-31-3
1. Hurst, George, 1927- 2. (hardcover version) Hurst Performance--History. 3. Automobile mechanics--United States--Biography. 4. Automobiles--Performance--United States--History. 5. Automobiles--Customizing--United States--History. I. Truesdell, Richard. II. Title.
TL140.H87F55 2012
338.7'6292872092--dc23
[B]
2012000641

Written, edited, and designed in the U.S.A.
Printed in China
10 9 8 7 6 5 4 3 2 1

Front Cover:
Two iconic Hurst cars–the 1972 Hurst/Olds Indy Pace Car and 1968 Hemi Under Glass. *The Hurst/Olds was one of the most prominent muscle car of late 1960s and early 1970s, and* Hemi Under Glass *was arguably the most popular wheelstanding drag car in history.*

Frontispiece:
Hood scoops were big in 1969, and this dual-snorkel Hurst addition clearly stated the H/O meant business. (Photo Courtesy Rich Truesdell)

Title Page:
The potent 421 engine with a Tri Power carb setup is nestled under the hood of the 1965 Pontiac LeMans convertible. It is also equipped with a Hurst shifter and wheels.

Back Cover Photos
Top:
Hurst was paid $200 for every SC/Rambler built. The original A-scheme paint was the most memorable. Everyone noticed when you saw one drive on the street back in 1969, and they still notice today. (Photo Courtesy Rich Truesdell)

Bottom:
Hurst built 82 Hemi-powered Darts for Chrysler in 1968. These lightweight drag cars terrorized the competition at the strip. Today, a restored example can top $250,000. This model is a recreation in honor of the original created by SS/AFX in Arizona. (Photo Courtesy Rich Truesdell)

Authors note: Many of the photographs in this book are very rare and some of them are of lower quality. They have been included because of their importance to telling the story.

OVERSEAS DISTRIBUTION BY:

Europe
PGUK
63 Hatton Garden
London EC1N 8LE, England
Phone: 020 7061 1980 • Fax: 020 7242 3725
www.pguk.co.uk

Australia
Renniks Publications Ltd.
3/37-39 Green Street
Banksmeadow, NSW 2109, Australia
Phone: 2 9695 7055 • Fax: 2 9695 7355
www.renniks.com

Canada
Login Canada
300 Saulteaux Crescent
Winnipeg, MB, R3J 3T2 Canada
Phone: 800 665 1148 • Fax: 800 665 0103
www.lb.ca

NIAGARA

Acknowledgments

A work of this size and scope has many parents, both literally and figuratively. In the case of this book, which was researched, compiled, written, and photographed over a period of more than three years, the list of those who made it possible is almost endless.

We would like to thank the following individuals for sharing their history, stories, and materials in our quest to accurately record the more than 50 years of the Hurst legacy. It starts with members of the Hurst family, especially Laurie Hurst and Bev Anderson.

In the course of researching this book, we both had the pleasure of interviewing Hurst co-founder Bill Campbell. And through a network of past Hurst employees, we were able to speak with Dave Landreth, Dick Chrysler, Bob Riggle, Joe Schubeck, Marty Danko, Don Lane, Walt Czarnecki, Jim Kerr, Pat Flannery Stevens, Linda Vaughn, Jim Wangers, Shirley Shahan Bridges, Bob Tarozzi, and Jack Watson. Hurst historians who contributed to our efforts include Mark Janaky, Tom Benvie, Eddie Stakes, Mike Pemberton, the Badgley family, and many members of The Hurst/Olds Club of America. We would also like to thank Joie Vaughn, Ron Flick, Dennis Kirban, Mark Beyer, Debbie and Larry Weiner, and Phil LaChapelle.

Appreciation is also expressed to those who own the cars displayed in these pages, and their ownership is cited in the text. Many have labored in the restoration and preservation of these fine cars that Hurst built. Special thanks go to Carol Trissel and the Bobbitt Estate for arranging the photography of the 1946 Lincoln Continental, the first documented Hurst conversion.

Special thanks are also due to Bill Sefton, who transported several cars from his collection in Arizona to our studio in California. This includes the Hurst *Hemi Under Glass* Barracuda, which graces the cover of this book.

We would both be remiss if we didn't mention the contribution of Pete Serio, who provided us unfettered access to his archive of original Hurst materials. Some of these materials are seen for the first time in almost 40 years.

Then there's our editor at CarTech, Paul Johnson. Paul persevered and guided this project through a process that ultimately stretched over more than three years. He believed in the project and his dedication resulted in our assembling this massive collection of research, stories, photographs, and documents into a cohesive historical view of this iconic corporation and its passionate associates.

Finally, we would like to thank the two men who instilled in us both our interest, passion, and enthusiasm for automobiles: our fathers, Elliott "Paul" Fletcher and Richard "Dick" Truesdell. Our fathers never had the opportunity to meet, but we know that, for both, a car was never just a way to get from point A to point B. We hope as you read this book and view the photographs we assembled that both men pointed us in the right direction.

Mark Fletcher
Richard Truesdell

Foreword

By Tomi Fay (Campbell) Forbes

My dad wrote the forward to the first edition of this book. He stated the following: "George Hurst was a remarkable man, a true visionary who helped define the automotive aftermarket in its infancy. Together, we launched a company that survives to this very day and in our time, launched several legendary products, most notably, the Hurst Shifter.

"As I look back on those years, I hope that a lot of the young men who bought the shifters and other items gained automotive knowledge as they skinned their knuckles improving their cars. Perhaps some went on to create some products of their own. Beyond the automotive products, to me, the most satisfying thing that came out of our work is the original concept of the rescue tools, which have helped many people all over the world.

"What's important about this book is that not only does it recognize George Hurst's contributions to the birth of the automotive aftermarket but it now recognizes many of those individuals who toiled in relative obscurity, who helped to build the Hurst brand. Many are being recognized to the general public for the very first time."

Dad always said, "If you love what you do, you will never work a day in your life." He lived by that motto. Not once in his 97 years of life did he cease to find wonder at the world around him or dampen in the excitement of learning something new. Every manmade object could be improved; he loved the challenge of solving engineering problems. In his 90s, when he could not fall asleep at night, he invented an object in his mind and then turned it on every angle to visualize it. Meanwhile, my mother, lying next to him, was reciting all the states, their capitols, and the presidents in chronological order.

Dad was a man of absolute integrity. He stated truthfully what he accomplished and generously gave credit where credit was due. He was accurate, yet humble about his work. Bill Widdemer, who ran the Detroit division, recounted, "George sketched out his idea on a paper napkin. Then your dad went to work figuring out how to engineer it." While George Hurst was garnering business, Dad was running the production line. Hurst-Campbell was a success because of the combined talents of both men. It could not have succeeded as it did without the attributes both George and Dad brought to the table.

Whenever the opportunity arose, my sisters and I declared, "Our dad invented the Jaws of Life." We want the world to know the true story. It has been my pleasure to count Mark and Rich as friends and to promote the story of Hurst-Campbell, Inc. in memory of my dad.

March 2020

Humble Beginnings

Birth of a Performance Empire

In this low-resolution archival photo, George Hurst is pictured next to an early engine conversion in a 1946 Lincoln Continental. It is reported that this was the first Buick V-8 conversion and it was completed about 1956 or 1957.

George Henry Hurst was born in Upstate New York in 1927. He was raised in Little Ferry, New Jersey, along with his younger sister Delores. George's early years were difficult, and never a subject of public conversation. As a young man, George found that he was mechanically inclined and spent much of his youth repairing bicycles in the neighborhood. At age 14, after completing the eighth grade, he started working for a local defense contractor.

At the age of 16, at the height of World War II, George convinced his mother to forge his father's name on papers so that he could join the Navy. George's Navy career has remained private, and few who served with him have shared their experiences in the service with George. He was trained as an aircraft machinist and suffered injuries to both his hands and feet due to an airplane explosion on the deck of an aircraft carrier.

By age 29, George Hurst had spent more than 10 years in service to his country. He was discharged and settled in Abington, Pennsylvania. Already married to his third wife, he began designing and performing engine conversions for his friends and former Navy friends from the nearby Willow Grove Naval Air Station. These motor mount components took into account torque, engine size, weight distribution, steering, and transmission requirements. Additionally, most of George's early conversions included larger brakes, transmission swaps, and heavy-duty suspension upgrades.

The year 1954 proved to be the seminal moment for what evolved into the performance powerhouse known as Hurst. George attended one of the first speed trials held at Daytona Beach, Florida, arriving behind the wheel of a new Oldsmobile 88. He watched both stock cars and custom hot rods at this event. Lee Petty, driving his own 1954 Oldsmobile, won the main event after Tim Flock was disqualified. After witnessing multiple racing accidents, George was determined to create a better and safer way for those drivers to race.

George immediately set about building a better system for engine conversions to provide increased top speeds while improving both safety and stability. He was very familiar with the growing trend of combining modern overhead valve V-8 engines into older, more affordable bodies. If the engines were not installed low, between the narrow frame rails of the older cars, handling and stability suffered. His years in the Navy had taught him the benefits of a well-designed solution for high-performance vehicles.

What started out as a hobby soon brought paying customers to his home-based garage business when enthusiasts recognized the performance potential for their own cars. The earliest conversions replaced the original factory motor mounts with heavy welded steel plates that kept the motor aligned within the chassis. George also created additional transmission adapters and related mounts.

In 1943, at the tender age of 16, George Hurst enlisted in the U.S. Navy. Reports say that his mother forged his father's signature, enabling him to enlist in the Navy even though he was not eligible. At the height of World War II, the minimum enlistment age was often skirted. (Photo Courtesy Bev Anderson)

Don Lane and Bill Campbell Join Hurst

Hurst stayed busy enough doing general automotive repair and these conversions; he was able to hire his first permanent employee in 1956. Don Lane, a young local, assisted George during the evenings in the basement garage of his home in Abington. The Hurst basement garage became the hang-out for many young hot rod enthusiasts west of Philadelphia. On many occasions, more conversion work was accomplished in the evening hours than during daylight.

Word soon spread that Hurst had already designed the components to swap out complete drivetrains, including engine, transmission, and sometimes rear ends. George was asked to supply these engine conversion components in kit form to other hot rodders so they could perform their own home-built conversions. As a result, a true "garage industry" was born on the East Coast just as a similar movement was gaining momentum among veterans nationwide, especially on the West Coast. The sudden surge in business required more space and included building an additional garage on the Hurst property early in 1956.

Although well designed, these heavy metal motor plates were welded and fabricated free-hand, so the manufacturing process was not consistent. George realized that the product quality would improve if he developed a jig system of manufacturing.

George was a talented mechanic, but not a schooled engineer. He had a solid understanding of all things mechanical, but he still needed an engineer to accurately design and document his product ideas. He placed a classified ad in the local newspaper seeking a certified engineer to design and create the jigs required for the expanding business. A skilled young engineer, Bill Campbell, answered the ad and started working for George as a second job during evenings and weekends.

Bill Campbell was the exact opposite of George Hurst in personality, profession, and business life. Disciplined and detail oriented, Bill introduced effective processes and principles into George's

This early Hurst engine conversion mount features heavy-duty construction and a drop between the frame rails to lower the center of gravity, improving handling. (Photo Courtesy Don Lane)

Don Lane (left), Bill Campbell (right), and an unidentified mechanic (center) are shown installing the Buick engine on to the Lincoln. The Hurst components are identified in white and include the two mounting plates attached to the frame, and the support bracket attached the front of the engine. (Photo Courtesy Don Lane)

George marked his early products with the Hurst name, an early example of George building his brand. (Photo Courtesy Don Lane)

garage-based business so the company could develop and sell viable speed parts. Most company meetings were held at the kitchen table and included George, Bill, Don Lane, and an ever evolving stable of young hot rodders from Eastern Pennsylvania.

Don and Bill recalled that payment for their work was rare, and often George traded for work on Don's car in order to keep current. Bill's interest did not involve his own hot rod, and soon the relationship matured into a business with a look to the future. Bill himself was rarely paid, and eventually was compensated by an equal partnership in the growing Hurst Motor Mount business.

Even during these early years, George's larger-than-life personality encouraged those in his business to get behind his products and ideas, and attracted potential customers to do business with Hurst. He was a flamboyant storyteller, and had a knack for turning the most mundane of get-togethers into one fine party. George was a magnet for youth and enthusiasm. Using his mechanical and engineering aptitude, he performed many modifications to customer cars, and a growing customer base of local rodders gathered each evening at the shop. His enthusiasm and ingenuity were contagious. He was able to convince investors of his company's goals, secure financing for his fledgling business, attract women, and satisfy his perpetual need for acceptance.

George Hurst stands next to a 1946 Lincoln Continental carrying an early Hurst engine conversion. The Lincoln engine was swapped in favor of a Buick V-8 around 1956 or 1957. (Photo Courtesy Don Lane)

George Hurst and Bill Campbell each possessed different and essential individual skills, and these combined skills propelled the company's success. Bill's engineering acumen produced innovative designs, so the products continued to improve, while George's ability to sell and motivate others provided vital sales and marketing firepower for the company. This "odd couple" partnership was a combination of talent that propelled the company to the forefront of the automotive business for more than a decade. It wasn't long before speed shops heard about Hurst Motor Mounts, and in late 1956, George directed Don to create their first advertising campaign and promotions for *Hot Rod* magazine.

A Couple Early Conversions

At about this time, George built a separate four-car garage on his property in Abington where he did powertrain conversions for the influential and wealthy of Eastern Pennsylvania. He specialized in replacing the flathead

George was an innovator in brake upgrades to match the additional power provided by his engine conversions. After all, a car with substantially more horsepower and torque requires better brakes to safely stop it. Here he is pictured with the upgraded brakes from the Buick-powered Lincoln. (Photo Courtesy Don Lane)

George inspects the finished conversion of the Buick-powered Lincoln hardtop. The Hurst conversion always included a change of the motor, transmission, rear end, and brakes. (Photo Courtesy Don Lane)

V-12 motors found in late 1940s Lincolns with 1950s-era Cadillac and Buick engines and transmissions. Often these conversions included the installation of stouter 1951 Lincoln Cosmopolitan or 1955 GM V-8 passenger car rear ends.

One of the first cars to get an engine conversion was a 1946 Lincoln Continental convertible belonging to one of the officers on the base. George pulled the flathead V-12, and replaced it with a new 1955 Cadillac Eldorado V-8 with factory dual carburetors. The well-engineered conversion was also well executed, and soon the car was being shown throughout the Philadelphia area. George added a few touches just for show: a brass-polished "Bat Wing" air filter, brass-plated valve covers, a polished brass radiator tank, and a custom-made chromed overflow tank complete with a hardware-store propane-tank pressure regulator valve. The final touch was the addition of an inscribed brass plaque stating: "Custom Conversion by George Hurst Abington, Penna." The owner treasured the car, and in 1956 the regional Classic Continental Owners Club awarded the owner its prestigious best engine conversion award. The trophy was inscribed with "Best Engine Conversion Lincoln Continental Owners Club Third Annual Meet, September 1956 Boyne Falls Michigan."

George was proud of this accomplishment, and retained the trophy

George is shown accepting the Best Engine Conversion award from the Lincoln Continental Owners' Club regional event in September 1956. Taken in front of the famous Dearborn Inn, Captain Smart (left) is standing next to George. (Photo Courtesy Pete Serio Collection)

1946 Lincoln Continental

This is the 1946 Lincoln Continental that started the Hurst legend. It still sports all of its Hurst modifications, including the 365-ci Cadillac V-8. In 2012 the estate of its last owner, Carl Bobbitt, put the car up for sale where it was spotted by co-author Mark Fletcher. (Photos Courtesy Thompson Photography)

George Hurst started his fledgling business in the garage of his Abington, Pennsylvania, home. But before long, the business outgrew the garage and he added on to it, shown here. This was a big step up for Hurst because he was now operating a stand-alone business separate from his residence. (Photo Courtesy Mark Fletcher Collection)

The attractive Best Engine Conversion trophy from the Lincoln Continental Owners' Club is shown up close. Noted Hurst memorabilia collector Pete Serio now has this trophy as part of his collection. (Photo Courtesy Richard Truesdell)

along with a picture of himself and Captain Smart standing in front of the car holding it. Hurst collector Peter Serio purchased both the trophy and the photo from George's estate in the late 1980s. After some research, we found the original car residing in Springfield, Ohio, preserved as a 55-year-old time capsule. We believe that only the interior has been redone, and over the years has traveled more than 30,000 miles.

A similar conversion was performed on Lawrence (Larry) Greenwald's car. Larry, a VP of a major corporation based in New York City, was a true car enthusiast already owning a first-year Corvette and a nearly new 1955 Chevy Nomad. George was contracted to remove the flathead V-12 from his 1946 Lincoln Continental convertible and replace it with something that offered a substantial boost in performance.

The original engine, transmission, and rear end were removed and replaced with a brand-new 1955 Cadillac 331-ci, 230-hp engine salvaged from a nearly new totaled car. Before the Lincoln was fitted with the new powerplant, the garage was burglarized and many items were stolen, including a like-new 1955 Cadillac engine. Fortunately, the insurance company reimbursed George for the loss, including the value of the engine.

George found a brand new engine, an even more powerful Cadillac Eldorado 365-ci V-8 that produced 285 hp, courtesy of its dual carburetors. Miraculously, the stolen engine was later recovered and used as payment to Don for his contributions at the shop. Don still has this engine today, installed in his 1955 Studebaker four-door hot rod.

The Lincoln/Cadillac conversion was done exceptionally well. Soon, George and his crew were contracted to create another hot rod Lincoln coupe, powered by a 1957 Buick V-8. George performed the conversion for one of his former commanders from the nearby Willow Grove air station. Throughout Hurst Performance's formative years, the Willow Grove base continued to play an important part in the Hurst legend.

A Partnership Made Official

A local insurance agent and mutual friend, John Bonner, was another catalyst in the upward trajectory of Hurst Performance. John suggested that Bill and George form a partnership. Together, these young hot rodders formalized their partnership at George's kitchen table, the same table at which they drafted many of the initial product designs, and Hurst-Campbell was born. The motor mount conversion designs were the major asset of the newly formed corporation. These kit designs encompassed motor conversions from installing early flathead Ford V-8s in Model As to installing Cadillac and Buick engines into 1940s Fords, Chevys, and Lincolns.

These core products were offered at the right time, as the hot rodding and drag racing scene increased in popularity. Therefore, they were essential to the company's financial success over the following decade. "Fast" is the best way to describe the growth of the Hurst-Campbell incorporation. Bill and George's business partnership started out similar to the way their products were used: spinning the tires, launching into fast production, and growing with a blur of movement and development mirroring the quarter-mile test bed for their products.

According to Campbell, Hurst-Campbell Corporation transitioned from a part-time cottage business into a full-time venture in early 1958. In addition to the engine conversion kits, Hurst offered dropped steering drag links to clear the lower V-8 oil pans and 12V electrical wiring conversion kits. While engine conversion kits, associated parts, and the shop were keeping Hurst-Campbell busy, the business was not profitable at this stage. Both George and Bill tried to take home $25 each per

The Hurst delivery van, a VW bus, sustained significant damage when an employee was involved in a traffic accident. Throughout his career, George was a stickler for safety, genuinely caring about the well-being of others. This freak accident led to Hurst developing front and rear bumper guards to protect passengers. The massive Hurst front and rear bumper guards were shown as products from the company's past in the 1969 Hurst catalog. (Photo Courtesy Mark Fletcher Collection)

week. Most weeks, it simply wasn't there to take. Bill had some savings put aside to supplement the unpredictable income from the partnership. He explained that, at first, he was able to feed his family a consistent diet of franks and beans, but by late 1959 the menu was simplified to beans alone. So, like many companies, the early years were very lean for all those involved.

Accidental Innovation

A coincidence led to the new company's first new product. George and Bill had borrowed a friend's Volkswagen panel van to haul welded engine and transmission conversion plates to the sandblaster prior to painting. During one such trip, the young man driving the borrowed van broadsided another truck at an intersection. The van's flat-nosed design afforded minimal frontal crash protection and, as a result of the accident, the driver suffered only a minor foot injury.

The injury disturbed George, and he quickly designed a heavy-duty bumper guard that attached to the strongest section of the front suspension, which encompassed the front bumper and encircled both headlights. This bumper guard assembly was made of a combination of 1-inch round tubing and heavy, flat, spring steel, which weighed more than 40 pounds. During the van's front panel repair, the first bumper guard was painted white and installed for future protection. Many people noticed the guard, and when the van was out on deliveries they asked where this protective bumper guard could be purchased. George asked Campbell to formalize the design, which added protection for the rear of the van. Soon Hurst-Campbell started selling them nationwide.

Motor Trend magazine installed a set on an employee's VW Microbus and ran an article under a feature called "Product Use Tests." The test, published in late 1958, stated that the units were sturdy and relatively easy to install. It also commented that, for $84.50, the product was well made, rugged, and gave excellent protection.

Soon bumper guard sales outpaced engine mount sales, and George quickly created a print advertisement to capitalize on the favorable review. The Volkswagen VW emblem was prominently displayed above the new Hurst-Campbell bumper guards. The ad copy utilized the emblem's stacked letters to start the phrases "Very Worried" (about damage), and that Hurst Bumper Guards worked "Very Well."

The units sold well through Volkswagen dealers across the nation. Soon the product, and George's clever advertisement, attracted the attention of Volkswagen of America. Hurst's advertisements spotlighted the light-duty European bumpers in comparison to their sturdy American counterparts. Additionally, the use of the VW logo was a flagrant violation of Volkswagen's registered trademark. Volkswagen sent Hurst Performance a cease-and-desist letter demanding that Hurst-Campbell stop using any reference to its product name and that all available brochure copies be recalled and destroyed at once.

Both Hurst and Campbell agreed that they did not have the resources for a court battle and immediately complied with the request. More than 500 bumper guard kits were produced and sold, but only a handful of the original units exist and are rarely, if ever, seen. Near the end of the production run of the bumper guards, Hurst-Campbell was about to launch a smaller version for the new Volkswagen Karmann Ghia, but the partners decided to sell the remaining stock and refocus their efforts on new products for American cars. Unknowingly, George Hurst and Bill Campbell just had their first of many influences on an international car manufacturer. In midyear 1959, Volkswagen introduced its own optional bumper guards and override bars for all its models.

Barely Hanging On

During its first full year as a corporation, Hurst-Campbell had skirted a major lawsuit and was struggling weekly to make expenses and payroll. They also had a California-based competitor selling cheap copies of the Hurst engine conversion kits, eroding sales to price-sensitive speed shops. George had recently separated from his third wife, owed thousands of dollars to their steel supplier, and now suffered the loss of the popular bumper guards. George and Bill had just experienced the smallest taste of success, and now were facing the potential bankruptcy of their fledgling one-year-old company. But despite all these challenges, Hurst and Campbell's resolve to make their company a successful business was unwavering.

Turmoil and Triumph

Hurst's Growing Pains 1959–1963

By the fall of 1959, George Hurst and Bill Campbell were $20,000 in debt, but had a steady stream of engine mount orders coming in. Hurst-Campbell had relocated from the small garage it had been working out of in Abington to another building in Glenside, Pennsylvania. George's third ex-wife had recently thrown him out of the Abington house and off the property the shop was located on. George remained undeterred and felt all they needed to succeed was more money.

George Hurst (left) inspects the Pontiac 389-ci V-8 with three deuces, 2-barrel carbs, which were factory installed on the 1961 *White Goddess* Catalina. Hurst gave away this rocket ship at the NHRA National Championship. (Photo Courtesy Pete Serio Collection)

CHAPTER 2

The ANCO Alliance

With a reputation for quality products and a nationally-known name as collateral, they went shopping for investors. Almquist Engineering in Milford, Pennsylvania, was an excellent candidate for a working partnership. Co-owners Ed Almquist and Ed Anchel had been inventing performance components while reselling performance parts through a catalog advertised in the back of *Hot Rod* magazine throughout the 1950s. Their product offerings included everything from body customizing accessories and car radios to spark plugs and performance parts.

Together, these four young men—George, Bill, Ed, and Ed—shared a passion for the emerging hot rod scene that they channeled into a business agreement. Unwilling to dilute the original partnership Hurst and Campbell had created, they formed ANCO as a new company handling both product marketing and sales, while the original Hurst-Campbell Corporation remained as the manufacturing arm.

Like George, Ed Almquist was an innovator, inventor, and promoter. In Almquist's book *Hot Rod Pioneers* (published in 2000 by the Society of Automotive Engineers) he stated, "George was the grand dreamer and Bill was the consummate engineer who turned dreams into parts. As a third party, I was either in the midst of total mayhem or in a perfectly sound 'idea factory.'"

One of the first issues the team addressed was to reduce the cost of the engine mount conversion kit to meet lower-cost competitors head-on. George and Ed developed a unique adjustable feature and christened the change Hurst Adjustatorque Motor Mounts. The changes did not provide any significant benefits, but they helped set Hurst apart

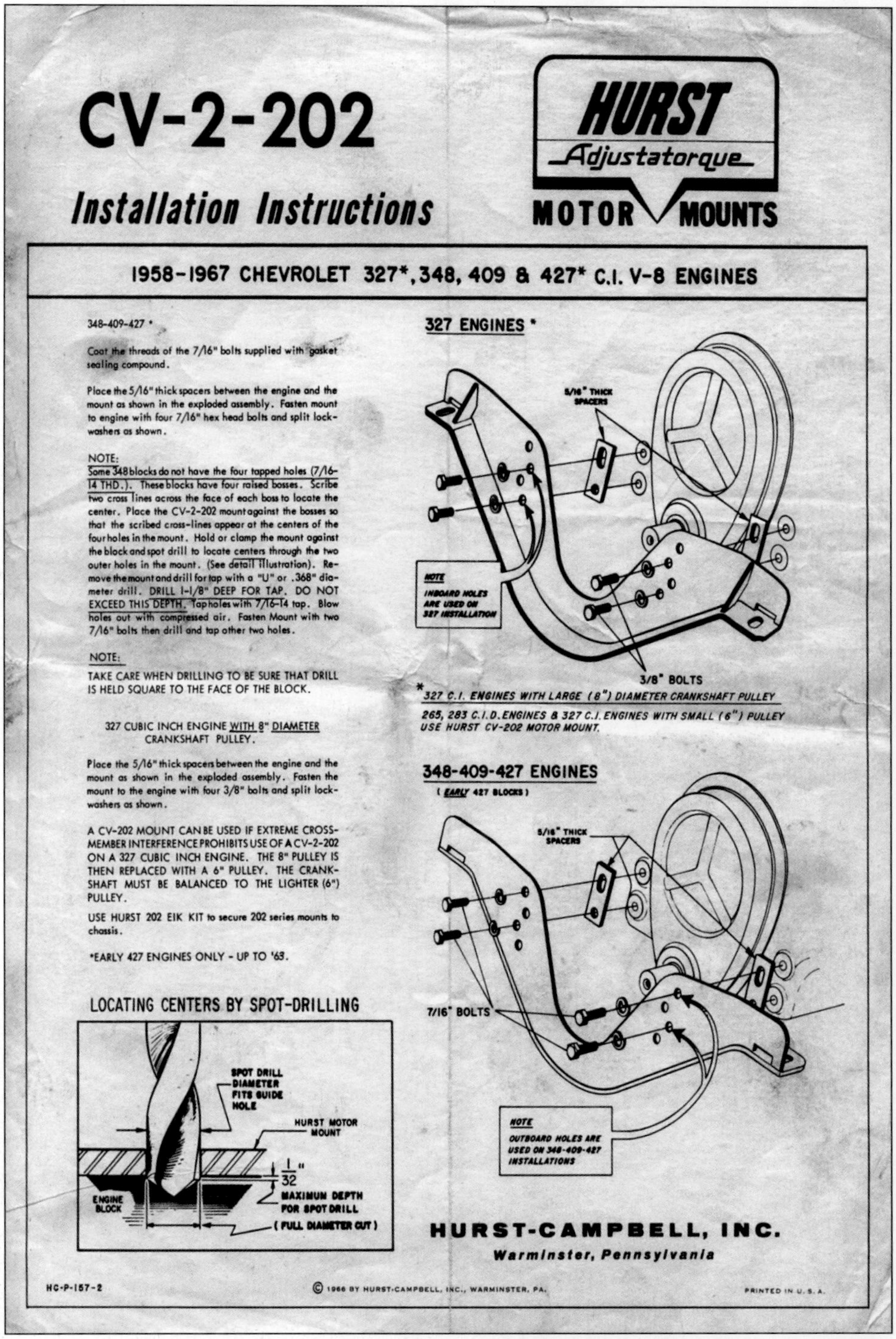

CV-2-202

Installation Instructions

HURST Adjustatorque MOTOR MOUNTS

1958-1967 CHEVROLET 327*, 348, 409 & 427* C.I. V-8 ENGINES

348-409-427 *

Coat the threads of the 7/16" bolts supplied with gasket sealing compound.

Place the 5/16" thick spacers between the engine and the mount as shown in the exploded assembly. Fasten mount to engine with four 7/16" hex head bolts and split lock-washers as shown.

NOTE:
Some 348 blocks do not have the four tapped holes (7/16-14 THD.). These blocks have four raised bosses. Scribe two cross lines across the face of each boss to locate the center. Place the CV-2-202 mount against the bosses so that the scribed cross-lines appear at the centers of the four holes in the mount. Hold or clamp the mount against the block and spot drill to locate centers through the two outer holes in the mount. (See detail illustration). Remove the mount and drill for tap with a "U" or .368" diameter drill. DRILL 1-1/8" DEEP FOR TAP. DO NOT EXCEED THIS DEPTH. Tap holes with 7/16-14 tap. Blow holes out with compressed air. Fasten Mount with two 7/16" bolts then drill and tap other two holes.

NOTE:
TAKE CARE WHEN DRILLING TO BE SURE THAT DRILL IS HELD SQUARE TO THE FACE OF THE BLOCK.

327 CUBIC INCH ENGINE WITH 8" DIAMETER CRANKSHAFT PULLEY.

Place the 5/16" thick spacers between the engine and the mount as shown in the exploded assembly. Fasten the mount to the engine with four 3/8" bolts and split lock-washers as shown.

A CV-202 MOUNT CAN BE USED IF EXTREME CROSS-MEMBER INTERFERENCE PROHIBITS USE OF A CV-2-202 ON A 327 CUBIC INCH ENGINE. THE 8" PULLEY IS THEN REPLACED WITH A 6" PULLEY. THE CRANKSHAFT MUST BE BALANCED TO THE LIGHTER (6") PULLEY.

USE HURST 202 EIK KIT to secure 202 series mounts to chassis.

*EARLY 427 ENGINES ONLY - UP TO '63.

LOCATING CENTERS BY SPOT-DRILLING

327 ENGINES *

*327 C.I. ENGINES WITH LARGE (8") DIAMETER CRANKSHAFT PULLEY

265, 283 C.I.D. ENGINES & 327 C.I. ENGINES WITH SMALL (6") PULLEY USE HURST CV-202 MOTOR MOUNT.

348-409-427 ENGINES

(EARLY 427 BLOCKS)

HURST-CAMPBELL, INC.

Warminster, Pennsylvania

HC-P-157-2 © 1966 BY HURST-CAMPBELL, INC., WARMINSTER, PA. PRINTED IN U.S.A.

As the company grew and matured, so did Hurst's products and development processes. The original engine mount plates were the foundation of the company, but the company needed a more price-competitive engine mount kit. To meet this goal, Ed Almquist and Hurst developed the Hurst Adjustatorque Motor Mount. This instruction sheet for the Ajustatorque shows how to install it on a Chevrolet small- or big-block. (Photo Courtesy Mark Fletcher Collection)

While this may not be the earliest Hurst shifter ad (which appeared in *Hot Rod* magazine in October 1960), it still shows a partnership with Ed Almquist's ANCO Industries. (Photo Courtesy Mark Fletcher Collection)

from its myriad of competitors that were also promoting similar products.

The associated hype and marketing created by these two dynamic leaders was a greater contribution to the new product line's success than the physical changes in the product. With the onset of larger engines available as optional upgrades from Detroit, the need for specially-designed engine plates and the complicated transplanting of power-trains was beginning to decline.

This was not the first time George was faced with a failing business venture. He was convinced he could increase product sales faster by meeting face to face with performance auto parts retailers, managers, and store owners than through the small ads he had placed in *Hot Rod* magazine. The company's product offerings were still variations of the Hurst-Campbell engine and transmission mount conversion kits George had initially built for the growing hot rod industry. At the time, George drove a bronze 1956 Chevrolet Bel-Air convertible demonstration car outfitted with the unlikely combination of a 1958 Buick Nailhead V-8 mated to a heavy-duty 1950 Lincoln 3-speed transmission. This drop-top Chevy included a custom chrome shifter arm projecting from the floor with an accentuated curve to clear the factory front bench seat. George departed Eastern Pennsylvania in the fall of 1959 with plans to travel west to acquire orders from speed shops for the winter. George started north, and soon found himself in Detroit at the legendary Gratiot's Speed Shop. As in past demonstrations, he showed the engine conversion and accompanying Hurst-Campbell products installed in his convertible. Although impressed by the conversion, the owner was more interested in the attractive chrome floor shifter and promised to be one of Hurst's first customers for a marketable product in kit form.

George continued west for the winter, taking Route 66 south all the way to California. He stayed in California until spring because his factory heater had been removed to accommodate the Buick Nailhead conversion, along with the creation of a multitude of unsealed holes in the firewall.

Many nights, George slept in his car and survived on prepackaged food in order to save on expenses. In the spring of 1959, George returned east to a shop at full production. He had traveled more than 11,000 miles while mailing back engine conversion kit orders totaling more than $100,000. During this excursion he had developed personal relationships with speed shop owners and hot rodders throughout the United States. These relationships were a beneficial foundation for the growth of not only Hurst-Campbell but also for the fledgling drag racing hobby that utilized empty airfields for head-to-head competitions.

George shared the speed shop owner's interest in the shifter with his partners at ANCO. Both he and Almquist simultaneously created competing designs of a floor-mounted 3-speed shifter. During testing, George's design was the better performer, but more complicated and expensive to manufacturer. Almquist and Anchel balked at the proposed $90,000 in manufacturing equipment start-up costs for the Hurst-designed shifter, and Hurst and Campbell chose not to market Almquist's less-precise shifter design, so a mutual agreement to disband the partnership was made.

Hurst Performance Products Floor Shifter

Hurst and Campbell needed to buy out Almquist and Anchel's interest in the company, but did not have the capital to repay the initial $20,000 investment. The solution came through one of George's friends who recommended making arrangements with long-time Hurst customer Larry Greenwald to provide funding for the buyout.

Greenwald, a well-heeled classic car guy, had initially hired Hurst to convert his 1946 Lincoln convertible to an upgraded powertrain. He had remained a friend and customer and was looking to invest in the fledgling shifter business. Greenwald not only repaid the outstanding $20,000 debt to Ed Almquist, but also invested in the tooling required to begin production of the Hurst floor shifters. For this investment, Hurst awarded him a 26-percent share of Hurst-Campbell. All three partners agreed to use the Hurst Performance Products name for marketing (in place of ANCO Industries), yet the original Hurst-Campbell corporate name was retained. Larry Greenwald's business arrangement with Hurst-Campbell went on longer than either of the company's namesakes. Hurst was also manufacturing conversion kits for modern cars, and these kits were featured in the October 1960 issue of *Hot Rod* magazine. The article detailed the complete Hurst kit for converting a 1960 Plymouth Valiant from the factory six-cylinder to a dual-carbureted small-block Chevrolet engine. This article brought Hurst products into the national spotlight and inspired Hurst to advertise products in *Hot Rod* magazine throughout the 1960s.

The OEM car manufacturers had spent years and considerable resources moving the shifter from the floor to the steering column so three people could fit across the front seat of their new vehicles. A complex and clunky steering-column-mounted, 3-speed shifter was developed during the 1950s that was barely adequate for daily driving. The components were lightweight and easy to shift, but the torque of the engine and transmission combination changed this geometry during hard driving, sometimes resulting in total failure of the mechanism.

The original Hurst 3-speed shifter had a tall, chromed, curved handle designed to clear the standard bench

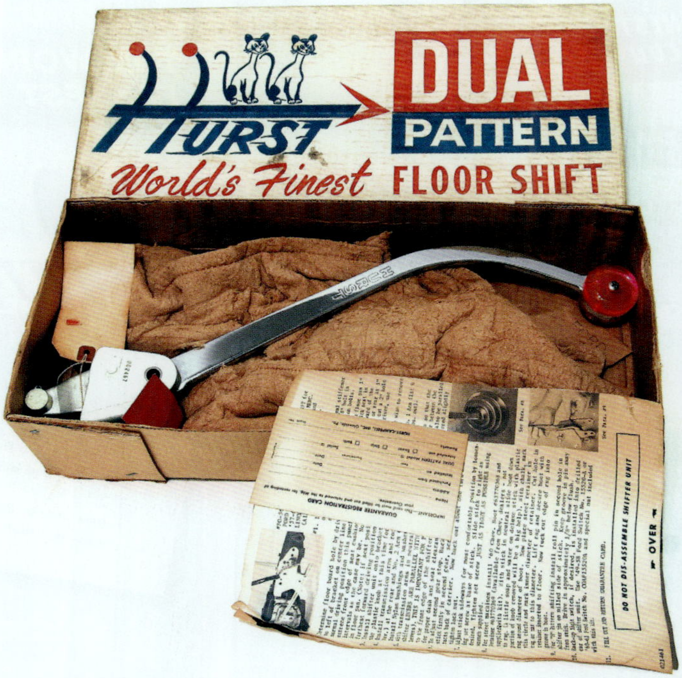

The original Hurst shifter used two brightly colored plastic pieces sandwiching the unique chrome handle to form the grip. This gave the appearance of a yo-yo. (Photo Courtesy Rich Truesdell)

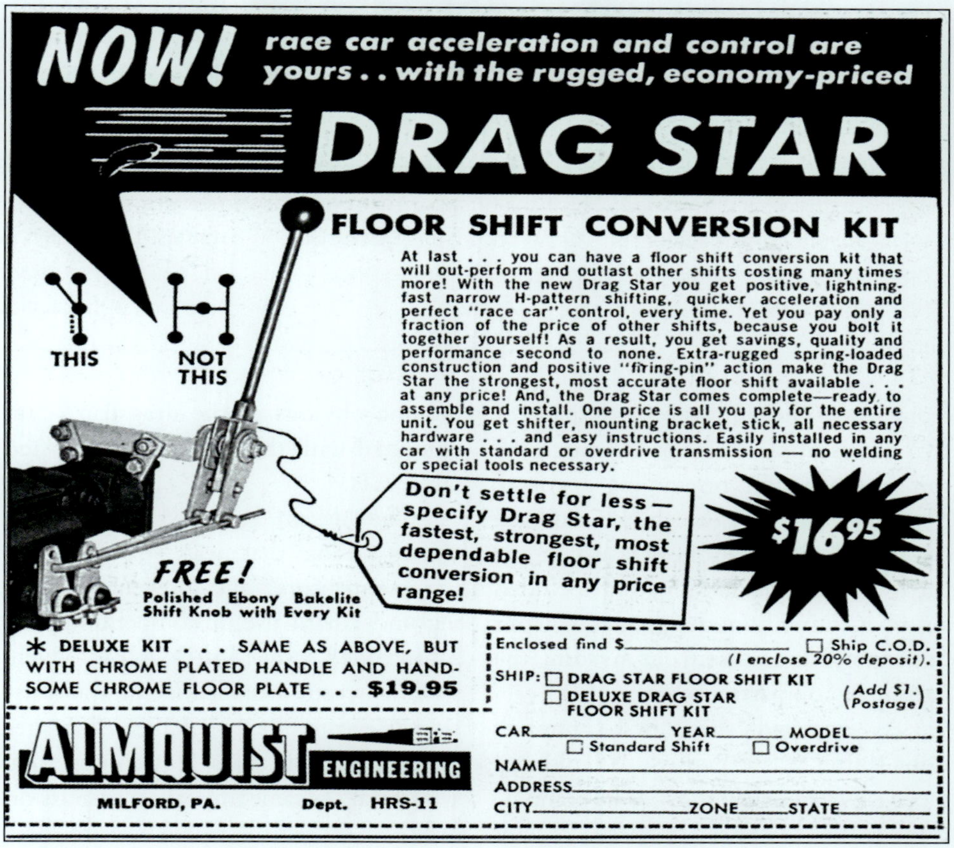

A difference in business philosophy and product development led to a parting of ways between Ed Almquist and George Hurst. After the business ties between the two had been severed in 1960, Ed Almquist promoted this lower-priced floor shifter conversion kit with limited success. (Photo Courtesy Mark Fletcher Collection)

Hurst made one of the strongest and most reliable shifters, and once racers and hot rodders recognized this, the company won over loyal customers. This early Hurst shifter sell sheet promotes the Hurst Dual Pattern shifter as "The World's Finest Floor Shifter Conversion." It also shows the applications and the price of $65. (Photo Courtesy Mark Fletcher Collection)

The first known Hurst floor shifter is shown on this cover of the 1961 Hurst catalog. Notice the "H" formed from two yo-yo-style shifter handles. The dual pattern was either the traditional "H" or a straight-line shift pattern. Even at this early stage in the company's history, Hurst was offering a warranty "Guaranteed for the Life of the Installation." (Photo Courtesy Mark Fletcher Collection)

front seats. The shift knob was made of two pieces of plastic bolted through the top of the handle resembling a yo-yo. The conversion of the shifter required cutting a hole in the floorboard of the car over the transmission, and included a rubber shifter boot designed to seal out both fumes and noise from invading the passenger compartment.

As expected, the Hurst-Campbell floor shifter was expensive to build and more expensive than most of its competitors. In the October 1961 issue of *Hot Rod* magazine, the Hurst 3-speed shifter is shown at $65, compared to Almquist Engineering's 3-speed shifter at $19.99. But the difference between the two became obvious at the dragstrip. Cars equipped with the Hurst shifter posted faster ETs.

The design included an internal shifter spring that was stronger than the competitors' and prevented binding under hard use or competition. The kit included a steel interlock pin which, when correctly installed in the transmission, prevented the simultaneous engagement of multiple gears. If two gears were selected at the same time, the transmission broke or caused the rear wheels to lock, sending the car into a slide. Hurst reinforced the image of this better product by introducing a Hurst lifetime warranty that repaired or replaced any failed shifter.

During the first few years of production, Hurst continually improved the product. Bill Campbell led and coordinated the product developments and improvements. He closely examined all shifters returned under warranty exchange. In fact, Bill spent a lot of time testing and analyzing shifters returned with bent shift rods.

After many experiments and tests, Bill learned that the shifter's innate weakness occurred at the various areas where the factory bent the shift rods to clear the transmission housing. These bends caused the metal to compress on the inside of the bend and stretch on the outside, reducing their overall strength.

PRICES FOR INSTALLATION KIT PARTS

Your standard discount applies

Item	LIST
BRACKET / BRACE / ADJUSTABLE LEG	8.26
ROD	2.68
ARM	1.06
BOLTS (BAG) CHEVROLET TYPE	5.11
BOOT & PLATE, WITH 4 SCREWS	3.95
BOLTS (BAG) FORD TYPE	3.18
BOLTS 0" - 1·½" ALL DIAMETERS	.19
BOLTS 1·3/4" - 4" ALL DIAMETERS	.31
NUTS ALL SIZES	.08
LOCKWASHER	.06
STARWASHER	.10
SPRING CLIP	.03
NYLON BUSHING	.07
BUTTON	1.09
INTERLOCK PIN	.57
U-BOLT WITH 2 FLEXLOCKS	1.27
TUBE SLEEVE #1859	1.29
KNOB (STANDARD) BLACK	1.00
KNOB (STANDARD) WHITE	2.00
KNOB WHITE IMPRINTED	2.60
KNOB DELUXE	4.00

HURST PERFORMANCE PRODUCTS, INC.
GLENSIDE, PENNSYLVANIA

This early Hurst price list shows individual component costs. At the time, in 1963, Hurst was still in Glenside, Pennsylvania. (Photo Courtesy Pete Serio Collection)

Bill discovered and patented a process that mechanically applied end-to-end pressure on the rod while the shifter bends were created. Through this process, the shift rods were able to retain their overall strength and no longer cracked at the bends. This production process remained in place throughout the Hurst shifter's lifespan, but was not used by any competitors' products.

Besides Ed Almquist and his competing shifter design, there were many others vying for space in this growing industry. Ansen, Midwest, and Foxcraft were a few of the start-up companies advertising in the pages of *Hot Rod* magazine in the early 1960s.

The Wangers Connection

The Automobile Manufacturers Association (AMA) placed a ban on new-car manufacturers directly sponsoring racing in 1957. Both Ford and Chrysler set up performance-oriented dealers in order to funnel "Severe Duty" or "Police Package" components to them for racing. Only General Motors strictly adhered to the ban, and doing so resulted in its being placed at a severe competitive disadvantage.

Jim Wangers, an ad man for McManus, John & Adams advertising agency, teamed with Ace Wilson of Royal Pontiac on Woodward Avenue in Detroit, Michigan, to create a Pontiac presence at the drag strip under the Royal Pontiac

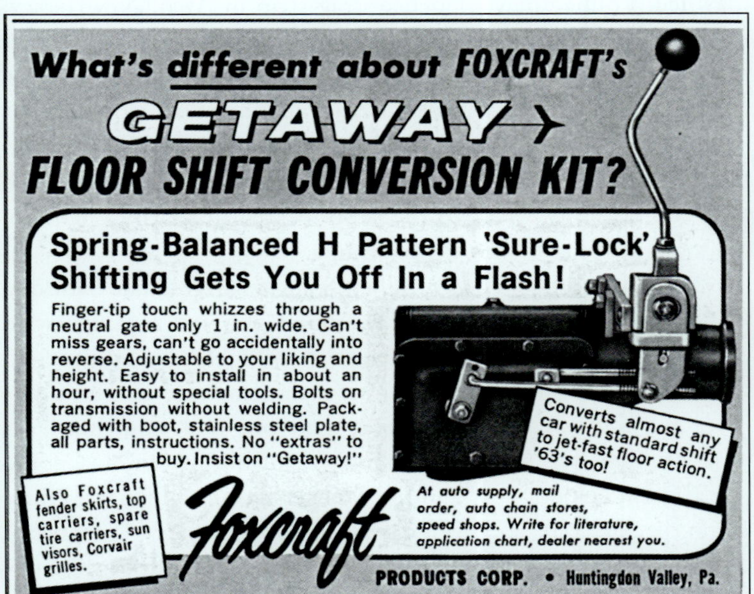

In the early 1960s, many different companies manufactured and sold floor shifter conversion kits. The Foxcraft company was a short-lived floor shifter manufacturer that competed against Hurst and was located in Hurst's backyard of Huntington Valley, Pennsylvania. (Photo Courtesy Mark Fletcher Collection)

Ace Wilson (left) of Royal Pontiac, drag racer and ad man Jim Wangers (center), and an unidentified man (right) are shown with *White Goddess*, a specially prepared and equipped 1961 Pontiac Catalina. Royal Pontiac gave this car the "Bobcat" treatment prior to Hurst awarding the car to the 1961 NHRA World Champion stock car driver. The treatment was a thorough high-performance makeover, giving the Catalina, fitted with a 421-ci engine and 4-speed transmission, enviable performance. (Photo Courtesy Pete Serio Collection)

banner. He campaigned one of Royal's Pontiac Catalinas with Pontiac's Super Duty 389 Tri-Power V-8 backed up with a 3-speed, column-mounted shifter. This car was extremely fast, despite the handicap of the steering-column-mounted factory shift linkage. Jim often commented that it was very difficult to shift from first to second gear with this car. His solution was to install steeper 4.56:1 rear gears, start in second, and shift only once.

During this drag racing foray, Jim supported the Pontiac Wide Track advertising campaign gaining momentum as the 1960s dawned. Pontiac may have legally maintained the ban on racing, but through Wangers and Royal Pontiac they were surely instrumental in designing and supporting Pontiac's racing image.

On July 3, 1960, Jim was racing the Royal Bobcat *Hot Chief 1* at the newly opened drag strip in Atco, New Jersey. While qualifying for the finals to be held on Sunday, July 4, Jim experienced a rear axle failure and contacted George Hurst for assistance. He phoned George and was asked to trailer the disabled Pontiac to the shop located in nearby Glenside, Pennsylvania.

When Wangers arrived late Saturday night, he found not just a garage with tools, but a crew of Hurst employees to help him fix the rear axle on the Catalina. This generous and thoughtful act sparked a friendship between George and Jim Wangers lasting a lifetime. Hurst offered to convert the factory "Spaghetti" 3-speed linkage to a Hurst floor shifter as well, but Pontiac did not offer the shifter,

Hildegard Hurst worked the Hurst Shifter Hospital in 1961 along with another "Hurst Girl." When racers bought the shifters, the Hurst mechanics installed them on their cars at the track. Later, this program helped repair cars that either failed the tech inspection or broke while racing. (Photo Courtesy Pete Serio Collection)

and therefore it was a non-stock modification. Hence, adding the Hurst shifter would have moved the Royal Catalina into a more competitive non-stock class. Wangers retained the factory column shifter and went on to win the 1960 National Hot Rod Association (NHRA) Top Stock Eliminator title.

George soon capitalized on the fledgling relationship and presented the Hurst shifter to Pontiac for the 1961 model year as an over-the-counter option. Wangers introduced the flamboyant George to Ace Wilson of Royal Pontiac as well as Bunkie Knudson of Pontiac's Super Duty program. Eventually, their racing collaboration brought them to the attention of Pete Estes who, at the time, directed the clandestine Pontiac racing effort. Estes was eager to meet George after reading an interview with him featured in *Hot Rod*. Pontiac was about to launch its new performance-oriented factory 4-speed with a floor shifter, and Estes asked Hurst to design and provide a product to keep the 1961 Pontiac Super Duty 421 and the Tri Power 389 cars in the NHRA winner's circle the following season.

Hurst Shifter Hospital

In 1961, Hurst also earned business with Chrysler, and a road test in the October 1961 issue of *Hot Rod* featured a Dodge Seneca equipped with a Hurst shifter. The car housed a 413-ci V-8 with cross-ram induction topped off with dual 4-barrel carbs. The article describes the new Hurst floor shifter as a factory-authorized, dealer-available option. The dealer parts catalog listing with a factory part number met the NHRA requirements as a factory stock component. This allowed for the addition of the Hurst shifter to all manual-transmission Chrysler and Pontiac models created after 1961 entered in stock classes. Longtime NHRA President Wally Parks, who was then the editor of *Hot Rod*, stated about the 1961 drag racing season, "Never before had so much high-level attention been focused on the drags."

Hurst didn't pioneer product support at the drag strip, but its fully equipped trucks and dedicated technicians brought shifter product support to a much higher level. Racers recognized if they had a problem with a Hurst shifter or needed an answer to a question that they would get the necessary help. It was one less thing for a racer to worry about. Here, Jack Watson (left) and an unknown helper work to set up the Hurst Performance Clinic on race day, circa 1961. (Photo Courtesy Pete Serio Collection)

Shortly after the George Hurst and Jim Wangers friendship began in 1960, Hurst was eager to capitalize on the relationship in order to get the performance shifters introduced to General Motors, and specifically Pontiac Motor Division. George felt he could offer Pontiac a better connection with the performance-oriented customer due to Hurst's racing and product knowledge. When racers failed tech inspections before races or broke components during racing, they were often done for the weekend because they couldn't haul all their tools to the track to fix breakages and other problems.

Hurst, in a brilliant marketing and public relations move, envisioned providing a rolling shop and a team of mechanics that could install shifters and perform minor repairs for the drag racing community on race day. George dubbed this the "Hurst Shifter Hospital." While discussing this with his friend Jim Wangers over drinks, George explained that the individuals capable of doing these repairs had to be mechanically literate, but young and single. This allowed the Hurst repair technician to travel most weekends and virtually live on the road.

Jim suggested that George speak with John (Jack) Watson, a young man who consistently hung out with the crew at Royal Pontiac. George subsequently hired Watson in 1961 to run the new Hurst Aid program at the racetrack. Jack was a young hot rodder himself and owned a Model A Ford with an early-1950s flathead V-8 and a Lincoln 3-speed transmission. Jack quickly became an integral part of the Hurst team working alongside Don Lane and others, assisting racers with small repairs in preparation to pass stringent tech inspections, adding Hurst shifters, and even welding up oil pans and suspensions that racers broke while running the quarter-mile.

This was the early 1960s, and drag strips were springing up across the country. National events were held on the same weekend in different areas of the country, and this created a problem because the Hurst support crew couldn't be in two places at the same. However, the Hurst Aid program continued to grow until Hurst supported a plethora of vehicles dispersed to the major events in promotion of the corporate products. Eventually, this fleet included a semi truck and trailer transporting a complete professional machine shop to Indianapolis, Indiana, and places as far west Bakersfield, California, and Renton, Washington.

Racing Promotions

George was an extravagant promoter, and in early 1960 started a contingency program that rewarded racers who won their division while using a Hurst shifter. In some cases, Hurst awarded more prize money than the tracks gave for winning a class purse. To a weekend warrior, the additional $100 to $500 was major money. Often the announcement of these promotions encouraged racers to purchase shifters on the spot, and with Hurst Aid at the track, racers received help installing them.

During the 1961 racing season, George gave away two cars to the winners of the World Championship at the Indianapolis NHRA championship and again at the summer national events. At the Indy NHRA nationals, Hurst decorated and gave away a new Wimbledon White 1961 Ford Thunderbird Hardtop. This car was not specially equipped for drag racing and, in fact, the car retained the standard full wheel covers.

This original 1962 Hurst ad appeared in *Hot Rod* magazine and identified the four different shifter offerings: the original 3-speed Dual Pattern Synchro/Loc, the 4-speed Competition Plus, the low-priced Mystery Shifter, and the Dual Gate auto transmission shifter conversion kit. (Photo Courtesy Mark Fletcher Collection)

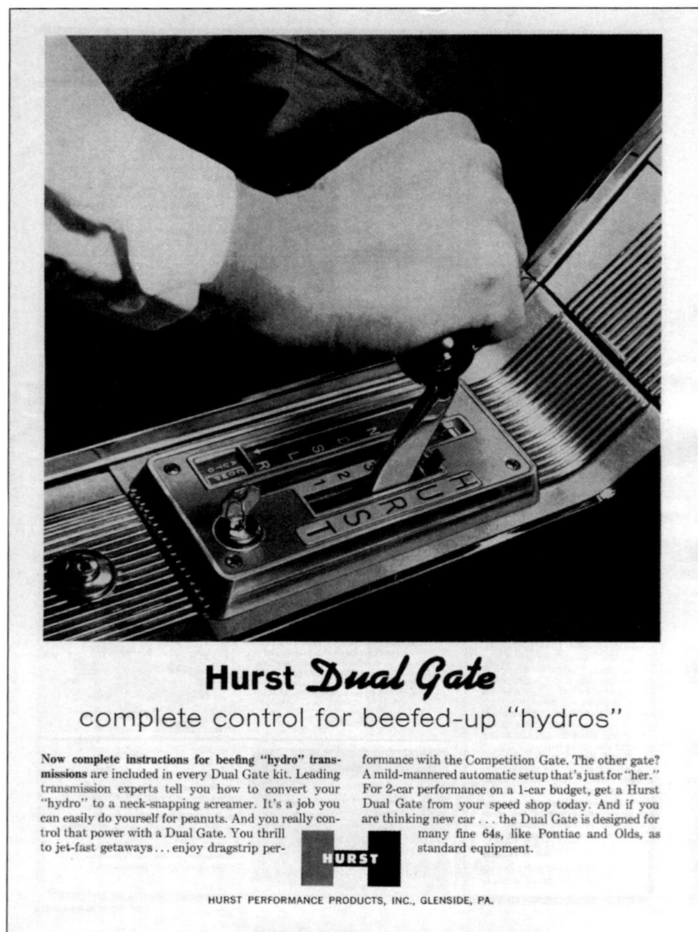

This early 1962 ad for the Hurst Dual Gate shifter was Hurst's first offering for the growing automatic transmission market. (Photo Courtesy Mark Fletcher Collection)

The 1961 Thunderbird was awarded to the season champion Jack Chrisman, who achieved a massive 550 points while running in the AA/D class. Jack used the car as a family vehicle for many years and then kept it in storage. The car recently surfaced in the same stock condition maintained by the Chrisman family for decades.

A Pontiac Catalina was the second car awarded at the 1961 NHRA nationals in California and was a collaboration between George Hurst, Jim Wangers, and Ace Wilson of Royal Pontiac, nicknamed *White Goddess*. Equipped with a 421 Tri-Power factory 4-speed with a Hurst shifter, the Catalina hardtop carried Pontiac's distinctive eight-lug wheels with wide whitewalls. This car received the full "Royal Bobcat" treatment including a performance tune-up, which was as simple as re-curving the distributor, adjusting the valve lash settings, and adding a few adjustment tricks to the otherwise stock carburetors.

This car was awarded to Bruce Morgan, who was crowned NHRA National Champion while piloting his black 1957 Chevrolet Bel-Air hardtop equipped with the high-performance Rochester fuel-injected 283-hp, 283-ci V-8. He came to the event with an almost perfect record for the season, winning every previous race of the season but one, in which he broke a fuel injection line. Bruce accepted the prize of the Hurst Catalina, but was soon critical of its performance and subsequently sold it. Morgan's action offended both Hurst and Wangers, and may have played into Hurst's decision to redirect the corporate prize awards for 1963, choosing to award smaller prizes to more category winners.

All this activity on the drag strips benefited Hurst-Campbell's business. For the 1962 model year, Hurst shifters were an over-the-counter option for all of the Big Three's performance offerings, which now included Ford as well as General Motors and Chrysler.

For 1962, Hurst again teamed with Pontiac to give away the new Grand Prix. Hurst bought these giveaway

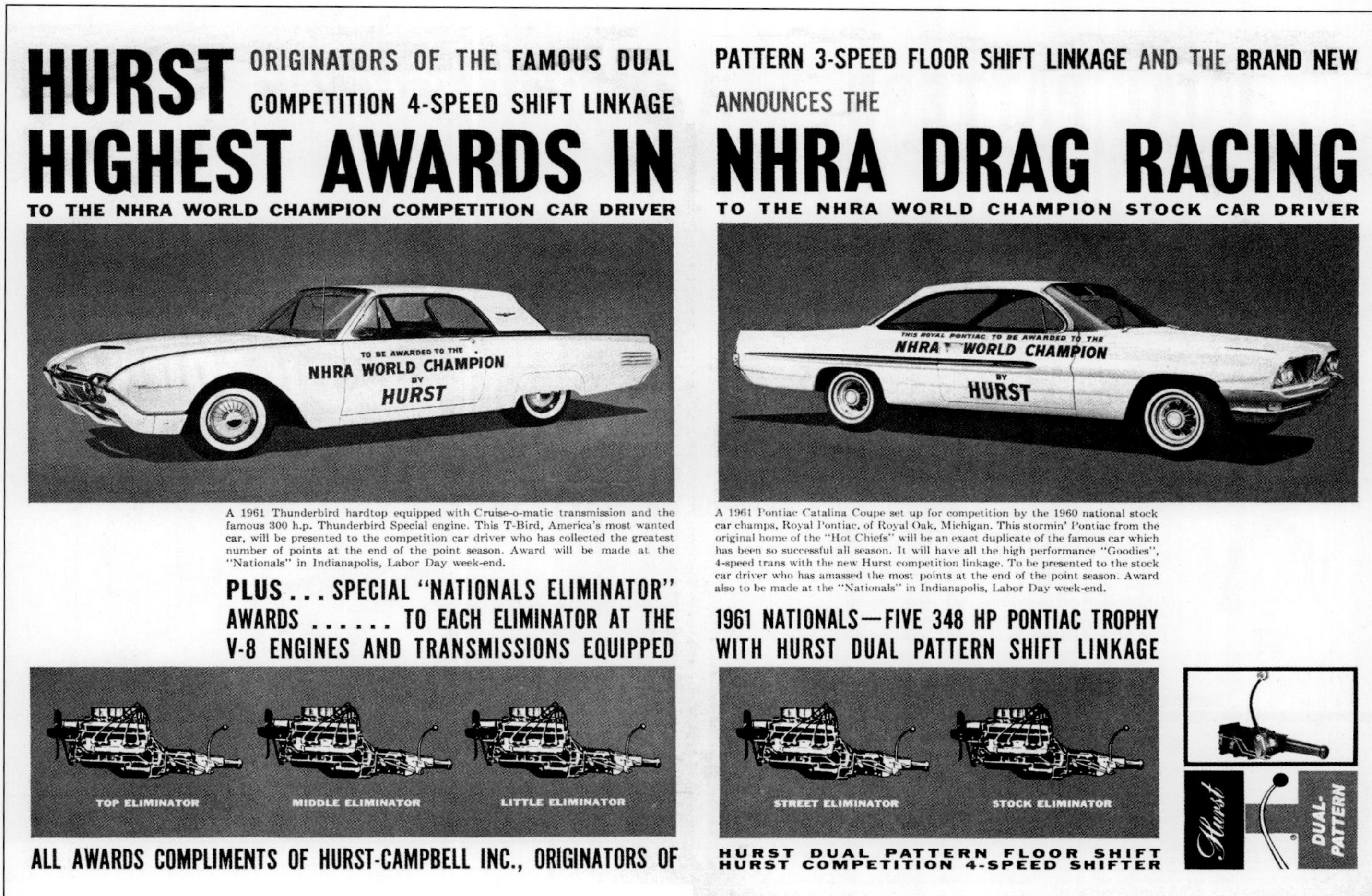

Hurst awarded a 1961 Thunderbird hardtop to the winner of the NHRA World Championship for 1961 (left). For the 1961 NHRA National event, Hurst gave away the *White Goddess* Pontiac Catalina, a factory Tri-Power carbureted hardtop specially prepared by Royal Pontiac (right). Hurst also awarded five 348-hp Pontiac mills, complete with 4-speed transmissions and Hurst Competition Plus shifters. (Photo Courtesy Mark Fletcher Collection)

cars through Jim Wangers and Royal Pontiac at dealer cost. Due to the sour publicity after the previous year's prize, Hurst decided to keep the car primarily stock and let the winner add his own performance goodies. The exception to this process was the inclusion of the dealer-optional Hurst 4-speed shifter and large Hurst lettering hand painted on the side of the car. George's fourth wife Hildegard was the inaugural Miss Hurst Shifter and presented the keys to the 1962 NHRA champion Tom Sturm. Coincidental to the 1961 *White Goddess* award fiasco, Tom drove to victory piloting a 1961 421 Catalina with a Hurst 4-speed shifter.

The use of a Hurst shifter was not a requirement for winning the award, but in this case it certainly didn't hurt. In an additional act of self-promotion, Hurst placed an ad in *Hot Rod* magazine congratulating the winner and emphasizing that a Hurst shifter assisted in the winning performance.

To promote the company and its products, Hurst gave away two cars during the 1961 race season and another in 1962. However, some criticized the lavish car giveaways for rewarding only a lucky few, while many racers competed using the shifters. Throughout his life, Hurst remained sensitive to criticism, and in 1963 he responded by awarding a smaller grand prize and more prizes throughout the classes. Hence, a Philco combination TV and stereo cabinet was given to the NHRA Nationals Mr. Stock Eliminator. He also awarded 70 Longines watches to the remaining class champions. In addition, other top competitors received a Hurst T-shirt with matching cap and an exclusive evening at Hurst's hospitality suite.

Jack Watson had quickly become the shifter expert at the racetrack, and soon the "Shifty Doctor" likeness was painted on one of Hurst's support vehicles at the racetrack. Watson was a colorful individual and shared Hurst's penchant for innovative thinking. They fueled each other's creative juices, most often serving as hosts for after-hours parties while traveling the race circuit.

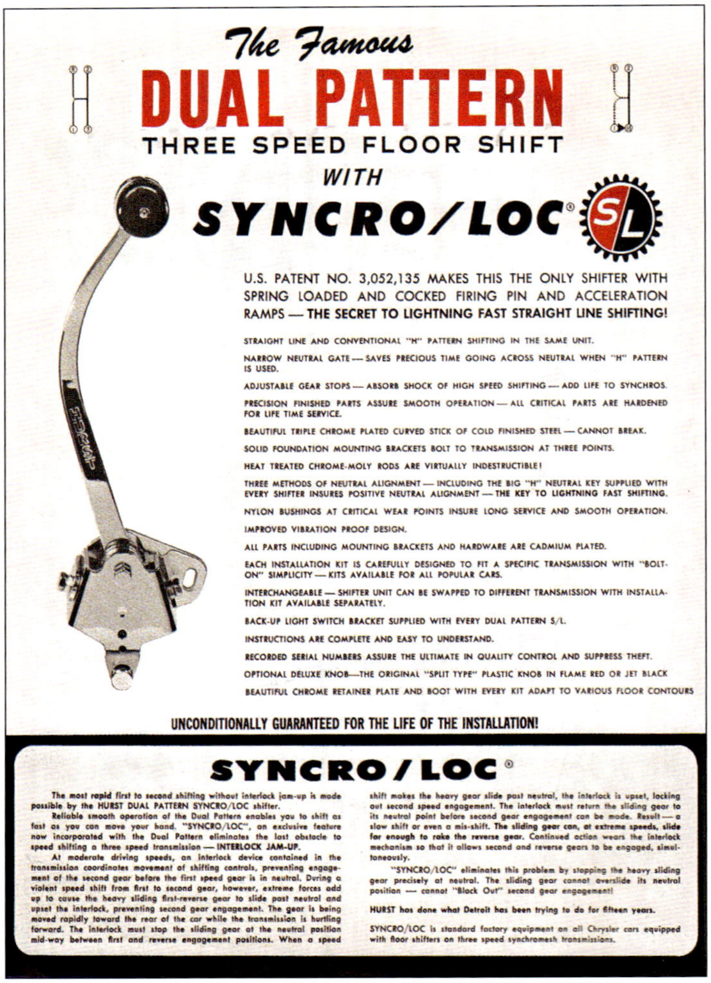

The original 1962 Hurst Floor Shifter Catalog page describes the patented 3-speed Synchro/Loc Dual Pattern shifter. (Photo Courtesy Mark Fletcher Collection)

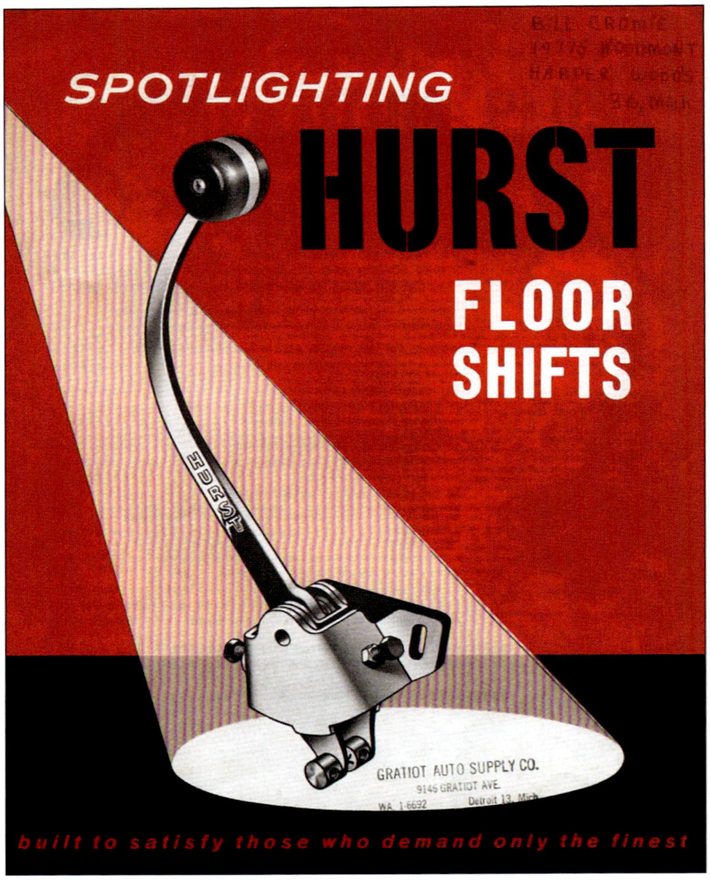

Gratiot Auto Supply in Detroit distributed this original 1962 Hurst Floor Shifter Catalog. Like many Hurst ads, the purpose was not only to promote and sell the products, but educate the customer and focus on Hurst's competitive advantages. Gratiot was one of Hurst's first and biggest floor shifter customers. (Photo Courtesy Mark Fletcher Collection)

Fireball Roberts Edition

This is a rare 1962 Pontiac Grand Prix, with the Fireball Roberts package. It sports gold spears with matching eight-lug wheels and is powered by a 421-ci Tri-Power V-8 mated to a 4-speed manual transmission with a Hurst shifter. (Photos Courtesy Rich Truesdell)

George's involvement and influence allowed him to meet many of the most successful racers in motorsports. George was often seen in the company of racers, such as Don Yenko, Smokey Yunick, Mickey Thompson, Dick Harrell, Tom McEwen, Joe Schubeck, and Don Garlits. Many who knew Hurst during this time believe he wanted to race himself, but the injuries he sustained in the Navy to both his feet and hands prevented him from competing.

ABC's *Wide World of Sports* interviews NASCAR legend Curtis Turner in 1963. He stands in front of a crowd that includes a spectator wearing the Hurst gold racing jacket and matching hat. (Photo Courtesy Pete Serio Collection)

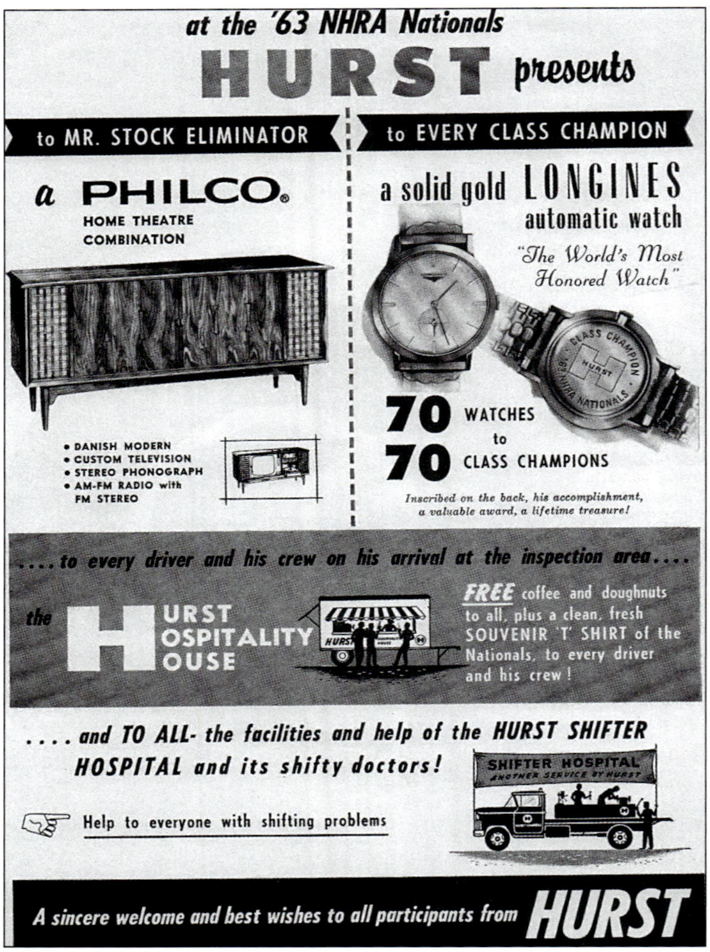

Hurst switched from awarding one grand prize to giving away many smaller prizes, including a new Philco home stereo and 70 winners of a Hurst-engraved Longines watch for the 1963 NHRA Nationals. (Photo Courtesy Mark Fletcher Collection)

In this 1966 Hurst armed forces ad, Jack Watson, Hurst's "Shifty Doctor" is featured. He headed up the company's product support program at major drag races throughout the country. George Hurst often created a persona around the key Hurst employees that were in the public's view. (Photo Courtesy Mark Fletcher Collection)

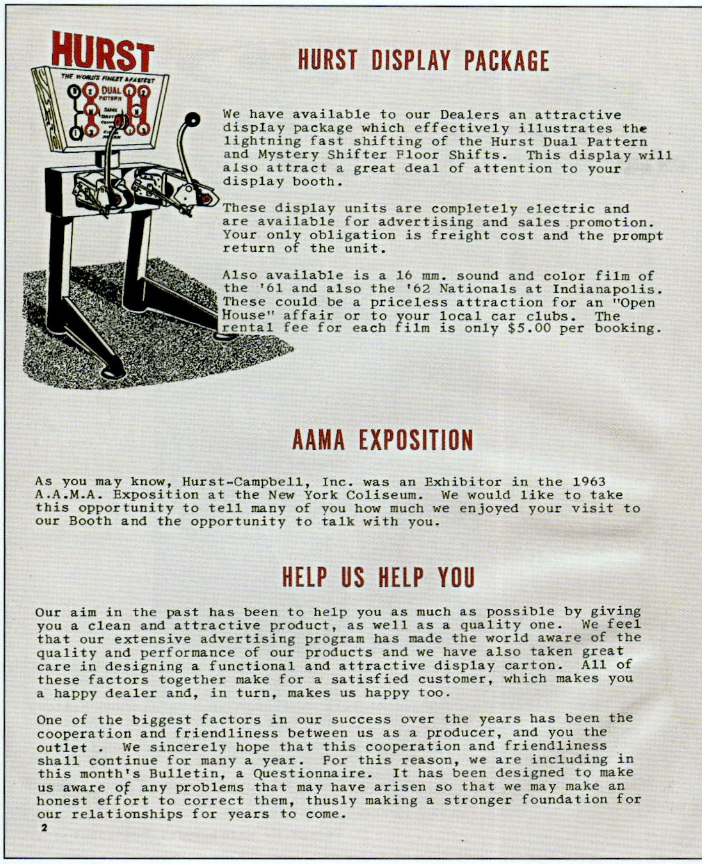

HURST

HURST DISPLAY PACKAGE

We have available to our Dealers an attractive display package which effectively illustrates the lightning fast shifting of the Hurst Dual Pattern and Mystery Shifter Floor Shifts. This display will also attract a great deal of attention to your display booth.

These display units are completely electric and are available for advertising and sales promotion. Your only obligation is freight cost and the prompt return of the unit.

Also available is a 16 mm. sound and color film of the '61 and also the '62 Nationals at Indianapolis. These could be a priceless attraction for an "Open House" affair or to your local car clubs. The rental fee for each film is only $5.00 per booking.

AAMA EXPOSITION

As you may know, Hurst-Campbell, Inc. was an Exhibitor in the 1963 A.A.M.A. Exposition at the New York Coliseum. We would like to take this opportunity to tell many of you how much we enjoyed your visit to our Booth and the opportunity to talk with you.

HELP US HELP YOU

Our aim in the past has been to help you as much as possible by giving you a clean and attractive product, as well as a quality one. We feel that our extensive advertising program has made the world aware of the quality and performance of our products and we have also taken great care in designing a functional and attractive display carton. All of these factors together make for a satisfied customer, which makes you a happy dealer and, in turn, makes us happy too.

One of the biggest factors in our success over the years has been the cooperation and friendliness between us as a producer, and you the outlet. We sincerely hope that this cooperation and friendliness shall continue for many a year. For this reason, we are including in this month's Bulletin, a Questionnaire. It has been designed to make us aware of any problems that may have arisen so that we may make an honest effort to correct them, thusly making a stronger foundation for our relationships for years to come.

2

Page two of a corporate Hurst Performance bulletin depicts a Hurst store display challenging consumers to compare the feel of the Hurst shifters. (Photo Courtesy Pete Serio Collection)

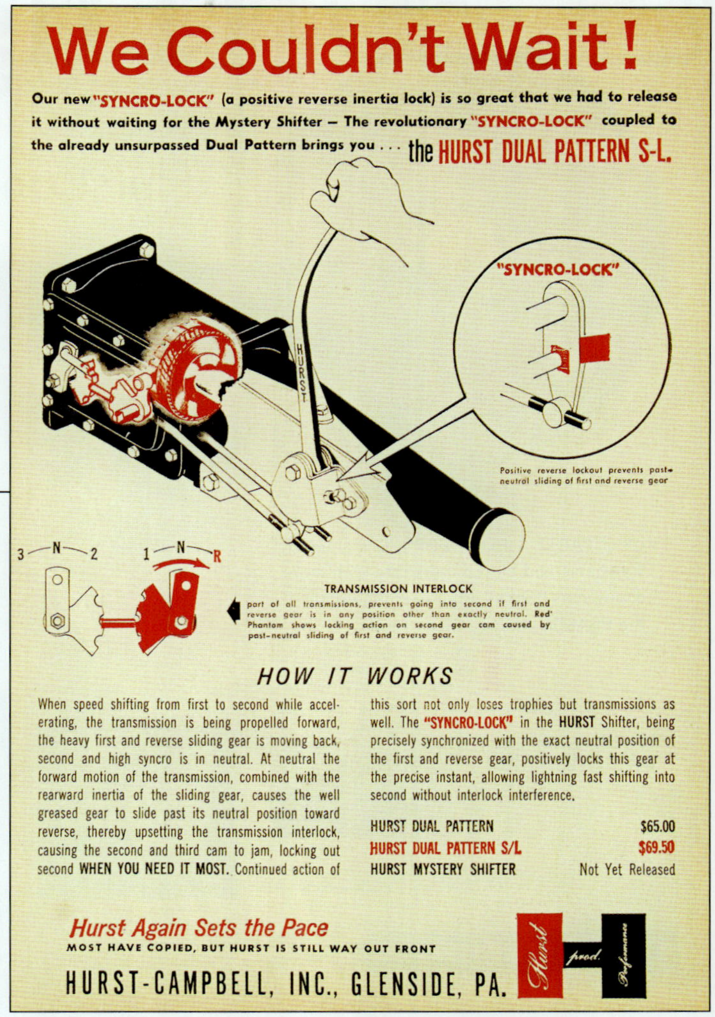

In 1963, Hurst placed an ad in *Hot Rod* magazine showing three product offerings and their prices. Note the Mystery shifter had not yet been priced. (Photo Courtesy Mark Fletcher Collection)

HURST PERFORMANCE PRODUCTS BULLETIN

VOLUME 1 | FEBRUARY, 1963 | NUMBER 2

MEET MR. BILL KENDRICK

Mr. Kendrick will now head up our Sales Department. We are proud of our acquisition, if I may call it that. Mr. Kendrick has had wide sales and management experience with companies like Bendix and Mallory Electric Company. He also has an extensive technical and engineering background, and will be most important. He is a NICE GUY interested not only in doing business, but in PEOPLE. His first task will be to analyze our distribution structure with the goal of cleaning up and re-organizing our system in a manner equitable to all. "Bill" has set out to help each and every one of you and if you have any doubts, why don't you call on him and see for yourself.

George H. Hurst, Jr., President

The cover of the February 1963 corporate Hurst Performance bulletin announces Bill Kendrick as the new Hurst Sales Manager. Prior to this, George Hurst managed the Hurst sales efforts. (Photo Courtesy Pete Serio Collection)

Shifting into High Gear

Hurst and Campbell Establish an Icon

By 1963, Hurst-Campbell was prospering, and it appeared George couldn't spend money fast enough on promotions to keep pace with the profits rolling in. Several lower-cost competitors had entered the shifter market, which minimally affected Hurst sales. To keep customers from defecting to competitors, George announced a lower-cost shifter with most of the features of the current offerings. He began promoting and taking orders for it before it was finalized, and therefore the new product was quickly labeled the "Mystery" shifter. The recipe was rather simple: remove costs so it could retail for half the price of Hurst's existing line.

Hurst created a giant display for the "His and Hers" Dual Gate shifter, and it was used at the first ever Speed and Custom Equipment trade show held at the Disneyland Hotel in 1962. Over the years, this trade show evolved into SEMA (Specialty Equipment Market Association), which is the biggest automotive aftermarket trade show. With this product and display, George tried to attract the attention of car manufacturers, and Hurst Performance succeeded as the "His and Hers" shifter was installed on the 1963 Pontiac Grand Prix. (Photo Courtesy Mark Fletcher Collection)

CHAPTER 3

This is the first Hurst Mystery shifter ad. Hurst needed a shifter to compete against lower-priced rival shifters. A simplified shifter with a threaded shifter handle and round plastic ball handle, yet still incorporating Hurst's renowned strength, was the goal of the new Mystery shifter, and it was achieved. (Photo Courtesy Mark Fletcher Collection)

Bill Campbell recognized that the most expensive single components, after the complicated shifter mechanism, were the heavy flat handles, which were specially designed for each vehicle. By using an adjustable-height round handle with simple bends, in combination with adjustable-length shifting rods, engineering was able to meet the cost reduction goals with a minimum of different part numbers. This product was extremely successful as an entry-level shifter for aspiring racers whose limited budget dictated their choices. The Mystery shifter quickly filled the void between the standard factory offerings and Hurst's top-of-the-line product.

In the spring of 1963, Hurst and Pontiac formed a business alliance and the Hurst shifter became standard on 4-speed-equipped models of Pontiac's GTO for 1964. For the first year of the new GTO production, the Hurst name

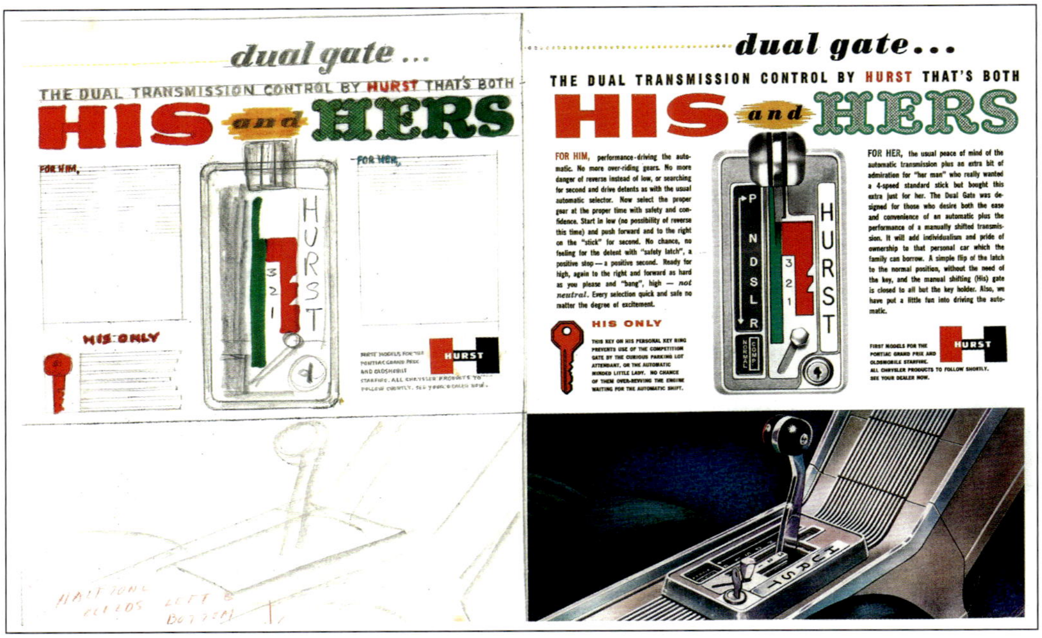

Hurst created this poster showing how the artwork for the "His and Hers" shifter evolved. The Hurst products, as well as the marketing and ad campaigns, had their own unique personality, and the enthusiasts who invested in Hurst products were rarely disappointed. Hurst was always developing and refining its products. (Photo Courtesy Mark Fletcher Collection)

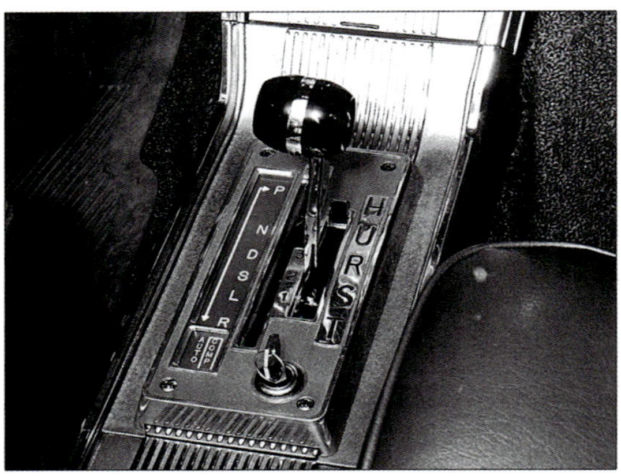

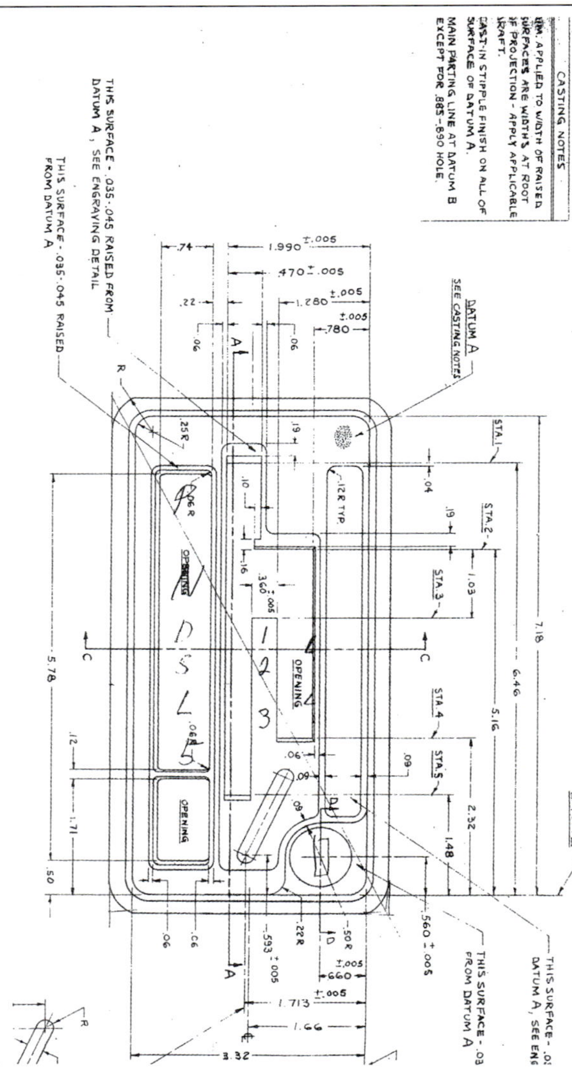

Hurst's "His and Hers" shifter was a Dual Gate shifter with Hurst's innovative marketing approach behind it. The shifter allowed the performance-minded driver to accurately select the correct gears up the line gate, while the other gate was a traditional gate pattern for common street driving. This is one of Hurst's original engineering designs side-by-side with the finished product. (Photos Courtesy Mark Fletcher Collection)

did not adorn the shifter because Pontiac management did not want branded aftermarket products on its vehicles. Hurst also offered the "His and Hers" shifter for the Grand Prix when it was equipped with the automatic transmission shifter installed in the floor console.

In comparison, the same model year Barracuda came with a Hurst-labeled 4-speed shifter. Jim Wangers felt Pontiac was missing a distinct marketing advantage by not allowing the Hurst name on the shifter. Through subsequent meetings with Pete Estes, Bunkie Knudsen, and John DeLorean, the Hurst name was prominently placed on the Hurst shifter for the 1965 GTO and every Hurst shifter manufactured since.

By the mid 1960s, Hurst manual shifters dominated on the drag strip as well as the street. Adding a Hurst competition shifter was often the first speed part a young enthusiast added to a new or used car. As many of these modified cars served double duty as daily drivers, owners made additional modifications for daily commutes.

Hurst was aware that not everybody wanted to work a clutch five days a week. Automatic transmissions were proving to be more reliable and, in many cases, matching the quarter-mile times laid down by manual transmissions. Hurst developed a line of floor shifters for automatic transmissions, the Hydro-Gate. These kits easily converted the shifter from a column mount to a floor mount and allowed the driver to manually shift the automatic transmission at the desired RPM.

Facility Expansion

Hurst shifter production was in full swing, and by this time George and Bill were working out of four separate buildings in the Glenside, Pennsylvania, area. One of the buildings was used for production of the steel handles and specially bent shifting rods. The handles were sent out to a local vendor for chroming. Upon their return, they were assembled into kits and boxed at the second location. They were then transferred to the third location, the warehouse from where they were shipped to speed shops, resellers, and the new car factories for installation on the assembly line.

A new facility was planned in nearby Warminster, Pennsylvania, on an 11-acre site directly across from the Johnsville Air Station where George was last stationed during his military service career. The new building was initially planned as a 52,000-square-foot facility combining all the processes occurring in the three separate facilities.

On January 7, 1965, George Hurst opened the new facility with much fanfare, marking an important milestone as the company's marketing team grew. Artist Bob Held, who had been with Hurst since 1963, became the art director. This team later included Bob Miller, Al Schoen, and Barbara Watson as marketing specialist, with Jack Duffy joining in 1965 as public relations director.

The Warminster facility allowed for administration, engineering, manufacturing, and warehousing to be housed under a single roof. Hurst's new home was dedicated to the late John Bonner, the longtime friend and insurance salesman who helped define the Hurst/Campbell partnership at George's kitchen table in 1958.

George Hurst was a dapper dresser and always enjoyed the company of women. (Photo Courtesy Pete Serio Collection)

From the beginning, Hurst's unique vision and passion for motorsports resonated throughout his company. Here, Linda Vaughn and George Hurst pose with a Playboy bunny next to a hotel pool. (Photo Courtesy Pete Serio Collection)

1964 Pontiac LeMans Convertible

By 1964 George Hurst was forging relationships with OEMs such as Pontiac to supply Hurst shifters as factory-installed options. This 1964 Pontiac Le Mans convertible is not only equipped with a Hurst shifter but a set of Hurst accessory wheels. (Photos Courtesy Rich Truesdell)

The Hurst team was actively involved with OEM projects for both Pontiac and Chrysler, and therefore Hurst needed a Detroit-area facility to directly communicate with engineers and coordinate projects from each company. Because they were often working on the next year's cars, this required a measured degree of security. For its Pontiac-related projects, Hurst had been using the service facility at Ace Wilson's Royal Pontiac in Royal Oak, but the automotive press was on to Royal Pontiac's strategic position within Pontiac, and confidential product information often leaked out.

To solve this problem, and to facilitate additional OEM projects, Hurst opened the Hurst Performance Research Center in Madison Heights, Michigan, which served as a skunk works of sorts. A portion of the shop space was closed off and segregated, so confidentiality of each manufacturer's project could be maintained. In fact, there were times when competing manufacturers had prototype vehicles in the same building within 30 feet of each other. When not being used for official business, OEM engineers commonly used these shop areas for customizing their own personal or company-provided cars. Often these cars ran head-to-head match races on nearby Woodward Avenue (see Chapter 6).

The new factory was dedicated to John Bonner, a longtime friend of Hurst and an insurance salesman. This is the complete fold-out press release and invitation to the new factory dedication in Warminster. (Photo Courtesy Pete Serio Collection)

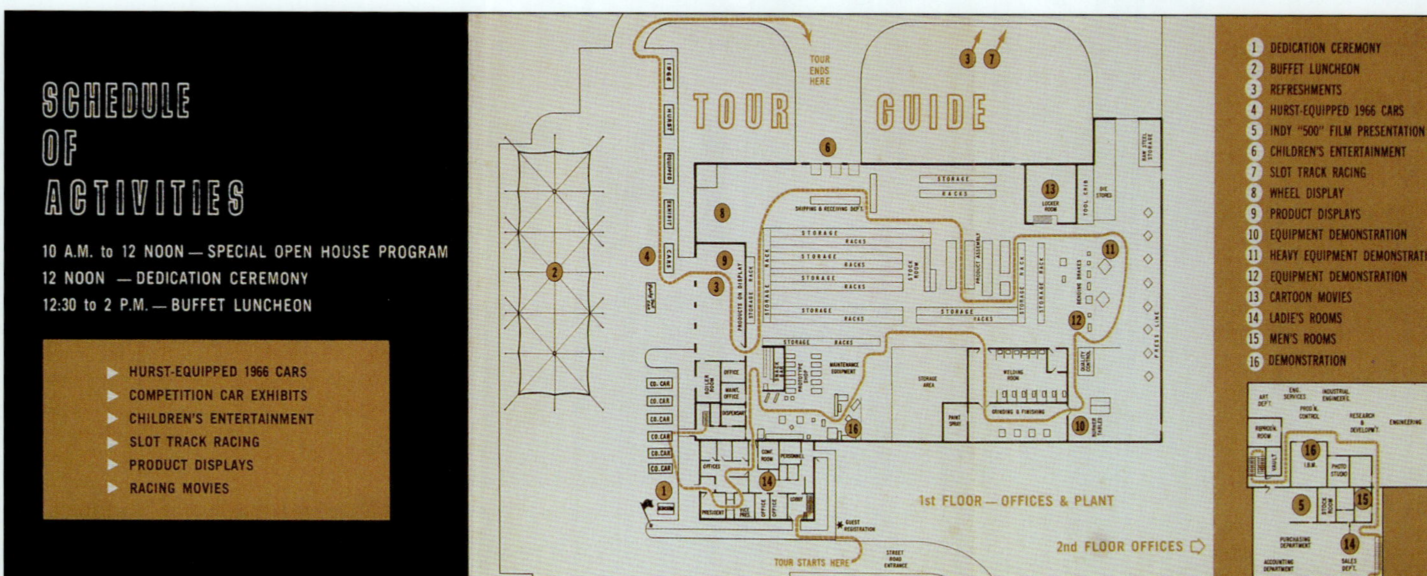

The press and local dignitaries were shown the new factory layout with a comprehensive tour. (Photo Courtesy Pete Serio Collection)

In the Heat of Battle

Hurst Competition Cars

Bill Shrewsberry lifts all four wheels of *Hemi Under Glass* off the ground in 1965. The more the crew tried to dial in the car and keep the wheels on the ground, the more difficult it was to drive. The Hurst group came to the conclusion that it was simply going to be a wheelstanding machine and went with it. Thereafter, *Hemi Under Glass* pulled up the front wheels for the length of the quarter-mile. (Photo Courtesy Bob Riggle Collection)

George Hurst was a hot rodder and racer at heart. From the earliest age, he worked on his own cars and developed ideas and products to make cars faster and better. Hurst Performance was launched from a passion to build better high-performance products, which led to the creation of the original Hurst engine mount plates, the foundation of the original business.

Hurst, a consummate promoter and salesman, recognized if he was going to build his aftermarket performance conversion and parts business, he needed his company to project a high-performance image through

The Indy Lotus team from left to right: George Hurst, Parnelli Jones, and co-sponsor J.C. Agajanian. (Photo Courtesy Pete Serio Hurst Collection)

In 1965, Hurst teamed with J. C. Agajanian to create *Hurst Shifter Special*, a modified Lotus Ford, to compete in the Indy 500. In fact, the car was a reworked 1964 Lotus, but the car proved to be somewhat fragile. When the chassis failed, a nasty crash resulted with legendary racer Parnelli Jones at the wheel. Hurst created a press kit for the #98 Lotus Indy race car. (Photo Courtesy Pete Serio Collection)

racing. Therefore, racing was always a top priority. Part of the core business involved marketing through racing to sell parts and, most importantly, shifters. In fact, Hurst directly or indirectly participated in Indy Car racing, NHRA drag racing, NORRA off-road racing, land speed runs, and other forms of motorsports.

Hurst Floor Shift Special

Hurst always looked for more high-profile ways to promote the company and its image in the eyes of the public. In 1964, he partnered with the legendary race car builder Smokey Yunick who had designed, developed, and built an unusual chassis for the 1964 Indianapolis 500 *Hurst Floor Shift Special*. This space-age configuration held the driver in a pod similar to a motorcycle sidecar suspended between the left-side tires. A 252-ci, naturally aspirated, DOHC four-cylinder Offenhauser engine powered this wild race car.

It is unclear if Hurst had any input into the unusual design, but both Yunick and Hurst were convinced that an asymmetrical design, enhanced by the driver's weight bias, would revolutionize the sport. The car was painted in Yunick's standard colors, in what also became the signature color combination for Hurst, black and gold.

Sprint, midget, and Indy Car driver Duane Carter, Sr. and rookie Bobby Johns were chosen to pilot the car. Both tested and practiced with the car extensively throughout May 1964 in preparation for the Memorial Day race. During testing, the design received extensive media attention. Wild speculation abounded as to whether the radical car had any scientific or engineering merit behind its design. While attempting to qualify the car, Johns lost control and slid the car backward into the outside wall of turn one, severely damaging it and removing it from further competition. No attempt was ever made to race the car again, as some felt it was an unsafe design.

The car was repaired and joined the collection at the Indianapolis Motor Speedway Hall of Fame Museum. It has also been loaned to the Honda Museum in Motegi, Japan, and was shown at both the 2010 and 2011 Amelia Island Concourse de Elegance events.

Even in the midst of failure, the overwhelming publicity of the stillborn Indy effort encouraged George.

Parnelli Jones was one of the best drivers of his era, and *Hurst Shifter Special* was definitely a competitive, albeit fragile, car. While he suffered a crash in practice, Jones drove the car to a second place finish behind eventual winner Jim Clark. Lotus provided the car for the 1965 Indianapolis 500 with Parnelli Jones. Hurst and J. C. Agajanian co-sponsored this effort. (Photo Courtesy Pete Serio Hurst Collection)

Hurst Shifter Special

For the 1965 Indianapolis 500, George Hurst teamed with J. C. Agajanian. Hurst and his team took a much more conventional approach than the previous year. The team built a modified 1964 Lotus-Ford adorned in signature gold Hurst colors. But the reworked Lotus proved to be somewhat fragile, and when the chassis failed with legendary racer Parnelli Jones at the wheel, a nasty crash resulted. The car was repaired and Jones started the 500 from the fifth position. Jones was one of the best drivers of his era and *Hurst Shifter Special* was definitely a competitive car, but Jim Clark was in a class of his own and pulled out a two-lap lead over Jones. Jones had his hands full for the last half of the race, racing wheel-to-wheel with Dan Gurney and holding off an impressive rookie named Mario Andretti. But Gurney's engine eventually failed, and Jones gained the upper hand against Andretti, finishing second.

Hemi Under Glass

While traveling together with Jack Watson, George sketched an idea combining two of Plymouth's newest product offerings for 1964. He used a bowling alley lounge napkin to show the concept of combining the new Barracuda with the 426 supercharged race Hemi. The engine bay was too small to house the massive elephant engine, so Hurst suggested moving it to the back of the car where there was plenty of room under the huge fastback window.

In the fall of 1964, Hurst procured a factory-fresh black 1965 Barracuda directly from Chrysler for the project. The car was delivered to the Hurst Performance Research Center in Madison Heights, Michigan. Dave Landreth, Jack Watson, Bob Riggle, Dick Chrysler, and others in the research center were enlisted to create this innovative and unconventional race car.

While in Hawaii in the fall of 1964, George relentlessly recruited Bill Shrewsberry of Pontiac AF/X fame to drive the new Hemi-powered Barracuda. As they spent a day together at sea, George outlined the value of relocating the engine into the backseat area and how this solved the traction issues plaguing many of the high-powered drag cars. Bill accepted the job despite a chance the car would never be built, but George invited him to Detroit six weeks later for the unveiling. Upon arriving, Shrewsberry immediately pointed out that the Corvette independent rear suspension could not handle the torque and weight transfer from the elephant engine. To prove his point while testing the car, Shrewsberry performed a hard launch and instantly shattered the rear suspension.

The car was initially envisioned as a competitive racer, but on the first

George Hurst came up with the idea of *Hemi Under Glass* in a discussion over drinks. Based on the Plymouth Barracuda, the engine was moved from under the hood to the rear of the vehicle for better weight distribution. The car was initially conceived and constructed to be a competitive drag car. But instead, it morphed into a wheel-standing exhibition car. Hurst later created this ad for *Hot Rod* magazine depicting the idea. (Photo Courtesy Mark Fletcher Collection)

A team of employees at Hurst Performance in Madison Heights, Michigan, built this one-of-a-kind wheelstander. The supercharged 426 Hemi was placed under the fastback's rear window, and the driveshaft connected directly to the rear axle, hence the name *Hemi Under Glass*. The car became arguably the most famous wheelstanding drag race exhibition car in history. The stock 273 V-8 was removed from the front, and attempts were made to get the Hemi engine through the door to test fit *Hemi Under Glass*. (Photo Courtesy Bob Riggle)

Hemi Under Glass in front of the Detroit-based Hurst Performance center in 1965. (Photo Courtesy Mark Fletcher Collection)

attempt with a replaced conventional rear axle, Bill stood the car on its rear bumper. With a little practice, Shrewsberry was soon able to run most of the quarter-mile on just the two rear wheels. In fact, Bill found that once the car's front wheels lifted, the air hitting the floorpans kept the car suspended until the brakes were applied and the front end came back to Earth. It was soon discovered that the dual carbs on the Hemi ran out of fuel before it covered half the track. A switch to Hilborn fuel injection solved that problem.

The finished car featured a supercharged, fuel-injected, race-prepped 426 Hemi mated to a Chrysler 4-speed transmission. The output of the transmission connected to a V-drive and then to the rear axle. Originally, the car had no way to steer once the front wheels were off the ground. The driver had to use the torque of the engine to make minor directional adjustments once in the air. Learning how to control this Plymouth changed the face of racing and the lives of both its pilots.

George immediately recognized the entertainment value associated with this stunt, and tasked Jack Duffy with booking *Hemi Under Glass* at racetracks where the event organizer was willing to pay Hurst a fee. The car traveled the race circuit as an exhibition vehicle, and not as a competitive drag car as originally conceived. Bill Shrewsberry and his crew were compensated with a portion of the proceeds paid to Hurst, out of which he paid for all travel expenses and overhead for his new mechanic Bob Riggle.

Jack Duffy, the marketing manager at Hurst Corporation, booked the car for events and made all necessary arrangements. It was transported on a specially prepared car hauler with either Shrewsberry or Riggle at the wheel. Chrysler provided, free of charge, spare and replacement parts. The racetracks often used Hurst promotional images of the car with its grille pointed toward the skies in their event promotional ads. Most venues paid the team between $500 and $1,000 to perform during a race weekend. At first the car was christened *A Bear of a Cuda* (Barracuda), but soon it was simply identified as *Hemi Under Glass*.

George was often introduced along with *Hemi Under Glass* at race weekends. He enjoyed his role as a dignitary and sponsor for many racing events, often driving the length of the track in a Hurst-lettered convertible with a bevy of pretty young models waving to the crowd. Hurst, ever the innovative promoter, recognized that attractive women could effectively market the company's shifters. So, in late 1965, he began a search for a full-time employee to serve as Miss Hurst Golden Shifter. In typical flamboyant George style, he placed an open ad in *Hot Rod* magazine announcing auditions at three separate racing events.

One of the contestants was Linda Vaughn, a vivacious young woman who had been both Miss Atlanta International Raceway and Miss Firebird Fuel. She won over the crowd with her charming personality and curvaceous figure. Equally important, Vaughn captivated

1967 Hurst *Hemi Under Glass* Plymouth

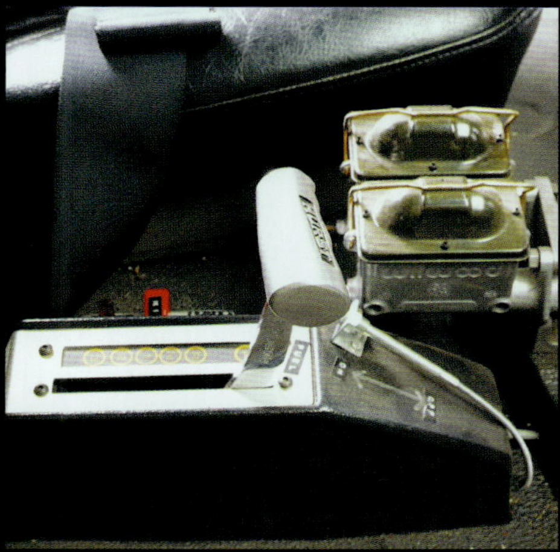

The Hurst "Hemi Under Glass" nomenclature was applied to many cars over the popular program's long run. This car, owned by noted collector Bill Sefton, is a version of the second-generation Plymouth Barracuda, as campaigned by Bob Riggle. (Photos Courtesy Rich Truesdell)

Crowds gathered and examined *Hemi Under Glass'* unique design between runs in the pits. Note the Plexiglas removable rear window. (Photo Courtesy Bob Riggle Collection)

George Hurst and won the contest. She became one of the first female ambassadors in the male-dominated sport of auto racing.

And like the *Hemi Under Glass,* Linda Vaughn became a consistent presence at the drag strip and part of the promotional machine to market Hurst products.

Bob Riggle

After running a Firebird service station in Ohio, Bob Riggle, a mechanic by trade, was hired in 1964. He interviewed over the phone and was told he would start his job by meeting Jack Watson at a rest stop along the Ohio turnpike. He was one of the Hurst mechanics who repaired racers' cars that failed tech inspection on race day. He was almost immediately assigned to *Hemi Under Glass* and explains that Bill was very hard on the Hemi's rod and main bearings due to over-revving the engine during performances. Shrewsberry was also known to openly brag about his driving talents and often suggested that no one else was capable of handling this "brute of a ride."

After the season had ended, Shrewsberry and Riggle worked on *Hemi Under Glass* at the Warminster plant. Bob recalls that George called Shrewsberry into his office for what Bill believed to be a renegotiation of the following season's contract. After 45 minutes, Shrewsberry walked out and announced he was leaving Hurst. He asked Riggle to go to Los Angeles as his mechanic for a new wheelstander, *L.A. Dart*, but Riggle chose to stay with Hurst. George then instructed Riggle to go to a local Chrysler dealer to pick up new 1966 sheet metal to freshen the look of the car to match the current year's production car.

During the cosmetic update of *Hemi Under Glass*, George asked Riggle if he felt he could pilot the beast. Riggle had helped build the car and had turned wrenches on it since its inception, but he had never taken it down the quarter-mile. "I failed to keep the car straight on the first two attempts. So, on the third try, I started in second gear and the car popped right up where I gave George the thumbs up. I then shifted into third and walked the car straight down the track," recalled Bob.

Riggle served as the driver for Hurst for four years and through two additional chassis changes. The next car was based on the all-new 1967 Barracuda fastback and included two significant changes that Riggle designed. The first was the inclusion of an automatic transmission, so Bob didn't have to concentrate

Riggle lifts all four wheels off the ground at Englishtown in 1966. The tracks paid Hurst upwards of $500 per day in order to entertain the crowds with this wheelstander. Eventually, a class of wheelstand cars developed, as well as match-type races between the wheelstanders. (Photo Courtesy Bob Riggle Collection)

on shifting the car and could focus on keeping it up on two wheels. The second was the installation of steering brakes on each rear wheel, allowing for minor directional changes as the car walked down the track. Late in 1969, Riggle bought the car from Hurst and continued *Hemi Under Glass* through two additional Funny Car renditions. Riggle finally retired the *Hemi Under Glass* moniker by the mid 1970s.

In the late 1990s, Bob Riggle found the remains of the original *Hemi Under Glass* languishing in Canada. The car was in rough condition and was only a rolling shell in 1966 trim. Since rediscovering it, he has painstakingly restored that car and created three additional *Hemi Under Glass* replicas. Until recently he still drove the wheel-standing cars at special events. Bob Riggle completed his last run at the wheel of the 1969 *Hemi Under Glass* at an Oldsmobile meet on August 24, 2019, at the Gilmore Museum in Hickory Corners, Michigan. This incorporated an uncountable total of performances over the historic 53-year run of Bob Riggle driving this spectacular exhibition car.

Hairy Olds

By late 1965, the wheelstanding *Hemi Under Glass* was booked solid, but was no longer a unique sight for the audiences. Not only did Shrewsberry go on to *L.A. Dart* fame, other wheelstanders were being campaigned to entertain crowds at the drag races. Bill Maverick's *Little Red Wagon*, *Mexican Jumping Bean* driven by "Mexican Pete," and Gary Watson's *Corvair Paddy Wagon* van were just a few of the wheelstanding cars now entertaining the race crowds. Soon, a day at the drags wasn't complete unless it had at least two wheelstanders racing side-by-side down the track.

George's personal car was a brand-new, front-wheel-drive 1966 Olds Toronado which, according to long-time Hurst employee Don Lane, was immediately outfitted with an optional Oldsmobile L69 Tri-Power off a 4-4-2. Recognizing the potential of the 425 engine, George decided to build a two-blown engine 425-powered race car in the lighter 4-4-2 body style. In the fall of 1965, as the crew started construction of this project, George searched for a racer who could handle both of the

Hurst shipped *Hemi Under Glass* to Hawaii on a United Airlines transport plane. The car and crew visited the naval hospital in Honolulu. (Photo Courtesy Bob Riggle Collection)

Hurst updated the sheet metal of *Hemi Under Glass* each year to match the Plymouth Barracuda road car. In this photo, the car is parked in front of the Detroit Hurst Performance center after being freshly updated for the 1967 model year. (Photo Courtesy Bob Riggle Collection)

Bob Riggle (driving *Hemi Under Glass*) and Chuck Poole (piloting *Chuckwagon*) were still entertaining the crowds with their wheelstanders in 1972. (Photo Courtesy Bob Riggle Collection)

By 1972, Bob Riggle had changed *Hemi Under Glass* to be a Hemi under a fiberglass body. Here he is having final adjustments made prior to a run. Riggle and his dedication to running and tuning the car helped make *Hemi Under Glass* the legend it is today. (Photo Courtesy Bob Riggle Collection)

According to Bob Riggle, George Hurst did not like the paint scheme of *Hemi Under Glass* in its 1968 trim. This was the view most spectators saw of the exhibition car. Riggle drove *Hemi Under Glass* in many events, but in the 1975 season he suffered a horrific wreck and called it quits. After years of retirement and a chance meeting with Linda Vaughn, who suggested he bring back *Hemi Under Glass*, Riggle found one of the originals and restored it in 1992. (Photo Courtesy Bob Riggle Collection)

2,500-plus-hp engines. George knew just the man and developed a plan before he called his friend and former racer, Joe Schubeck, the owner of Lakewood Industries in the Cleveland, Ohio area.

When George asked former drag racer Schubeck to meet him for dinner, he purposely did not disclose his reason for the meeting. Joe had always been impressed with what George Hurst had accomplished and felt that Lakewood Industries was a potential merger candidate with the growing Hurst-Campbell organization. Joe met George Hurst, Jack Duffy, and Jack Watson over dinner at the Cleveland airport. George greeted him warmly as "Gentleman Joe" and outlined his

In this particular photo, Linda Vaughn (left) is shown at the Indianapolis Speedway leaning on the 1967 Grand Prix convertible. (Photo Courtesy Pete Serio Collection)

The Hurst Grand Prix convertible on February 26, 1967, at Daytona International Speedway. Note the Hurst company photographer. Mario Andretti built a large lead and triumphed over the competition to take the victory. Andretti went on to become the only driver in history to win the Daytona 500, Indy 500, and Formula 1 world championship. (Photo Courtesy Pete Serio Collection)

Hurst always brought a contingent of vehicles to the Indianapolis 500. This 1968 photo was included on the front of their catalog. The H/O was equipped with a 455-ci V-8, and it was more than a match for many of the muscle cars running the streets at that time. (Photo Courtesy Mark Fletcher Collection)

Kaiser Jeep wanted to portray a high-performance image for its line of off-road vehicles, and it wanted to generate more sales, so it enlisted Hurst Performance to come up with a car that broke new ground for the company. Hurst photographed the Jeep with models dressed in each of the armed services uniforms circa 1968. It is rumored that this Jeep was destroyed in a rollover accident. (Photo Courtesy Bob Riggle Collection)

concept for the most outrageous exhibition Funny Car imaginable. It consisted of a dual-engine, dual-controlled, four-wheel-drive Olds featuring two gas pedals, a single brake pedal, two shifters, and double everything else.

He proceeded to explain the controls and the procedure for an exhibition run. Starting with a front-engine-only burn-out, he was then to start the back engine as he re-staged the car at the Christmas tree. At the helm of the dual-engined, 5,000-plus-hp nitromethane drag car, he would rocket down the full distance of the quarter-mile in a cloud of smoke.

Joe had a few concerns about the number of controls, and realized there was more to do than one man could handle. Jack Watson put his fears to rest by describing the new Hurst Line Lock system that hydraulically locked the brakes with a touch of a button mounted right on the shifter. This freed up both feet so he could mash the gas pedal to the floor prior to launch.

The year before, Schubeck had retired from Top Fuel racing to concentrate on his business and explained he wouldn't have the time to run a car and his business. George told him that he had assembled a crew and transporter to haul, prepare, and repair the car. Joe's only responsibility was to meet them at the track, race the car, and then fly back to Cleveland to manage his growing business.

But running the car was only part of the spectacle that Hurst staged with the program, and George continued to explain the production he had envisioned. He described how Joe would wear a fire suit fashioned into a tuxedo, complete with top hat. He would play the role of "Gentleman Joe" and the new Miss Golden Shift Girl, Linda Vaughn, would play his associate. As he climbed into the car for a run down the strip, Linda would exchange his top hat and cane for a helmet, sending him off in royal style.

Hurst was already building the car when Joe was asked to drive it, referred to as "4-4-Two Much" at the time. Dave Landreth, Dick Chrysler, Jack Watson, George DeLorean (brother to John DeLorean of Pontiac), Paul Phelps, Ray Sissner, and John DeJohn all had a hand in building the car.

The car featured a full tube frame, surrounded by 1966 Oldsmobile 4-4-2 sheet metal. Dual supercharged, blown, fuel-injected Olds Toronado 425-ci

The 1968 Hurst Catalog cover had a photo montage of Hurst's expanding line of automotive speed products and its involvement in the racing hobby. (Photo Courtesy Mark Fletcher Collection)

engines were mated to twin Turbo 400 automatic transmissions combined with two Toronado front-wheel-drive transaxles. The rear-mounted engine sat above a reversed front suspension system that had the steering components welded into place, but retaining the independent action, while huge Toronado disc brakes provided stopping power. To keep the weight balanced and provide cooling to the rear engine, John DeJohn of the Hurst team designed the coolant to flow from the front radiator through the tube frame and back.

The car was introduced at the spring NHRA race in Bakersfield, California, on March 5, 1966. *Hairy Hauler*, a special enclosed truck, was built to carry the twin-engined Olds from race to race. At the event, the spectacle was pulled off in true Hurst style. Linda traded out Joe's top hat and cane and sent him off in grand style for his run. And true to its name, Joe described the first drive as "hairy."

"The two major contributing factors," said Joe, "was that all this power was being transferred to the four 10-inch racing slicks, causing the car to hydroplane most of the way down the track. This, combined with the intense torque generated by each engine, caused both front wheels to want to walk around the pivot point of the front suspension." In essence, this created a severe toe-in condition, and the front end plowed all the way down the track.

At the third race in Palmdale, California, Joe was explaining this to his crew chief, Bob "Animal" Lathrum when a young boy, about 12 years old, approached them. He asked, "Why not start with the wheels toed out, so that when you accelerate the wheels go straight?" The solution was so simple and obvious that both wondered why they hadn't thought of it before. At rest, the front suspension was toed out, and under power it aligned itself. As a result, Joe gained far greater control and confidence driving the car. But toeing out the front end was just the first step in sorting out the issues. They continued to experiment until they found the right combination of stronger steering components, revised steering geometry, and this overcompensated front-end alignment.

Even with many improvements, the car was still a handful to drive and Joe constantly fought to keep it going in a straight line. Early in the Hurst *Hairy Olds* program, Joe lost control on a run and slid into a guardrail during an event. The car only suffered superficial

Hairy Olds was another brain child of the ever unconventional George Hurst. This twin-engine, four-wheel-drive beast was certainly aptly named. Its cockpit had dual shifters and dual gas pedals to control two massive fuel-injected and supercharged 425-ci Oldsmobile V-8s. (Photo Courtesy Mark Fletcher)

The original *Hairy Olds* was recreated and is now displayed at the Oldsmobile Museum in Lansing, Michigan. This wickedly heavy and enormously powerful exhibition car posted its maiden run on March 5, 1966, at the Bakersfield Fuel and Gas Meet. (Photo Courtesy Mark Fletcher)

Hairy Olds used two blown Oldsmobile 425 engines, each with an estimated 2,500 hp. The line locks that locked the front wheels for burn-outs made the car driveable because the driver could take his foot off the brake and use both feet to depress the individual gas pedals for each engine. (Photo Courtesy Mark Fletcher)

Dick Chrysler was the traveling mechanic for the original *Hairy Olds*. He had a lot of work to do to keep this spellbinding exhibition car running. To make it four-wheel-drive and do four-wheel burn-outs, the car was fitted with two Tornado transaxles. (Photo Courtesy Mark Fletcher)

damage, so it was repaired and repainted in time for the next race day. But the incident demonstrated that *Hairy Olds* was indeed hairy to drive.

A far more serious accident took place during the second season at Niagara Raceway in upstate New York. The car wore new sheet metal to look like a 1967 Olds 4-4-2. Schubeck did his usual spectacular warm-up presentation. But he noticed that the track was still slick from an earlier rain. While warming up the car at the line, he performed a smoking burn-out with the front engine only. Once stopped, he started the rear engine and backed to the starting line with both engines running.

He staged and set both shifters into drive and pushed the line-lock button so both feet could be used on the dual gas pedals. He raised the RPM of the two 2,500-hp, 35-percent methane-fed Olds engines in unison, released the line locks, and shot down the wet track. He expected to cover the 440 yards in less than 10 seconds, but the car had a surprise in store for him. *Hairy Olds* started the run on the ragged edge of control with tires spinning and smoking, but about 200 yards down the track, the front magneto failed and the front engine shut down.

The front suspension was no longer loaded under the massive torque of the front end and immediately toed the wheels inward. The front end started to plow, and Shubeck lost control of the drag car. *Hairy Olds* headed off the track toward spectators in the bleachers and disaster seemed imminent. The former Top Fuel racer said he had thrilled the crowd during the burn-out and launch, yet these same fans continued to applaud him as he barreled toward them in the stands at more than 100 mph. With the front engine dead and the slick conditions on the track, he fought to regain control of the car as it left the asphalt. The car caught a cable hidden in the standing grass near the edge of the track, which prevented it from reaching the stands, averting a tragedy.

The frightening incident shook Schubeck, and he lost confidence in the car. For him, *Hairy Olds* ultimately proved to be too hairy to drive. He climbed out of it and told his mechanic Bob Lathrum to load it up and take it back to Hurst and Watson. The car was severely damaged and was never run again. Subsequently, Hurst dismantled it for parts. After two years and two heart-pounding wrecks, Joe didn't want to take any more chances.

As an interesting note, Oldsmobile sponsored the exhibition car, and as part of the deal, Schubeck was given the use of a one-off 1966 Olds Toronado station wagon which was used as a push vehicle for the monstrous *Hairy Olds*. For two years, Joe used this car and requested to purchase it at the end of the contract. The car carried no serial number and was driven on manufacturer's plates, so he was forced to return it to Oldsmobile in Lansing, Michigan. He was later told the car survived, but has never seen it again.

Baja Boot

By 1967, professional off-road racing was a legitimate and popular form of motorsport on the West Coast. The automakers and, of course, Hurst recognized that this new kind of racing was an important market for high-performance products and vehicles. Everything from privately entered motorcycles to OEM-backed, purpose-built off-road machines entered these 500- to 1,000-mile desert races. Hurst saw opportunity in this emerging market niche to

The *Hairy Olds* crew assembles for a photo. Shown from left to right, George Hurst, Bob Lathrum, unknown woman, Joe Schubeck, Linda Vaughn, Dick Chrysler, and Jack Watson. (Photo Courtesy Joe Schubeck Collection)

Joe Schubeck fills the Hurst *Hairy Olds* with smoke at Niagara Raceway in 1967. This was just prior to the accident that destroyed the car and caused Joe to retire from racing. (Photo Courtesy Joe Schubeck Collection)

sell its performance products and shifters and chose to participate.

This time Hurst teamed with Vic Hickey, one of General Motors' performance engineers, to build the Hurst *Baja Boot*. Hurst Performance had been providing space at its Madison Heights, Michigan, facility for his engineering team to work on its own projects and Hurst chose to build *Baja Boot* there.

Similar to *Hairy Olds*, *Baja Boot* was built with a full-tube construction on a 112-inch wheelbase. A Chevy 350 powered the mid-engined racer, which carried a Turbo 400 automatic transmission connected to a Dana transfer case and a Corvette independent rear axle. Equipment included a Hurst-supplied Dual Gate shifter, telescoping steering wheel, and power steering. Perching on huge Goodyear 16 x 12-inch off-road balloon tires measuring 36 inches in diameter kept *Boot* connected to Mother Earth. Four-wheel 11-inch Hurst-Airheart disc brake units stopped the vehicle. The result was a well-balanced all-terrain vehicle with four-wheel-drive, immense power, and extreme suspension travel.

Hickey, Drino Miller, and Al Napp, along with the help of the Hurst team, built the car in less than 30 days under a veil of secrecy. The team completed the car for a newly sanctioned race that became the preeminent event in off-road racing—the grueling Mexican Baja

Joe Schubeck (left) was a courageous driver to helm the Hurst *Hairy Olds* while mechanic Bob "Animal" Lathrum spun the wrenches on the wild and difficult-to-drive machine. Both men remained friends throughout their lives. (Photo Courtesy Joe Schubeck Collection)

Hurst recognized the market potential of the emerging off-road sport and getting a strong foothold in it. Vic Hickey and the Hurst team developed *Baja Boot*. This early photo of *Baja Boot* shows it equipped with oversized Goodyear tires. (Photo Courtesy Pete Serio Collection)

At the start of the 1967 Mexican 1000 (soon to be Baja 1000), George Hurst watches *Baja Boot* begin its journey. It was a less than auspicious beginning for the off-road racing program. Drino Miller and Al Napp drove *Baja Boot* in the event, but after 237 miles a broken rear suspension ended their race. (Photo Courtesy Pete Serio Collection)

Hurst presented a press folder for *Baja Boot*'s first event in November of 1967. (Photo Courtesy Pete Serio Collection)

1000. Officiated by the National Off Road Racing Association (NORRA), *Baja Boot* entered the inaugural race on October 31, 1967, on a course running from Tijuana, Baja California, to La Paz, Mexico, covering almost 850 miles. Drino Miller and Al Napp drove *Baja Boot*, but about 237 miles into the race, the car suffered a rear suspension failure, ending its first outing far short of the finish line. The winning team of Vic Wilson and Ted Mangels, in a VW-powered Meyers Manx dune buggy, covered the desert trek in 27 hours and 38 minutes.

Steve McQueen and Bud Ekins also competed in this race and recognized the performance potential of *Baja Boot*. After some late-night negotiations in a hotel lounge with George Hurst, Jack Duffy, and Vic Hickey, they made arrangements to prep and race the vehicle in additional desert events. Steve and Bud entered *Baja Boot* in the Las Vegas–based Stardust 7-11 off-road race in June 1968. They were confident this vehicle was a contender as they were able reach speeds of more than 100 mph across the rough terrain. The pair was running at that pace when they noticed a huge tire pass them up on the race course. It was their own rear wheel that had come loose when the axle broke, and hence they were knocked out of the race.

Hurst and the crew worked night and day to get this innovative machine to the starting line on October 31,1967, and *Baja Boot* showed speed and definite potential. But unfortunately, *Baja Boot* (or *Boot I*) did not make it to the finish line of the Baja 1000. (Photo Courtesy Pete Serio Collection)

The following year, a second Hurst *Baja Boot* was constructed with an improved and beefier suspension. Subsequently, McQueen ended up owning and campaigning *Baja Boot II* along with the original version. After a few more DNFs, it finally won the Baja 500 in 1969 with Bud Ekins and Guy Jones at the wheel. The two cars were raced throughout the 1970s. The original *Baja Boot* has been fully restored, and is now in the hands of exotic car collector James Glickenhaus in New York.

The relatively unknown designer, Vic Hickey, went on to work with General Motors on innovative vehicles and landmark projects. He was directly involved in the suspension design of the first lunar rover and was the project director for the original military High Mobility Multipurpose Wheeled Vehicle, better known as the Humvee.

Goldenrod

Hurst was not going to be left out of the quest for ultimate speed. George teamed with brothers Bob and Bill Summers to set the unlimited speed record at the Bonneville Salt Flats. The Summers brothers built a streamlined 32-foot-long, speed-run vehicle christened the Hurst *Goldenrod*.

A promotional photo of the Hurst *Goldenrod* land speed record car, a 30-foot-long wheeled missile housing four naturally aspirated fuel-injected 426 Hemis. Pat Flannery wrote the record speed of 409.277 mph on the tailfin in lipstick after the record run. (Photo Courtesy Mark Fletcher Collection)

Weighing 6,000 pounds, four naturally-aspirated, fuel-injected 426 Hemis connected to a complex four-wheel-drive transmission system. Like other speed-run vehicles of the day, the Summers had innovatively engineered quite a

Crews prep the Hurst *Goldenrod* prior to its run at the Bonneville Salt Flats. Note the four in-line Hemi engines that were loaned by Chrysler for the speed run. Collectively, these engines produced about 3,000 hp. Of the four engines in the car, two were ganged to a drive axle running to the rear while two were mated to a drive axle running to the front of the car. (Photo Courtesy Bob Riggle Collection)

unique vehicle. In fact, two engines were ganged to drive the front wheels, while the other two were ganged to drive the rear wheels. Each pair of the engines was connected to a transmission and transfer case, and these transfer cases fed into a single driveline running the length of the vehicle. The transaxle for the front wheels was positioned ahead of them. Interestingly, a pair of these engines was fitted to the chassis in reverse. To feed these 426 elephant engines, the car carried three gas tanks. A center tank fed the two mid-mounted engines, while a tank on each end of the vehicle fed the other two.

Bill and Bob (Butch) Summers had created *Goldenrod* in less than a year with an investment of more than $175,000.

This engineering marvel recorded a wheel-driven record of 409.277 mph in the winter of 1965, running pure methanol in the four almost-stock Hemi engines loaned by Chrysler for the record attempt. After returning the loaned power plants back to Chrysler, they retained the car for many years, often showing it during special events at the Salt Flats. The brothers sold the car to the Henry Ford Museum in 2002 where it has been fully restored and still resides today.

Mobile Economy Run

Pontiac had been participating in the Mobil Economy Run for decades. Prior to the EPA setting fuel economy estimates based on running a car on a dynamometer, The Mobil run created huge bragging rights and sales for Detroit automakers. The Mobil Oil officials purchased a new car from a Southern California dealer randomly off the lot, driving it coast to coast and calculating its mileage. The cars then had the engine compartment sealed and a special fuel tank was mounted in the trunk in order to accurately measure fuel consumption. Sometimes each new-car manufacturer shipped specially built models with thinner tires and economy-calibrated carburetors throughout the Southern California market prior to the event. This way, no matter which car was chosen from the dealer's lot, it was prepared for the run.

In 1967, George Hurst and Doc Watson were asked to help prepare the Pontiac cars. It was reported that they were able to hide fuel bladders in the windshield pillar posts on the Bonnevilles that were chosen. When the cars achieved an unprecedented 25 mpg, Mobil officials investigated and quickly disqualified the Pontiac team. John DeLorean was embarrassed over the fiasco, but never admitted to having any knowledge of the cheating. This was the beginning of the end for the contest, and 1968 was the last year of the cross-country economy competition.

In 1967, four of the wheelstanders gathered together at the Los Angeles Coliseum. Clockwise from the left, Bill Maverick's *Little Red Wagon*, Bill Shrewsberry with the *L.A. Dart*, Chuck Poole's *Chuckwagon*, and Bob Riggle with the *Hemi Under Glass*. (Photo Courtesy Bob Riggle Collection)

Hemi Under Glass is one of the most famous if not *the* most famous wheelstanding cars of all time. With Bob Riggle at the controls, *Hemi Under Glass* rode its rear wheels down the quarter-mile and often was the feature attraction at hundreds of drag races and events from 1965 to 1975. Bill Sefton owns this fully restored 1968 *Hemi Under Glass* as well as the other two sheet-metal-skinned *Hemi Under Glass* cars.

The interior of *Hemi Under Glass* is spartan, just as you would expect from a competition car. When driver Riggle first started piloting the car, he had to look out the side window to figure out his position on the track during a run.

Riggle switched to a Camaro body in 1973, but kept the *Hemi Under* (fiber) *Glass* name. (Photo Courtesy Bob Riggle)

AMC Gets Serious

American Motors and Hurst Join Forces

AMC never followed the pack from Detroit and had its own distinct culture, and as a result its cars stood out among other American models. In the early 1960s, AMC didn't embrace the muscle car market as the Big Three had done, and it wasn't until 1967 that AMC truly committed itself to competing for the youth buyer in the muscle car wars. As a result, AMC soon discovered it was late to the game. It needed help to get the company's products up to speed, and Hurst filled that role. Together Hurst and AMC produced some stand-out muscle cars and competition cars—SC/Rambler, Rebel Machine, and Super Stock AMX.

Hurst was paid $200 for every SC/Rambler built. The original A-scheme paint was the most memorable. Everyone noticed when you saw one drive on the street back in 1969, and they still notice today. (Photo Courtesy Rich Truesdell)

CHAPTER 5

Bill Kotula of Michigan now owns the Craig Breedlove AMX. In the early 1970s, AMC gave the car to Arizona-based Randal Rambler. Built from one of the first AMXs off the assembly line, it was specially prepared to set speed records and averaged 140 mph for over 24 hours, breaking the old record by 38 mph. (Photo Courtesy Rich Truesdell)

But let's start at the inception of the AMC Corporation in the mid 1950s.

The merger of the storied Nash and Hudson nameplates in 1954 created American Motors Corporation (AMC), but AMC had little interest in either producing performance cars or racing in sanctioned events. The lone exception came in 1957, when AMC installed its then-new 255-hp, 327-ci V-8 in the intermediate-size Rambler with a, 108-inch-wheelbase and called it the Rebel. With just 1,500 units built, the Rebel was the fastest production car produced in the United States that year—with the exception of the Corvette—and was the precursor of the modern muscle car.

While Ford, General Motors, and Chrysler actively embraced the emerging muscle and pony car markets, AMC was late to the party because it simply wasn't a priority for company management. In fact, AMC CEO Roy Abernethy stated in a 1964 ad that "The only race we are interested in is the human race." While resisting the Big Three's mantra of "Race on Sunday, Sell on Monday," it did make a half-hearted attempt midway through the 1965 model year to appeal to the emerging performance market.

AMC released the midsize Marlin as a sporty two-door "fastback" design. It was similar in appearance to both the early Barracuda and the 1966 Charger. The Marlin came standard with a 232-ci six or one of two V-8s displacing 287 or 327 ci. None of these older engine design offerings were competitive with the more modern "thin wall" castings that the Big Three offered in their pony cars. Overall, it was an abject failure in the marketplace and was discontinued after only three years with only 17,419 units sold.

AMC didn't have a suitable small-block V-8 to fit between the wheel wells of its American compact. Midway through the 1966 model year, this was remedied when an all-new 290-ci V-8 became available. It was first introduced in the Rogue, a top-of-the-line, two-door hardtop. The 290-ci V-8 served as the foundation of all AMC performance engines to follow. As years rolled on, displacement of this block enlarged to 343, 360, 390, and 401 ci. (A 304-ci version was also introduced, but only for mainstream applications.) And the American chassis evolved into three of AMC's best-known performance vehicles: the American-based SC/Rambler, the Javelin pony car, and the two-seat AMX sports car.

After a run of success in the early 1960s, AMC was bleeding red ink by mid decade. This led to the ouster of Roy Abernethy who was replaced in January 1967 by Roy G. Chapin Jr., son of the founder of Hudson Motors. Abernathy's departure signaled a new direction for AMC that included both the production of high-performance cars as well as participating in a variety of motorsports.

The new intermediate Rebel and full-size Ambassador models for 1967 were expected to lead a sales resurgence, but AMC continued to lose money and market share to its stronger rivals. So, new models and a new change in direction was needed. The new leadership

Hurst was one of the sponsors for the Car Craft Speed Spectacular Javelin. Three teams of three mechanics prepared each 343-ci V-8-powered Javelin. Craig Breedlove drove each car at Bonneville Salt Flats. (Photo Courtesy Mark Fletcher)

team of Roy Chapin Jr. (CEO), Victor Raviolo (Vice President Automotive products), R. W. (Bill) McNealy (Vice President of Marketing), and Carl Chakmakian (Director of Performance Products) was confident that designer Richard Teague's upcoming Javelin/AMX product line would be a contender in the muscle car wars, and that it would prove to be a viable option when compared to the Big Three's offerings. But to reach out to the all-important youth market setting the trends, a new marketing approach was needed.

Racing was the hot button for reaching these trendsetters, and AMC needed to race to reach its potential customers. Aftermarket companies, Hurst included, competed in most forms of sanctioned racing. In the days before 24-hour cable sports networks, *ABC's Wide World of Sports* brought racing into the homes of automotive enthusiasts from coast to coast. NASCAR, NHRA, and the emerging Trans-Am racing series offered venues for AMC to tell its story and promote its performance cars.

AMC's Chapin had a personal interest in racing and recognized that the company needed a shift in marketing strategy, so it built a high-performance car for the youth market. Rambler's reputation of product reliability was

The engine compartment of the Hurst Javelin shows the supercharger sitting atop the original 390-ci engine. (Photo Courtesy Mark Fletcher Collection)

well known, and while AMC's five-year, 50,000-mile warranty helped move the mainstream metal, it didn't lure young buyers into AMC showrooms. Something more was needed.

AMC took its first step in the fall of 1967 when the all-new Javelin pony car was introduced. Sized right and well styled, the Javelin was a competitive car in the muscle car market, and it stacked up well against the Barracuda, Camaro, Cougar, Firebird, and Mustang, not needing to make any excuses.

The Javelin was initially a moderate success, but lacked big-block motivation between the shock towers. Its biggest engine displaced just 343 ci, which was far below the displacement of top offerings from AMC's competitors. This shortcoming was addressed in January 1968 with the introduction of a 390-ci version of the AMC small-block V-8, the top engine option for the midyear AMX two-seater.

To get the launch of the AMX off to a flying start, AMC delivered a pair of AMXs—one with a 290-ci engine, the other with a 390—to world land speed record holder Craig Breedlove. Together, the two cars set 106 FIA speed and endurance records. AMC heavily promoted these records during the launch of the AMX, which sold a modest 6,725 units in the abbreviated 1968 model year. Some of these AMXs were privately campaigned in SCCA road racing and NHRA/AHRA drag racing competitions. Both dealer and privately sponsored AMXs were often seen painted in the same red, white, and blue (RWB) paint scheme pioneered on the Breedlove AMXs.

1969 Super Stock AMX

During the summer of 1968, R. W. (Bill) McNealy, Vice President of Marketing at AMC, approached Dave Landreth, who at the time was the Vice President of the Hurst Performance Research Center in Madison Heights, Michigan. During these discussions, McNeely asked Landreth to work in the newly formed AMC Performance Group. Landreth turned down the offer, but recommended a young Hurst employee named Walt Czarnecki for the job. At the beginning of the 1969 model year, Czarnecki started working for Carl Chakmakian in AMC's Marketing and Performance group. Winning put AMC cars in front of potential customers, and that was the department's goal.

AMC's recent financial struggles, new product line, and pursuit of racing also caught the attention of a few young rebels in Detroit. George Hurst and Doc Watson were looking to expand the Hurst Performance Research business and make use of the center's now empty

AMX Super Stock Announcement Letter

In a letter dated November 4, 1968, AMC announced the AMX Super Stock program to specific dealers that had sponsored local drag racers. AMC required 50 individual orders to move forward with the project, which was the minimum needed to homologate the car. The dealers were asked to commit to buy each car, but there were no other details provided other than a promise from AMC that the cars would be prepared for the Super Stock class. The Super Stock AMX cost no more than $5,000 and the trust in Hurst's reputation to build heavyweight contenders. AMC needed 50 firm orders in 30 days or the program would be canceled. AMC had not even published a statement of work for Hurst Performance at this time and literally had nothing at risk if the orders did not come. Over the next 30 days, 40 dealer commitments were obtained and a follow-up letter dated December 2 asked the dealers for an additional 10 orders.

This letter also detailed the equipment on the Hurst Super Stock AMX package, which included:

- Functional cold-air induction hood scoop
- Special manifold and carburetor (AMC PN 4486228)
- Competition clutch and explosion-proof bellhousing
- Performance-modified cylinder heads
- Battery relocated to trunk
- Modified suspension for drag racing application
- Wheel wells altered to accommodate drag slicks

The letter went on to state that these cars would be shipped without the federally mandated emission systems, as these AMXs were intended specifically for drag racing only. They were not street-legal, nor were they eligible for the factory five-year, 50,000-mile warranty.

garage. After the success of Chrysler's Hemi Dodge Dart and Plymouth Barracudas, George saw an opportunity to build a winner in the NHRA Super Stock and the AHRA Formula One C/Stock class. The two-seat AMX was already participating in these classes.

Early in the 1969 production year, Hurst and Watson met with AMC's newly formed performance group of Bill McNealy, J. W. Voepel, Carl Chakmakian, and Hurst's own transplant Walt Czarnecki. At this meeting in the fall of 1968, Hurst and AMC agreed to a two-pronged attack for 1969. The first part of the plan: AMC would field the AMX for professional drivers in Super Stock drag racing. The second part: AMC would install Hurst Competition Plus shifters on the 1969½ AMX and Javelin models equipped with a 4-speed manual transmission for amateur drag racers use. (AMC Performance served as the intermediary between Hurst and AMC dealers who were racing AMC products.

Shirley Shahan stands next to her Hurst SS/AMX, *Drag-On-Lady*, in 1969. She switched from running a Super Stock Dodge to racing a fully race-prepped AMX in 1969. (Photo Courtesy Eddie Stakes Collection)

AMC had limited development funds and, in turn, it appears it invested very little in the Hurst SS AMX project.)

The purpose of this project was to make sure the AMX met the NHRA homologation requirements. In 1968, Super Stock rules greatly restricted what dealers and privateers who campaigned the AMX could change or modify and remain in the class. The factory built 50 race-prepared cars, so the Super Stock AMX met the requirements as a "stock" car.

With 50 guaranteed dealer orders in hand, AMC made a financial investment of a single Frost White production 1969 AMX 390 delivered to Dave Landreth at the Hurst Performance Research Center, in Madison Heights, Michigan, in early December 1968. Over the next 60 days, Hurst extensively modified the AMX into racing trim and unveiled it to the Southern California Dealers Association at the Riverside drag strip in February of 1969.

A well-known female drag racer, Shirley Shahan, who was under contract with the Southern California Dealers Association, piloted the prototype down the quarter-mile drag strip. She came onboard to drive an AMX instead of the Super Stock Dodge she had raced in 1968. The AMX she drove on this February day was very similar to the 52 others being modified by Hurst in a rented facility in Ferndale, Michigan. One noticeable difference was the hood scoop on the prototype car, which was later changed to match the production unit.

Her contract stipulated that she would receive $500 per month, the use of the Southern California Dealers Association co-op Javelin (and the subsequent Hurst Super Stock AMX), a fresh AMC to drive every 5,000 miles, and free parts. Husband H. L. Shahan turned the wrenches and Shirley handled the driving

H.L. Shahan helped Hurst develop the Super Stock AMX prototype, which became the standard for the other 52 units built. Most were raced in the SS/E-G classes where the cars enjoyed success against some fierce competition, such as the Cobra Jet Mustang, big-block Camaros, and Super Stock Dodges. (Photo Courtesy Mark Fletcher Collection)

duties in a team successful effort that saw her establish a new SS/D stock record in 1969.

The American Motors agreement with Hurst was similar to the Hemi Dart and Barracuda program of the year before. American Motors sequentially built the 52 cars on the east line in Kenosha, Wisconsin, as standard Frost White 390-ci, 4-speed cars. They all had the standard charcoal vinyl interior and carpeting, with standard bucket seats, factory dash, instrumentation, and headliner. The most notable difference was the heater and AM radio delete. The assembly performed three unique changes. First, assembly workers removed all sound-deadening materials and hood insulation. Second, the non-emission exhaust manifolds reserved for automatic cars were installed. All related emission components were omitted. Third, all cars were equipped with a 4.44:1 rear axle ratio that previously had only been available as a dealer-installed option.

The production run started with serial number A9M397X213560 and concluded with A9M397X213611. They rolled off the assembly line the last week of January 1969 and were delivered to Hurst. The agreement was for AMC to ship 26 cars to the Hurst Performance Research center in Madison Heights. Doc Watson recalls that AMC attempted to deliver the second half of the order, only to have the cars turned away due to space issues at Hurst. Pictures of the AMXs during the conversion show that the cars were delivered with rocker moldings and four standard black wheels that were reported to be Javelin spare tires.

Hurst removed the following components: front sway bar, one of the two factory horns, lower body rocker moldings, factory air cleaner assembly, intake and exhaust manifolds, carburetor, space-saver spare and jack, underhood battery tray, and assorted brackets and braces. (The ever-frugal AMC corporation requested these discarded components to be returned to them for use on the production line.)

Hurst created a production line for the cars in the warehouse. Each AMX was given a unique build number, and a handwritten checklist was placed on the windshield to track each car. The underhood list showed the following eight steps to each conversion: pistons, heads, flywheel, clutch, intake, carbs, linkage, and ignition.

A second more comprehensive 20-step check-off sheet has also been found in some of the Hurst Super Stock AMX cars.

The factory 390 and 4-speed transmission were pulled from each car.

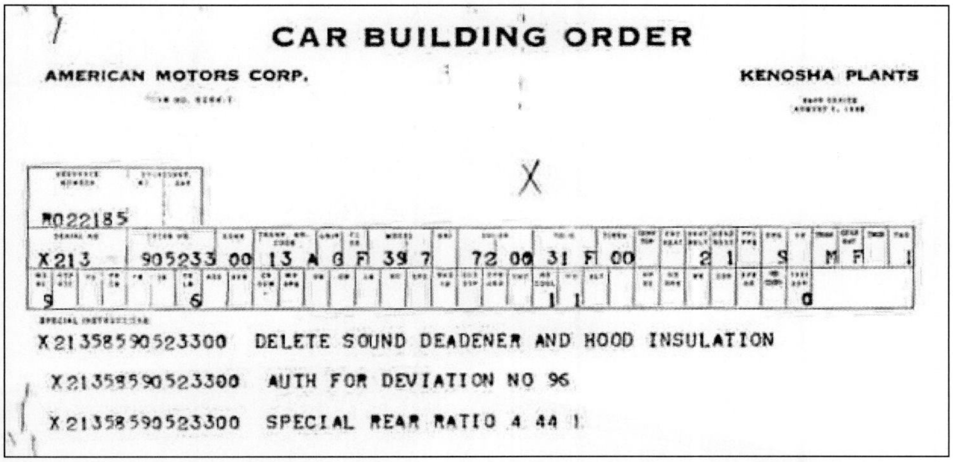

CAR BUILDING ORDER

AMERICAN MOTORS CORP. KENOSHA PLANTS

X

M022185

X213 905233 00 13 A G F 39 7 72 00 31 F 00 2 1 S M F 1

X21358590523300 DELETE SOUND DEADENER AND HOOD INSULATION

X21358590523300 AUTH FOR DEVIATION NO 96

X21358590523300 SPECIAL REAR RATIO 4 44 1

Each SS AMX was specially prepared with three unique build requirements. The sound deadener, hood insulation, and emission control system were deleted at the factory. A stout 4.44:1 rear axle ratio was installed. Other than these modifications all SS/AMXs were production line prior to being modified by Hurst. (Photo Courtesy Tom Benvie collection)

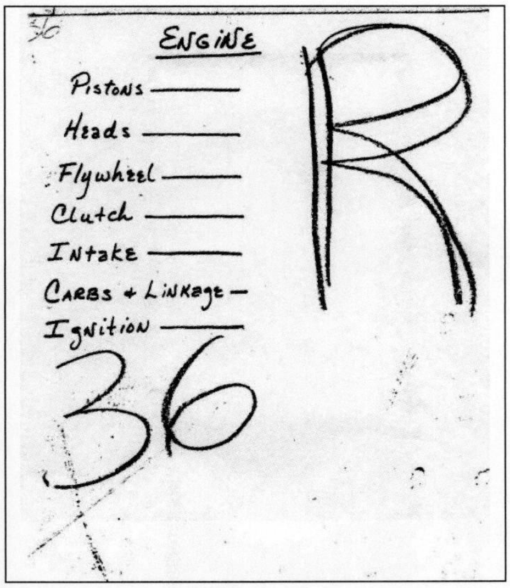

Hurst used a checklist to track the changes to each engine prior to its install into the finished race-prepared car. This check sheet was from Hurst car number 36. (Photo Courtesy Tom Benvie Collection)

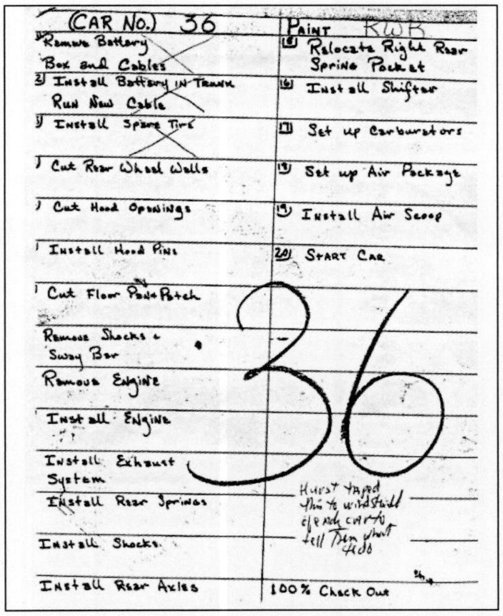

These hand-written cards were taped to the windshield of each SS/AMX's while Hurst preformed the conversions into race prepared cars. (Photo Courtesy Tom Benvie Collection)

1969 AMC Hurst SC/Rambler B-Scheme

One of the wildest Hurst efforts was in conjunction with American Motors Corporation. A total of 1,515 AMC SC/Ramblers were built in two different paint schemes. Owned by co-author Mark Fletcher, this is an example of the more restrained "B" scheme. (Photos Courtesy Rich Truesdell)

AMC dealers that committed to purchase the Super Stock AMXs also sponsored most of the racers running them. Chuck Milner Rambler in Shreveport, Louisiana, campaigned this car as *Chuck's Luck*. (Courtesy Eddie Stakes)

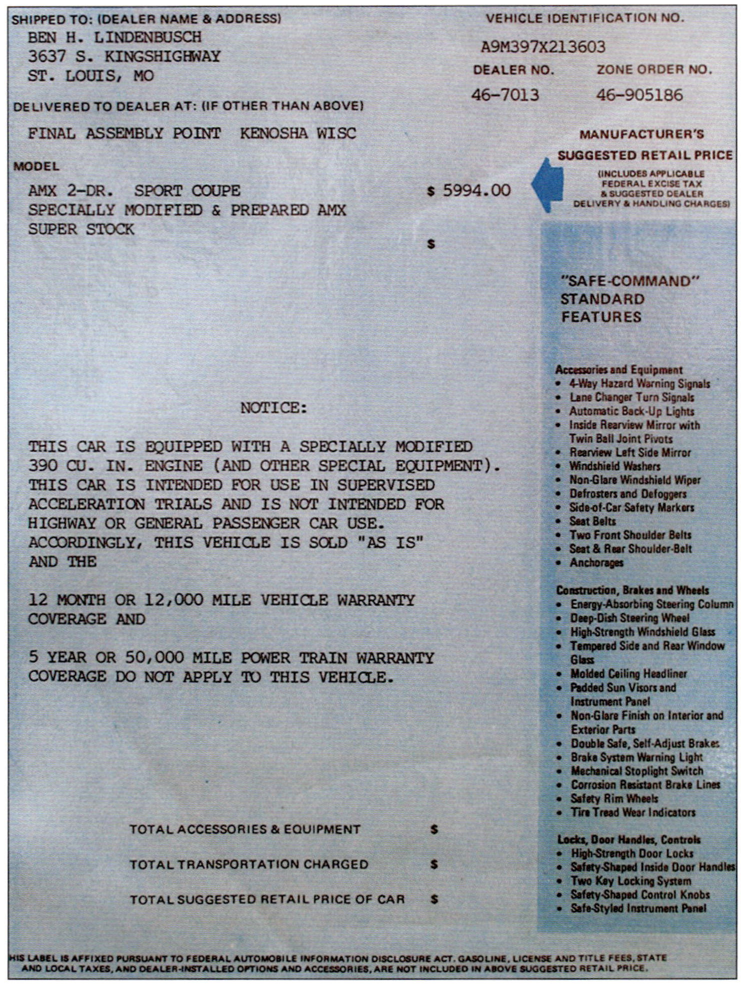

SHIPPED TO: (DEALER NAME & ADDRESS)
BEN H. LINDENBUSCH
3637 S. KINGSHIGHWAY
ST. LOUIS, MO

VEHICLE IDENTIFICATION NO.
A9M397X213603

DEALER NO. 46-7013
ZONE ORDER NO. 46-905186

DELIVERED TO DEALER AT: (IF OTHER THAN ABOVE)
FINAL ASSEMBLY POINT KENOSHA WISC

MANUFACTURER'S SUGGESTED RETAIL PRICE
(INCLUDES APPLICABLE FEDERAL EXCISE TAX & SUGGESTED DEALER DELIVERY & HANDLING CHARGES)

MODEL
AMX 2-DR. SPORT COUPE $ 5994.00
SPECIALLY MODIFIED & PREPARED AMX
SUPER STOCK $

NOTICE:

THIS CAR IS EQUIPPED WITH A SPECIALLY MODIFIED 390 CU. IN. ENGINE (AND OTHER SPECIAL EQUIPMENT). THIS CAR IS INTENDED FOR USE IN SUPERVISED ACCELERATION TRIALS AND IS NOT INTENDED FOR HIGHWAY OR GENERAL PASSENGER CAR USE. ACCORDINGLY, THIS VEHICLE IS SOLD "AS IS" AND THE

12 MONTH OR 12,000 MILE VEHICLE WARRANTY COVERAGE AND

5 YEAR OR 50,000 MILE POWER TRAIN WARRANTY COVERAGE DO NOT APPLY TO THIS VEHICLE.

TOTAL ACCESSORIES & EQUIPMENT $
TOTAL TRANSPORTATION CHARGED $
TOTAL SUGGESTED RETAIL PRICE OF CAR $

"SAFE-COMMAND" STANDARD FEATURES

Accessories and Equipment
- 4-Way Hazard Warning Signals
- Lane Changer Turn Signals
- Automatic Back-Up Lights
- Inside Rearview Mirror with Twin Ball Joint Pivots
- Rearview Left Side Mirror
- Windshield Washers
- Non-Glare Windshield Wiper
- Defrosters and Defoggers
- Side-of-Car Safety Markers
- Seat Belts
- Two Front Shoulder Belts
- Seat & Rear Shoulder-Belt
- Anchorages

Construction, Brakes and Wheels
- Energy-Absorbing Steering Column
- Deep-Dish Steering Wheel
- High-Strength Windshield Glass
- Tempered Side and Rear Window Glass
- Molded Ceiling Headliner
- Padded Sun Visors and Instrument Panel
- Non-Glare Finish on Interior and Exterior Parts
- Double Safe, Self-Adjust Brakes
- Brake System Warning Light
- Mechanical Stoplight Switch
- Corrosion Resistant Brake Lines
- Safety Rim Wheels
- Tire Tread Wear Indicators

Locks, Door Handles, Controls
- High-Strength Door Locks
- Safety-Shaped Inside Door Handles
- Two Key Locking System
- Safety-Shaped Control Knobs
- Safe-Styled Instrument Panel

HIS LABEL IS AFFIXED PURSUANT TO FEDERAL AUTOMOBILE INFORMATION DISCLOSURE ACT. GASOLINE, LICENSE AND TITLE FEES, STATE AND LOCAL TAXES, AND DEALER-INSTALLED OPTIONS AND ACCESSORIES, ARE NOT INCLUDED IN ABOVE SUGGESTED RETAIL PRICE.

The original sticker price of the SS AMX was not cheap. The dealer cost for the car was $4,870. For the cost of one SS/AMX you could purchase two 1969 SC/Ramblers, and they came with a warranty. (Photo Courtesy Rich Truesdell)

While out of the car, the pistons and heads were swapped in favor of high-performance units. An Edelbrock cross-ram intake and two Holley carbs were installed. The ignition system was changed, and a heavy-duty Schiefer steel flywheel and 10-inch Borg and Beck clutch were installed with the Lakewood blow-proof bellhousing. A stock 2.23:1 low super BorgWarner T-10 transmission and Hurst Competition Plus Shifter with separate reverse lockout were also part of the package. This was then re-installed into the vehicle. Hurst did not have to worry about placing the correct engine back into its original car, as AMC did not stamp engines with the vehicle identification number (VIN).

Hurst requested 50 extra sets of heads from American Motors so it could send them to Crane for porting and polishing. This assembly process allowed a faster conversion and quicker delivery to the dealers. However, AMC didn't supply the heads, so Hurst removed the heads from each AMX, and sent them to Crane. Once Crane had performed the work and returned the heads, the Hurst team re-installed them on the Super Stockers.

Domed and forged J&E 12.3:1 pistons replaced the stock pistons, while the stock crank, rods, cam, and oil pan were retained. Crane enlarged the combustion chambers from the stock 50 cc to 58 cc. They incorporated 2.065-inch intakes with 1.74-inch exhaust valves. The ignition systems were upgraded to a Mallory unit with mechanical tach drive distributor. The combination of these changes provided an advertised increase of 25 hp from the stock 315 hp. The NHRA estimated output at a more realistic 405 hp and later increased this rating to 420 hp. AMC underrated the horsepower on its next Hurst project as well.

In addition, Hurst performed several changes in the conversion facility. The floor was modified so the Hurst Competition Shifter with a separate reverse lockout lever could be installed. The rear end was an AMC Corporate 20 (12-bolt cover) Twin-Grip with Henry's Hi-Tuff forged axle shafts in order to eliminate the anemic stock keyway system that commonly allowed for spun axles. Rear springs were exchanged for Rockwell units and the right rear spring pocket was relocated. Rear shocks were exchanged for Monroe 50/50s. The fronts were changed to Monroe 90/10 racing shocks. A metal hood scoop was installed to cover the two holes cut in the hood for velocity stacks mounted on the Holley carbs and Edelbrock cross-ram intake manifold. The rear wheel wells were cut

This Powder Puff race poster promises that Hurst girls Linda Vaughn and Nikki Phillips will be on hand to watch Shirley Shahan and five others compete on a Wednesday night in July of 1969. (Photo Courtesy Mark Fletcher Collection)

The owner added this Hurst Equipped dash emblem to his 1969 SS/AMX. (Photo Courtesy Rich Truesdell)

from the standard 29-inch opening to a radius of 32 inches to accommodate larger racing slicks for traction. Interestingly, some cars were designated for the AMC racing red, white, and blue paint while others were delivered in the factory Frost White paint.

A popular rumor is that Hurst installed a modified three-piece crossmember enabling the pan to be dropped out the bottom for inspection and service of the crank, rods, and main bearings. But there is no documentation to support this claim. Racers most likely made the crossmember modification themselves, as not all documented cars had this conversion, and those discovered vary in design and application.

AMC introduced factory-approved performance parts under the Group 19 banner in its 1969 parts catalogs distributed to its dealers. Carl Chakmakian and Walt Czarnecki's embryonic Performance Division introduced the Group 19 parts used in each of the 52 Hurst AMXs because engine components required AMC part numbers for Super Stock homologation.

Initially, the completed AMX Super Stock cars were returned to AMC in Kenosha, Wisconsin, so they could be shipped with regular production cars. However, due to the delay in completing the cars, along with the impatience of the dealers and their racers, Hurst shipped the cars directly to the designated dealers. Locked inside the trunk was a stash of parts, including two air velocity stacks, Hurst T-handle, and various decals from the component manufacturers used in the Hurst conversion. The MSRP was $5,994, or about $2,000 more than a fully-equipped new 390 AMX. The dealer cost was approximately $4,870, keeping AMC's initial promise of being less than $5,000.

By mid March, Hurst had completed the conversions and started shipping cars to dealers. At that time, the NHRA season was well under way, and dealers and their racers were obviously eager to start competing with their cars. Many were disappointed to find that the cars still had the factory cam, crank, and rods, and that the engine had not been blueprinted. Each needed to perform their own performance engine build in order to be competitive in the Super Stock class.

The Hurst Super Stock AMX promptly made a name for itself as a fierce competitor. Those fortunate drivers also found their own names in *Hot Rod*, *Super Stock*, *Popular Hot Rodding*, *Car Craft*, and other magazines. Most were raced in the SS/E-G classes where they competed with the likes of Sox and Martin. This class was full of successful and now-famous drivers who had dominated the class with Super Stock Dodges, Cobra Jet Mustangs, and big-block Camaros. With Shirley's husband, H.L. Shahan, tuning her car, she enjoyed a degree of success with a run of 10.97 seconds at a speed of 125.69 mph at the 1969 Orange County Raceway Super Stock meet. On the East Coast the S&K AMX driven by Fred Dellis set an AHRA World record with an 11:08 elapsed time at 127.11 mph.

In 1969, Hurst performed two major conversions for AMC. The Hurst crew built the SC/Rambler at the AMC factory in Kenosha, Wisconsin, but the company also converted 52 Super Stock AMXs at the Hurst facility in Ferndale, Michigan. (Photo Courtesy Rich Truesdell)

Jeff Malacaine owns this Hurst Super Stock AMX that has been restored to how it was raced in 1969. The driveline for these cars was heavy duty. It featured a Schiefer steel flywheel and 10-inch Borg and Beck clutch, Lakewood blowproof bellhousing, and BorgWarner T-10 transmission. (Photo Courtesy Rich Truesdell)

The *Pete's Patriot* AMX has been restored to its as-raced condition. (Photo Courtesy Mark Fletcher)

Shirley Shahan drove one of the original Hurst SS AMXs for the Southern California Dealers Association in 1969. (Photo Courtesy Mark Fletcher)

1970 Super Stock AMX

Only a few months later, AMC introduced the updated 1970 AMX with a different hood and grille to the public. In order to maintain a consistency between the track and the showroom cars, AMC sent a 1970 update kit to each of the Super Stock AMX dealers.

This kit included the 1970 hood, front bumper, grille, fender extensions, lights, and wiring. It also included the rear quarter end caps and the taillight panel. Inside, the conversion included a new dash assembly and two high-back bucket seats. The idea was that these parts would change the appearance of the 1969 Hurst AMX to look like a new 1970 model.

If updated to the 1970 configuration, the cars could be equipped with the upgraded 1970 dog-port heads and larger head bolts, which provided better flow and an estimated 25 more hp. Some cars were converted, but the NHRA caught on and quickly banned the cars from racing as 1970 models.

AMC did not upgrade the front suspension from the 1969 trunnion to the new-for-1970 upper ball joint design. This easily identified AMC's rouse, and most of the cars were converted back to 1969 trim in order to continue racing.

SC/Rambler

AMC reserved the Rambler name for its smallest car in 1969. This was the last year for the Rambler, and this designation was allocated for the American body. AMC was feeling the pinch from import competitors, especially Volkswagen, Datsun, and Toyota. Each offered a small fuel-efficient car for less than $2,000. AMC countered with a lightweight Rambler two-door sedan equipped with a 199-ci six-cylinder engine mated to a 3-speed manual transmission resulting in a whopping gain of 20 mpg. This base stripper came with rubber floormats and a very short list of available options. At $1,998 it was the lowest price American-built automobile available.

AMC and Hurst met in the fall of 1968 to discuss the Super Stock AMX and the subsequent partnership that manufactured 52 Hurst cars. During these meetings Dave Landreth shared an idea that he and Jim Wangers of Pontiac GTO fame had developed. They had envisioned an AMC super car similar to the original 1964 GTO. Five years had passed since the introduction of the big-block Tempest, and the public's perception of fast cars included the expectation of a more dynamic appearance. The compact-size Rambler American and Rogue two-door hardtops shared a similar overall appearance to the early GTO but were 600 pounds lighter. The concept was to install the same 390 AMC engine that propelled the Super Stock AMX into the lighter 1969 Rambler Rogue two-door hardtop and add an attention-getting red, white, and blue paint scheme. AMC then offered these 500 modified Rogue hardtops to the public.

Walt Czarnecki took the idea to AMC's engineering department. The engineers were concerned that the Rogue chassis could not handle the power of the 390-ci V-8, especially in two-door hardtops. In 1967, when AMC slotted the

Shirley Shahan speaks with Mark Donohue (right) and Roger Penske (left) in the pits during the 1970 Trans-Am season. (Photo Courtesy Mark Fletcher)

Pete's Patriot, *Drag-On-Lady*, and another SS/AMX in 1970 AMX trim are displayed at the 2009 AMO national convention in Denver, Colorado. These cars weighed in at 3,050 pounds because they were stripped of all unnecessary equipment, such as anti-roll bars, radios, horns, and so forth. (Photo Courtesy Mark Fletcher)

343-ci, 280-hp, V-8 into American series, the unibody chassis suffered from flexing. Likewise, the 1967 Rogue suffered from flex in the unibody after severe and repeated drag racing launches. AMC had added subframe connectors under all Americans starting in the 1968 calendar year to add more chassis rigidity and meet more stringent federal crash requirements. The additional reinforcement also strengthened the car against the increased torque that the larger V-8 bore upon the car. With engineering's green light, the SC/Rambler was born.

Hurst was responsible for design and marketing, and it was agreed that AMC would maintain manufacturing on the assembly line. AMC put the car together from existing parts bins.

The components included:

- Power front disc brakes
- AMC Corporate 20 12-bolt rear differential with 3.54:1 gears
- Twin-Grip differential with AMX-style torque links
- 20:1 quick-ratio manual steering
- BorgWarner Super T-10
- 4-speed with Hurst Performance Shifter
- Hurst T-handle
- AMX-designed handling package with severe-duty front sway bar, front and rear springs and shocks
- Heavy-duty cooling system with seven-blade fan and shroud
- Stock Rogue interior in charcoal vinyl fully reclining split bench seats
- Deluxe wood grain three-spoke steering wheel
- Factory Magnum 500 rally wheels painted bright blue
- Goodyear Polyglas redline tires

Unique SC/Rambler performance parts included functional hood scoop, hood pins, and teardrop-shaped mirrors that were identical to the ones used on the 1968 Mercury XR7-G Cougar and the 1969 Hurst/Oldsmobile.

The car sported three special SC/Hurst emblems placed in front of the production Rambler moniker in addition to the front fender's AMX 390 Crossed Flag emblem. A Sun ST-635 chrome tachometer was strapped to the steering column for a boy racer look. The exhaust system consisted of stock manifolds with a full air-injection system, and two Thrush Hush glass-pack mufflers that barely reduced the decibel level of the combustion process.

Similar to the arrangement with the Super Stock AMX, AMC gave Hurst a single production-line Rogue with a 390 in order to develop the prototype. The plain-Jane two-door hardtop was lightning fast, but did not stand out in a crowd. George Hurst was a fantastic promoter, and what this car needed was presentation. The car was a brick in the wind and needed something special in order to stand out.

The SC/Rambler was introduced in what was to become the "A" paint scheme. Being painted red, white, and blue from the factory was a major departure from the normal conservative AMC marketing. (Photo Courtesy Mark Fletcher)

A giant hood scoop resembling a mailbox helped the car shed its econo-car image. Red-painted sides (similar to the two-tone trim on the 1967 Rogue) accented the car, while a wide, bright blue decal stripe over the full length of the vehicle helped give it a distinctive look. The final touch was an arrow pointing toward the hood scoop, denoting that this Rambler was equipped with the 390-ci V-8. This over-the-top paint scheme distinguished the SC/Rambler from its American and Rogue counterparts. To balance the taxi cab appearance of the all-charcoal interior, special red, white, and blue striped headrests were added for some panache.

"We took a bar of soap and made it into French perfume," stated AMC's Walt Czarnecki on the SC Super Car Hurst Rambler. Linda Vaughn reminisced about the SC that George Hurst gave to her in 1969, "We took it out in the parking lot at the Warminster plant and lined up Coke cans." She then dropped the clutch and popped the front wheels right over the can without hitting it. She only kept the car about six months as she "preferred the refinement offered by the Hurst/Olds."

This complete racing package was nationally advertised at $2,998, with a full five-year, 50,000-mile drivetrain warranty. The SC/Rambler was competitive with its direct rival in the low-buck, stripped-down muscle car marketplace, the 335-hp 383-ci Plymouth Road Runner. Weighing almost 600 pounds less than the cartoon budget-priced Mopar, the SC/Rambler was more than competitive, both in price and performance.

Hurst and AMC were eager to race the car in the NHRA F stock class. To qualify for this category, the car needed more than 10 pounds per horsepower. For this reason, the official factory curb weight was listed at 3,160 pounds, a full 160 pounds more than its real curb weight. In addition, the horsepower rating was the same as a stock 390-ci V-8 found in the Javelin and AMX, which lacked the benefit of the mailbox-size hood scoop Ram Air and the low back pressure exhaust system. Real peak horsepower was closer to 335 to 340 in full-factory dress. The only available option was the factory-installed AM radio. Air conditioning was not an option.

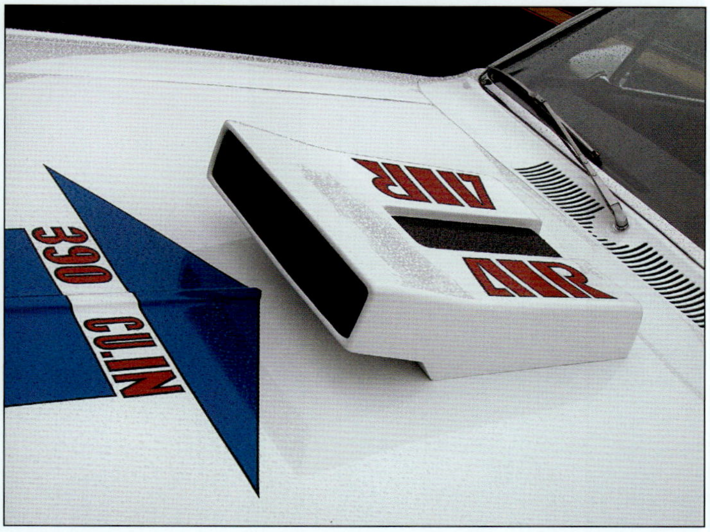

Hurst-designed graphics told the air where to go. A similar arrow and the block letters almost made it into production on the 1969 H/O hood. (Photo Courtesy Rich Truesdell)

AMC created a three-color flyer that was handed out to potential customers at the local dealers. Not every dealer chose to sell the SC/Rambler, as it was a big departure from the normal AMC product offering. (Photo Courtesy Mark Fletcher)

Once again, Hurst went to Demmer for the unique hood scoop. The accompanying hood graphics were similar to those proposed to Olds for the 1969 H/O on the prototype car.

According to the contract, AMC paid Hurst a royalty of $200 per car. AMC invited George Hurst to drive the first SC/Rambler off the assembly line. When the first car was scheduled to roll off the assembly line, it was 20 degrees in Kenosha, and George did not care for cold weather. He had remembered his cold cross-country trip from 10 years before, so he sent Dick Chrysler to represent Hurst at the SC/Rambler's unveiling.

Conversions started in early February 1969 with a planned production run of 500 units. All assembly was done on Kenosha's east production line, which produced all Rambler Americans, Javelins, and AMXs. Rumor swirled that Hurst installed the specific parts at a separate location. In reality, the SC/Rambler was fully assembled on the AMC production line with the black pinstripe outlining the red sides being done by hand on the third floor of the plant, prior to shipping directly to the dealer.

AMC's original plan was to build only 500 units and AMC had more than 1,700 dealers, so many dealers did not receive an SC/Rambler. Some of the more conservative dealers said they could sell the car if it had toned-down graphics. Simultaneously, the initial dealer frenzy for the 1969 AMX production had slowed from a peak of 325 per week in October to a low of 123 units per week in February. Therefore, AMC did not meet its forecasted sales goals of 10,000 AMXs for 1969, and as a result, AMC had an overstock of more than 1,000 390 V-8s that were already scheduled by year's end. Management decided to extend the original production by 1,000 units, and add a second production run (with a more conservative paint scheme), which was received with a flurry of follow-up orders.

Collectors have referred to the second more sedate paint scheme, designed by head AMC design engineer Dick Teague, as the B-scheme. It was an all-white car without the bold blue over-the-top stripe, graphic hood lettering, or full red sides of the previous A-scheme of the first 500 cars. The bright blue wheels remained with a matching lower body-side stripe covering the bottom 6 inches. The requisite red stripe was located above the blue with a white border separating the two colors. These stripes were applied in the form of a decal set, with the red and blue bordered in black pinstripe.

The earliest documented B-scheme car was built during the week of March 15, 1969. Owners of surviving SC/Ramblers can track their cars on the 1512 Registry. For many years, many enthusiasts believed that AMC built the first 500 cars in the original A-scheme paint job, including the bold blue over-the-top stripe. It was reported that AMC then built 500 B-scheme SC/Ramblers, followed by the last batch of 500 units, which were produced in the original A-scheme. The registry, combined with original owner and documentation of known histories, proves this is wrong.

The first 45 days of production were all A-scheme versions. Once the production of B-scheme cars commenced in mid March, production of A- and B-scheme SC/Ramblers was intermingled and continued until the third week of June. Final production came to 1,512 units. The toned-down B-scheme paint treatment accounted for a little less than one-third of total production. Actual build numbers were not broken down by paint. It is estimated, based on reported paint choices on the 1512 Registry, that only about 20 percent (300) of total production was B-scheme SC/Ramblers.

At the time, AMC was the only American auto manufacturer to advertise

NOW SOME OF THE GOODIES CAN'T BE SEEN.

Take that 10½" heavy-duty clutch, for example. Or the Twin-Grip differential with 3.54 to 1 cogs. There are even heavy-duty U-joint spiders and special rear-axle torque links.

Then there are heavy-duty springs and shocks . . . a larger-diameter front sway bar . . . heavy-duty cooling system . . . power disc brakes (in front) . . . and special 20:1 ratio AMX-type manual steering.

Of course you'll also find all of the regular Rogue safety and comfort equipment including the Weather-Eye Heating and Ventilating system, plus electric windshield wipers.

That's it. The SC/RAMBLER from Hurst and American Motors.

There is one more thing, however.

It lists for exactly $2998!*

We think that makes the SC/RAMBLER unbeatable on *every* count.

1969 SC/RAMBLER SPECIFICATIONS
(See regular sales catalog for basic Rambler Rogue specs)

- 390 Cubic-inch AMX V-8 Engine (315 HP).
- 4-speed all-synchromesh close-ratio transmission.
- Special Hurst 4-speed shift linkage with T-handle.
- Sun tach mounted on steering column.
- Dual exhaust system with special-tone mufflers and chrome extensions.
- Functional hood scoop for cold-air induction.
- "Twin-Grip" differential.
- 3.54:1 (11-39) axle ratio.
- 10½" diameter clutch.
- Power disc brakes (front).
- Rear axle torque links.
- Handling package (larger-diameter front sway bar plus heavy-duty springs and shocks).
- Heavy-duty cooling system (heavy-duty radiator, "Power-Flex" fan and fan shroud).
- A 20:1 AMX manual steering ratio.
- Special application of new Red, White and Blue exterior colors.
- Two hood "tie-downs" with locking safety pins and cables.
- Custom "teardrop" racing mirrors (one each side).
- Custom-finished grille.
- Custom SC/RAMBLER-Hurst emblem on front fenders/rear panel.
- Mag-styled steel wheels, 14" x 6" specially painted blue to compliment exterior color scheme.
- Five E70x14 Goodyear Polyglas™ wide-tread, red-line tires.
- Sports steering wheel.
- Custom-upholstered head restraints in red, white and blue vinyl.
- All-vinyl charcoal seat upholstery with full carpeting.
- Individually-adjustable reclining seats.

*Manufacturer's suggested retail price federal taxes included, state and local taxes, if any, destination charges excluded. All items of equipment mentioned, included.

SC/RAMBLER HURST

American Motors, whose policy is one of continuous improvement, reserves the right to discontinue or change specifications, models, equipment or prices at any time without incurring obligation.

The SC/Rambler carried limited slip differential in the 12-bolt rear end, and the power was fed to it through a BorgWarner Super T-10 4-speed. (Photo Courtesy Mark Fletcher)

A Rambler that does the quarter mile in 14.3.

American Motors and Hurst have collaborated on the custom-built SC/Rambler.

It's a limited production car; only 500 units are planned at this time.

Enough to qualify the SC/Rambler for stock classes in drag racing.

The price is $2,998.[1] Which is very little money when you see what it buys.

1. 390 cubic inch AMX V-8 Engine.
2. 4-speed all-synchromesh close-ratio transmission.
3. Special Hurst 4-speed shift linkage with T-handle.
4. A Sun tach mounted on the steering column.
5. Dual Exhaust system with special-tone mufflers and chrome extensions.
6. Functional Hood Scoop for cold-air induction.
7. Twin-Grip differential.
8. 10½" diameter clutch.
9. 3.54:1 axle ratio.
10. Power disc brakes (front).
11. Rear axle torque links.
12. Handling package (heavy-duty front sway bar plus heavy-duty springs and shocks).
13. Heavy-duty cooling system (heavy-duty radiator, power-flex fan and fan shroud).
14. A 20:1 manual steering ratio.
15. Special application of new Red, White and Blue exterior colors.
16. Two hood Tie-Downs with locking safety pins and cables.
17. Custom Tear-Drop racing mirrors (one each side).
18. Custom Grille.
19. Custom SC/Rambler-Hurst emblem on front fenders/rear panel.
20. Mag styled wheels, 14" x 6", painted specially to complement exterior color scheme.
21. Five E 70 x 14 Goodyear Polyglas™ Wide-Tread tires.
22. Sports steering wheel.
23. Custom-upholstered head restraints in Red, White and Blue vinyl.
24. All-vinyl charcoal seat upholstery with full carpeting.
25. Individually adjustable reclining seats.

There's more, but you get the idea.

With this car you could make life miserable for any GTO, Roadrunner, Cobra Jet or Mach 1.

American Motors'/Hurst SC/Rambler

1. Manufacturer's suggested retail price includes all items listed and federal taxes. State and local taxes, if any, and destination charges excluded.

AMC advertised a 14.3-second quarter-mile time for the Hurst-prepared SC/Rambler, weighing in at 3,160 pounds and equipped with AMC's largest V-8, the 340-hp 390. They went on to list the go-fast components that were included in the $2,995 list price. (Photo Courtesy Mark Fletcher)

SC/Rambler was built for straight-line acceleration, but it was designed to take curves as well. The car featured an AMX-designed handling package with a heavy-duty front sway bar, and front and rear springs and shocks. (Photo Courtesy Rich Truesdell)

AMC's recipe was big cubes, high horsepower, and light weight in this little Rambler hardtop. A giant hood scoop screamed high performance to all onlookers. Hurst built 1,512 SC/Ramblers without the optional power steering or air conditioning. (Photo Courtesy Rich Truesdell)

The SC/Rambler was designed with the luxury of a taxi cab. Standard charcoal interior allowed AMC to keep the price at an attention-getting $2,998 per car. The only option available was the AM radio. (Photo Courtesy Rich Truesdell)

The Hurst Rambler was offered in two paint schemes. The original A-scheme (rear) was considered too loud for some buyers. AMC designer Dick Teague tamed down the graphics, which were offered as the B-scheme mid run. The B-scheme is owned by co-author Mark Fletcher, and the A-scheme is owned by AMC collector Bob Hodson. (Photo Courtesy Mark Fletcher)

Off-Road Rambler Racers

AMC was determined to compete with the Big Three in major forms of racing. The Super Stock AMX was built for NHRA Super Stock competition. Craig Breedlove, piloting the AMX, set many endurance and speed records. AMC was also competing in Trans-Am road racing. While AMC didn't post a victory, Javelin racers had a string of impressive results. But AMC was not considering a foray into off-road racing until actor/racer James Garner approached the company about fielding the Rambler in off-road competition.

Garner and AMC came to agreement, and for three years, Garner and his American International Racers (AIR) were under contract to race the Ramblers in off-road competition. The first race the team entered was the Baja 500 on June 11-12, 1969. The following race story appeared in the 1969 dealer newsletter, *The AMC Redliner Report*.

> Ensenada, Baja California, Mexico: An American Motors SC/Rambler from James Garner's American International Racing team won the PASSENGER CAR category June 11th-12th in the Baja 500 Off Road racing event, an automotive enduro race that stands as a challenge to both vehicle and driver.
>
> A specially prepared team of bright red, white and blue American Motors' sedans was entered in Category I and IV. Category I is open to production two-wheel-drive vehicles while Category IV is open to four-wheel-drive experimental vehicles.
>
> This race is sanctioned by NORRA (National Off Road Racing Association) and is considered one of the toughest endurance races in the world, negotiating hundreds of miles of rocky, dusty terrain through the remote Baja (lower) California peninsula.
>
> Veteran Grand Prix race driver Bob Bondurant of Santa Ana with his co-driver, Tony Murphy of Los Angeles roared across the finish line in a SC/Rambler after 19 hours and five minutes of racing around a treacherous 550-mile long course that circles the upper 1/2 of the Baja California peninsula and return to the finish line in the center of the resort city of Ensenada. "The performance of our SC/Rambler was truly remarkable," declared Bondurant. "We experienced no mechanical trouble despite the tremendous pounding our car took on the course."

Other AMC off-road racers enjoyed success in the Baja 500 as well. Bondurant and Murphy led two more American Motors SC/Ramblers home, taking the win, while teammates nailed down third, fifth, and thirteenth place in Class I, which was halted after 30 hours of rugged racing. Ed Orr of Studio City, California, and J. W. Wright of North Hollywood, California, finished third, while Walker Evens of Riverside, California, and Don Simpson of Hemet, California, were fifth. Dick Hansen of San Diego, California, and Johnnie Crean of Riverside, California, finished thirteenth. Adding to this impressive victory was Carl Jackson and Jim Fricker's fourth-place finish in an experimental four-wheel-drive SC/Rambler in the Category IV Class. Jackson and Fricker circled the hazardous, bone-crushing course in 17 hours and 30 minutes!

Elmer Waring, chief Inspector for NORRA's technical crew, paid tribute to the American International Racing Team Crew that prepared the Jackson-Fricker 4X4 SC/Rambler: "This four-wheel-drive vehicle was a real 60-day wonder, for it was created in two months and placed into competition against units with years of development and dozens of open competitive events. Carl Jackson, Jim Fricker, and the SC/Rambler four-wheel-drive were outstanding."

Actor James Garner's AIR Racing ordered 12 SC/Ramblers. Two were converted to four-wheel-drive and raced in the Mexican Baja 1000 in 1969. (Photo Courtesy Mark Fletcher Collection)

The Hurst-inspired Rebel Machine had its own AMC press kit and brochure promoting the car as anti-establishment. (Photo Courtesy Mark Fletcher Collection)

an elapsed quarter-mile time for one of its cars. The only SC/Rambler magazine ad published in the March and May issues of *Motor Trend* boldly stated, "A Rambler that does the quarter-mile in 14.3." It went on to state that American Motors and Hurst collaborated on the custom-built SC/Rambler. During the press launch in February of 1969 at Orange County Raceway in Southern California, the press tested the claim and ran the SC/Ramblers down the track. In stock trim, and with non-professional drivers, the SCs averaged 14.2 seconds in the quarter- mile, beating AMC's published claims.

With a factory-delivered quarter-mile time of 14.3 seconds, the SC/Rambler was squarely positioned to compete with its rivals, such as the Chevelle LS6, Mustang 428 Cobra Jet, and the Dodge Dart equipped with the 440 wedge. Dale Young of *Super Stock and Drag Illustrated* magazine covered the quarter-mile in 12.67 seconds with an SC/Rambler, which was equipped with the dealer-available Group 19 cam kit, Doug Thorley headers, a 4.44:1 rear gear ratio, and larger racing slicks. This clearly put the SC/Rambler in with the big boys. The cost of membership for entry into this prestigious club was less than $1 per pound with an MSRP of just $2,998, making the SC/Rambler one of the certifiable bargains of the muscle car era.

Many young family men walked into their local American Motors dealership wanting one of the limited-production Hurst Ramblers, only to drive out with a slightly less performance-oriented and much more practical Javelin, Rebel, or Ambassador. Hurst had once again helped build a struggling brand's image by converting the mundane into the insane, and that is what the car buyer of 1969 wanted.

Television and movie actor James Garner, owner of American International Racing (AIR), signed on with AMC to campaign a number of specially prepped Americans in off-road racing for 1969. Garner's team received 10 SC/Ramblers to compete in the Mexican Baja 500 race as part of the deal. It is rumored that Garner also received two additional street-trim SCs for promotional use. Garner, who had campaigned two L88 Corvettes at Daytona the year before, was unable to drive in the race due to a movie filming commitment in Spain. Of the 10 AIR-prepared SC/Ramblers entered, seven finished the grueling race, with three crossing the finish line in the top five.

Two of AIR's SC/Ramblers were converted to four-wheel drive. Automotive historian Fred Phillips in Calgary now owns one of these cars. He bought it on eBay in 2005, and it has been preserved in its unrestored condition.

1970 Rebel Machine

The success of the Hurst and AMC collaboration continued into the 1970 model year. Again, AMC turned to Hurst to help package and merchandise an overlooked production car. The Hornet replaced the American, so the 1970 canvas was bigger, in the form of the midsize Rebel line. Taking a more pedestrian cue in appearance from the previous year's SC/Rambler, the all-white car featured a red stripe flowing from the leading edge of the front fenders, across the rear quarter hips, where it joined a blue and white stripe connecting over the trunk lid.

This stripe decal, produced by 3M, was reflective for a distinct nighttime presentation. The hood had a bright blue painted insert with a flat and wide hood scoop, which incorporated a lighted 8,000-rpm tachometer. The lower rockers were also finished in bright blue, similar to the SC/Rambler B-scheme of 1969. A grille surround, painted red, white, and blue to match the rest of the package, finished the car's appearance. Each Rebel Machine also received a set of unique stamped-steel Kelsey-Hayes 15-inch rally wheels, which had a tall-domed center cap and a unique non-removable trim ring.

All Rebel Machines came from the factory with bucket seats and floor-mounted shifter. For 1970, the dealers had the choice of the standard BorgWarner

Hurst designed the 1970 Rebel Machine as a follow-up to the successful 1969 SC/Rambler in the corporate red, white, and blue. (Photo Courtesy Mark Fletcher Collection)

Super T-10 4-speed or an M-12 3-speed automatic. Both were mated to the new-for-1970 390-ci, 340-hp engine. This engine featured a Rebel Machine–only intake and factory Ram Air scoop, contributing to the 340-hp output, AMC's highest rating ever.

Unlike the 1969 Hurst SC/Rambler, more creature comforts were available, including tilt wheel, power steering, and even power-robbing air conditioning. Sometime early in the production year, the choice of any factory color also became available. When ordered in a color, the stripes were not included, although the hood scoop with tachometer remained. The hood center and scoop were finished in flat black with a bright silver pinstripe along the paint seams. Even a vinyl top was optional.

In 1970, AMC manufactured 1,936 machines of which approximately 1,000 were painted white with the Hurst-designed graphics. However, at the time, high-impact colors were all the rage, so the other cars were painted in

The midsize Rebel Machine was meant to compete with the Road Runner and Ford's Fairlane, but it also had a little attitude along the lines of the GTO Judge. Success was limited though, with only 1,936 produced, of which 596 were ordered in regular production colors, and 1,340 in the AMC red, white, and blue. (Photo Courtesy Rich Truesdell)

The patriotic red, white, and blue design was carried over to the Rebel Machine package. The AMX 390 engine had a 340-hp rating due to improving design to the cylinder heads, intake, and the Ram Air system. The tachometer was built into the back of the hood scoop, making it difficult to read in the rain. (Photo Courtesy Rich Truesdell)

Only 596 customers ordered their 1970 Rebel Machines in regular factory colors rather than the bold red, white, and blue colors we have become most familiar with. (Photo Courtesy Rich Truesdell)

an assortment of bold, brash colors, such as Big Bad Orange, Big Bad Blue, and Big Bad Green. While the 390 V-8 was available in other 1970 Rebels, only the Rebel Machine was fitted with matching free-flowing exhaust manifolds and low-restriction mufflers that proved to be quieter than the SC/Rambler's rowdy glass packs. The same 3.54:1 Twin Grip rear axle was connected to a four-link trailing arm suspension with coil-over rear springs. Handling was enhanced with the addition of huge front and rear sway bars. Power front disc brakes were standard, as was the two-spoke wood grain steering wheel.

Interestingly, even though the Hurst team helped design and implement this car for AMC, it had no external Hurst designation and was never publicly accredited to Hurst Performance. At its introduction, AMC rated the Rebel Machine at 10.7 pounds per horsepower, positioning the car for the NHRA F-stock class. At a curb weight of 3,650 pounds, the Rebel Machine competed directly against the Big Three's intermediates, such as the Ford Torino Cobra and all the GM A-Bodies, which included the Chevelle LS6 and GTO Judge 455. It also competed against the 426 Hemi or 440 Six-Pack Dodge Super Bee and Plymouth Road Runner.

For 1970, the competitors' gloves came off. General Motors had eliminated the previously self-imposed 400-ci limit for its intermediates. Ford had its 428-ci Cobra Jet in the Mustang and the Torino/Fairlane lines. At Chrysler, the elephant Hemi engines were installed in both the Dodge Challenger and Plymouth 'Cuda. AMC still offered a great value at $3,495, but against the larger displacement competition, only 1,936 buyers opted for the distinctive looking Rebel Machines.

1971 Hurst Jeepster

The fourth and final Hurst-AMC collaboration was not well publicized and, as a result, is the least well known. In February 1970, AMC took on the Jeep line from Kaiser and felt that a flashy image would help it compete with the International Harvester Scout line. Once again, the marketing department turned to Hurst and the result was the Hurst Jeepster.

Jeep had been successful as a utilitarian rough-road and off-road product. The goal was to create a Jeep that drew attention in suburban driveways as well as on the trail. In 1967, Kaiser revived the Jeepster, and it was scheduled for a cosmetic refresh for 1972, but it needed a sales boost for 1971.

Hurst chose a familiar white canvas to start with, and added a hood scoop similar to the 1970 Rebel machine's scoop with the built-in 8,000-rpm tachometer. To distinguish the Hurst Jeepster from its more proletarian stable mates, Hurst added red and blue stripes wrapping over the cowl, along with another set of stripes across the tailgate and downward on each side of the taillight, and required the Hurst emblem on the right lower tailgate.

Hurst Jeepster was a cosmetic package that included exterior striping, an oversized hoodscoop, and Hurst badges. All of the Hurst packages were delivered on factory white jeeps. (Photo Courtesy Russell Witkop)

AMC did not switch from the then-current Buick drivetrain to its in-house offerings until the following year. The 1970 Hurst Jeepster Commando came equipped with the Dauntless 225-ci Buick V-6, sporting 160 hp and a healthy 235 ft-lbs of torque. The Dauntless V-6 was mated to a 3-speed manual transmission with Hurst T-handle shifter, or the optional automatic when ordered. It featured a console-mounted Hurst Dual Gate shifter reminiscent of the original GTO version. The Hurst Jeepster gold low-back bucket seats, sports steering wheel, roof rack, and Goodyear G70 x 15 raised white-letter tires mounted on wider steel wheels finished the package.

Again, this was a Hurst design that was fully assembled on the regular production line; in this case it was the Jeep facility in Toledo, Ohio. The package sold fewer than 100 units, and although they are difficult to find today, values have remained surprisingly affordable for a Hurst product.

All Hurst Jeepsters were white with red and blue stripes across the cowl and lower tailgate. (Photo Courtesy Russell Witkop)

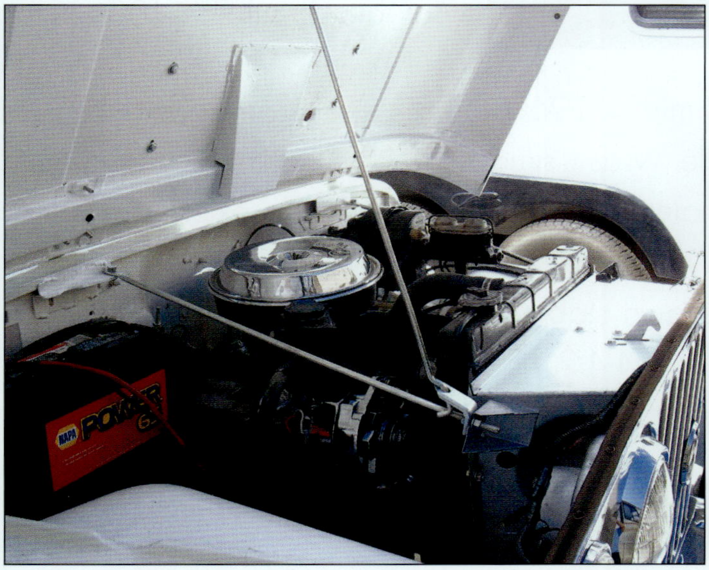

Power for the Hurst Jeepster came from the standard GM V-6. The owner has added chrome valve covers, air cleaner, and alternator. (Photo Courtesy Russell Witkop)

Hurst added the Dual Gate shifter to the optional console in what was an otherwise spartan interior. (Photo Courtesy Russell Witkop)

A Legend is Born

Hurst Teams with Oldsmobile

By the mid 1960s, Oldsmobile was struggling to maintain its competitive edge in the muscle car market. From its own stable at GM, Oldsmobile's 4-4-2 had to compete against A-Body siblings of the Pontiac GTO and Chevelle. These muscle cars were outselling the 4-4-2, and Oldsmobile had been denied its request to build a "Pony car" on the F-Body platform. While Chevrolet collaborated with Yenko and Ford worked with Shelby, Oldsmobile didn't have a high-performance partner. In addition, Oldsmobile was looking to circumvent the GM corporate edict of engines no bigger than 400 cubic inches in GM intermediate-size cars. But a larger engine could be installed in a car modified through an external partnership, and that was impetus for the alliance with Hurst. This strategic alliance led to the creation of one of the most memorable and notable muscle cars of the era—the Hurst/Olds.

The huge 13-inch-wide Ram Air scoops hidden under the bumper drove air into intake of the massive 455 mill. Phil LaChapelle owns this first-year 1968 H/O. (Photo Courtesy Rich Truesdell)

CHAPTER 6

The spoiler was designed to lay flat to the trunk during typical street driving, but when the brakes were applied, it deployed. A driver override switch was installed so that the spoiler could be raised for added stability at speed. No measurable benefit was ever achieved. (Photo Courtesy Hurst/Olds Club of America)

One Thing Leads to Another

In January 1966, Dick Chrysler started working part-time at Hurst for $1.50 per hour. He was a local hot rodder who had run his share of races both on and off the track. Through his job at Hurst, he had the opportunity to meet different car engineers who worked on secret projects at the Hurst Skunk Works located in Madison Heights.

In Detroit at the time, the "Thursday Night Drags" was the worst-kept secret. Most of these participating car manufacturers left their best street-prepared performance car at the Howard Johnson parking lot at the intersection of 10 Mile Road and the new I-696 freeway in North Detroit each Thursday afternoon. Drivers were either manufacturer engineers or local street racers with ties to the various OEMs. Often, Dick was the designated test pilot for the cars from Pontiac Engineering.

By early Thursday evening, up to a dozen new cars appeared at the Howard Johnson's parking lot. Drivers gathered their keys and then cruised 10-Mile Road. In those days, racers, muscle car owners, and factory engineers cruised Woodward Avenue and the surrounding freeways until finding a suitable challenger. In reality, the factories used this area and night as unofficial testing for prototype and preproduction cars. Stoplight races were common, but all-out racing had to wait. After an hour of street jousting, the dueling cars moved to the new and underutilized I-696 freeway for the real match-ups. While slower cars blocked traffic from behind on I-696, the factory cars paired off and ran against each other on the straight, open road. There was no measured quarter-mile, and either driver signaled the end of the race by backing off the throttle.

While working full time at Hurst, Chrysler was also street testing cars for Pontiac. In the fall of 1967, Chrysler recalled that one particular 1968 Cutlass driven by an Olds engineer was impossible to keep up with out of the hole. Dick was driving a new 1968 GTO 400 4-speed, possibly equipped with the Ram Air IV engine (no designation was displayed). The Olds accelerated hard but ran out of steam once it topped 100 mph. Just as Dick began overtaking the car, the driver backed off the throttle and ended the competition. Dick later discovered the car had an experimental 7-speed automatic transmission with extremely deep rear gears.

"Most times the Pontiac offerings were in the thick of the race," said Chrysler. "The most difficult competitors were the Chrysler Hemi cars or a memorable 427-powered Mercury Comet that consistently dominated the evenings. Responsibilities came with this fun; the designated drivers were required to fill out the log books kept in the glove box before returning the car to the hotel. The following morning, the cars were gathered by engineering teams and the log book was reviewed before additional tuning and development occurred prior to the following week's race."

Chrysler had learned a lot during his time as a test driver for Pontiac. On the streets of Detroit, he saw first hand that Oldsmobile had strong cars, but the competition was often stronger. In a short time, Hurst and Oldsmobile capitalized on each other's strengths and formed an alliance.

Since Hurst installed the first 4-speed shifters in the 1961 Pontiac Super Duty Catalina, Hurst Performance had developed a fruitful and mutually beneficial relationship with Pontiac, and Chrysler was an integral part of it. Without the relationship with Pete Estes and Pontiac management, it's uncertain whether

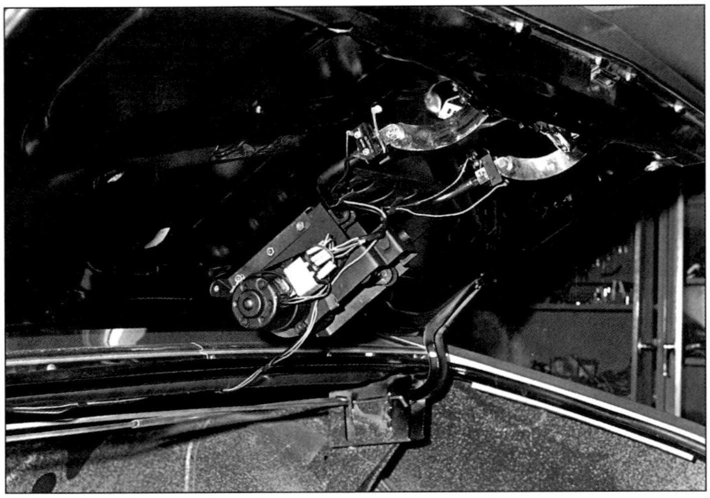

An off-the-shelf windshield wiper motor, with actuators that ran through the trunk lid, deployed the spoiler. Unfortunately, the spoiler never proved to be functional so it was scrapped. (Photo Courtesy Hurst/Olds Club of America)

The headlight doors were inverted GTO doors that dropped behind the front bumper. (Photo Courtesy Hurst/Olds Club of America)

Hurst would have built a performance and business partnership with Oldsmobile. When Pontiac passed on building a Hurst special-edition Firebird, Estes recommended that Hurst offer it's high-performance car-building services to Oldsmobile. From that initial meeting with Oldsmobile brass, Hurst became a preeminent muscle car builder and Oldsmobile had one of the leading muscle cars of the era—the Hurst/Olds.

1968 Program

In the fall of 1967, George Hurst, Jack Watson, and Jim Wangers met with then GM Vice President Pete Estes and Pontiac's John DeLorean in the GM Detroit office. George proposed creating a special-edition Firebird to circumvent General Motors' self-imposed limit of 400 ci for compact and intermediate-size cars, including the Chevy Camaro and Pontiac Firebird. The larger displacement engines were only allowed in the Corvette and GM full-size cars as well as its trucks. George and Wangers shared their idea for Hurst to create 100 special Firebird hardtops with the Pontiac Catalina's 428-ci Tri-Power carburetor engine transplanted in place of the original 400-ci V-8.

After listening to Hurst's and Wangers' proposal, Pete Estes turned to George and asked, "We are selling every Firebird we can make. Why would we want to do this project?" However, he explained to George that the boys in Lansing were unhappy that Oldsmobile was not given an F-Body car based on the Camaro and Firebird platform. Estes said he would arrange a meeting between Hurst and Oldsmobile General Manager Harold Metzel and Chief Design Engineers John Beltz and Ted Lucas to discuss George's idea in relation to helping Oldsmobile gain market share with the growing performance-oriented market.

George knew John Beltz well, as he had been the chief engineer for the Toronado and had worked with the Hurst team in Ferndale on the development of the Hurst *Hairy Olds* drivetrain. Beltz

This 1968 H/O proposal car appears as it was shown to Oldsmobile during the winter of 1968. Note the large W-31 ram scoops below the front bumper and the directional signals that have been relocated to the center of the front bumper. (Photo Courtesy Hurst/Olds Club of America)

insisted on using the Toronado front-wheel-drive powertrain both front and rear to dispel the criticism and perceived weakness of the internal chain-drive design.

In November 1967, George and Jack Watson had their first meeting with John Beltz. Notes from the meeting were used to develop a prototype car based on a 1968 Oldsmobile 4-4-2 two-door coupe sporting 13-inch-wide W-30-style dual-Ram Air scoops mounted below the front bumper. Watson and his Madison Heights—based Hurst performance research center team started by removing the 400-ci engine and replaced it with a new factory-crated 455 Toronado engine.

"Doc" Watson with the first H/O prototype. (Photo Courtesy Hurst/Olds Club of America)

The prototype was painted in Hurst's traditional black with gold accents, with the Dazzler Hurst wheels wrapped with redline tires. The factory grille and matching headlight doors were removed and replaced with custom units made from an extruded aluminum fluorescent light cover. This gave the appearance of a one-piece grille, but included hidden headlights. GTO headlight doors were installed upside down, and tucked the open headlight covers behind the front bumper. A Hurst Dual Gate shifter was installed in a mini console between the bucket seats.

On the deck lid, an electrically actuated rear spoiler operating like the flaps of an airplane wing was added. A switch on the brake pedal engaged a windshield wiper motor connected to two cantilevered arms under the trunk lid that raised and lowered it. During testing of the spoiler, Jack Watson asked Don Lane to look out the back window while he piloted the Olds at more than 100 mph on a road in front of the Warminster plant. Don Lane recalls that "the expectation was the design would cause a downward force on the back of the car and increase the rear-wheel braking capabilities. The high-speed test only succeeded in proving that no measurable braking improvement was achieved." An override switch was also installed on the dash to extend the spoiler and theoretically improve stability at high speed. This was never documented, and Oldsmobile never seriously considered the spoiler for production units.

Building the Hurst/Olds

The Oldsmobile Cutlass and the optional 4-4-2 model sales were not keeping pace with GTO and Chevelle brethren. Oldsmobile was looking for a way to change its image and capitalize on the youth market that purchased new cars more often than previous generations. Hurst documents show the proposal was first presented to Oldsmobile in December of 1967 as the "Ultimate Youngmobile." The conservative Oldsmobile management team gave it mixed reviews.

The prototype was trimmed in Tiger Gold, which was a Pontiac-only color. Peruvian Silver was the Oldsmobile flagship color, and all involved felt it helped differentiate the car from the GTO design. The covered headlights looked similar to the Pontiac Grand Prix or GTO grille, and this proposal was rejected for production. Additionally, the complex and ineffective rear spoiler was never seriously considered for production. The written Hurst proposal stated that Hurst would install the crate-engine 455s rather than the factory 400 V-8s. Hurst had been hoping to receive an order of at least 100 of these special-production cars, so in January he was ecstatic to receive a verbal commitment for a 500 build run for springtime delivery.

Hurst's first order of business was to find a facility within a few miles of Oldsmobile's Lansing production line. Jack Watson was able to procure temporary use of a vacant portion of Demmer Corporation's tool and die facility located just three miles away from the Oldsmobile plant.

Oldsmobile delivered the cars to Hurst's rented space at the Demmer manufacturing facility in Lansing. In a covert rebellion to General Motors' cubic-inch limitations, each car had the 455 engine installed at the Lansing factory assembly

First Front-Wheel-Drive Cutlass

By Rich Truesdell

In February 1968, Hurst and Oldsmobile were in full production of the first-year H/O program. Oldsmobile engineer Dale Smith asked Hurst to assist in the development of an experimental vehicle. The plan was to combine the proven Toronado front-wheel-drive components into the lighter Cutlass 4-4-2 body. Dave Landreth received the car in Ferndale, Michigan, where the Hurst team immediately started altering the car's firewall and front floor to accommodate the powerful 455-ci front-wheel-drive package.

What started life as a special-order gold 4-4-2 coupe was soon transformed into a midsize front-wheel-drive vehicle. It was 11 more years before a front-wheel-drive Cutlass was built for production by Oldsmobile, part of the ill-fated X-car program.

The floor was altered to show off the removal of drive-shaft and associated tunnel. Dave Landreth, Paul Phelps, and Doc Watson were all instrumental in the build, and it was completed in less than 30 days. The car was evaluated in the March 1968 issue of *Super Stock* magazine, which highlighted the changes in the car. Oldsmobile borrowed the vehicle back for an internal feasibility evaluation. After a thorough testing, most corporate engineering prototypes were destroyed so as not to expose the manufacturer to any product liability.

However, George was somehow able to keep the car when he moved to Southern California in 1971. He later parted with the unique car, and it was later sold to Bill Hess from Southern California who later relocated to Oklahoma. Bill kept the car and drove it as regular transportation, and Bill's teenage children even learned to drive in this one-off vehicle. Soon he had more than 100,000 miles on the clock and he chose to put the car aside for safekeeping. During the 20 years he drove the prototype in normal traffic, few people identified it as anything special. The key giveaway was the presence of the unique FWD wheels found only on an early Toronado.

I located the owner and the car through rumors of its existence, much of it on the Internet. I was able to view and verify that this is the one and only car built by the Hurst team in early 1968. This altered vehicle has survived and provided the owner with many years of reliable transportation, a true testament to the ingenuity and craftsmanship that the Hurst team put into each custom and promotional car.

I was present at the revealing of this hidden treasure that had been in hibernation close to 20 years. The car is all original, with the exception of regular maintenance items. Even the black pinstriping remains atop the Hurst-applied gold lacquer paint. The car is a true survivor and is ready to be restored and displayed as a unique American-built midsize front-wheel-drive sedan.

The current owner of this rare, front-wheel-drive, Hurst-converted 4-4-2 purchased it in 1970 in Southern California.

The inset photo shows the Fouranado when it was uncovered to coauthor Richard Truesdell in 2011. He ran across the car (now restored and owned by Fred Mandrick of Scottsdale, Arizona) at the 2020 Dr. George Car Show in Indian Wells, California, just before this book was printed. (Photos Courtesy Richard Truesdell)

The Olds Toronado engine and front-drive components fit snuggly in the 4-4-2 engine compartment. The engine compartment shows more than 100,000 miles of trouble-free driving for this Hurst-converted hot rod. (Photo Courtesy Rich Truesdell)

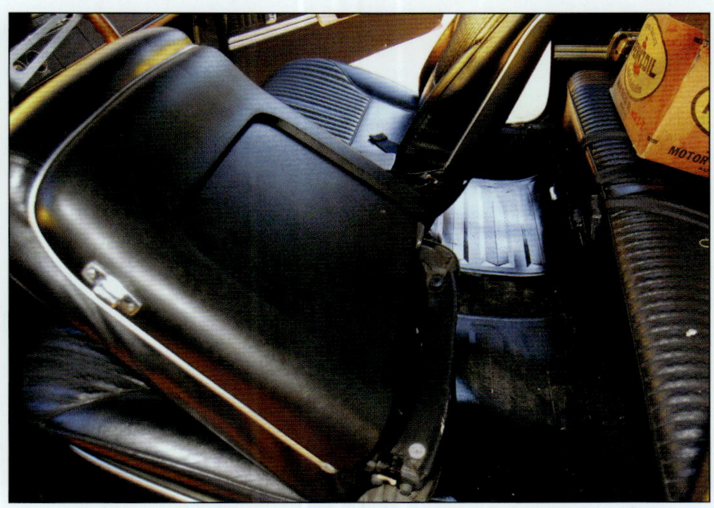

The tunnel hump was removed by the Hurst team during the build process in 1968 as evidenced in this photo of the rear floor area. (Photo Courtesy Rich Truesdell)

A 1968 H/O in front of the Demmer office in Lansing, Michigan. (Photo Courtesy Mark Fletcher Collection)

line. Dave Landreth's recollection that no engine swaps were performed during the conversions with the Oldsmobile-designated serial numbers matching the engine stampings are proof of the clandestine build process. The Toronado W-45 455 was the standard engine, and it featured the W-30 camshaft that helped produce 390 hp, with the transmission fed into a 3.91:1 rear axle. These cars have the coveted "D" heads, which designate the HP option. In addition, 153 cars were ordered with air conditioning, but these received the milder W-46 optioned 380-hp 455 with the C-coded heads and a final-drive ratio of 3.08:1 rear gears.

The factory console and floor shifters were installed between the required bucket seats. When the cars were delivered, they were equipped with power steering, power disc brakes, F-41 suspension, 12-bolt Positraction rear end, and optional air conditioning. The well-appointed interior featured bucket seats and real wood grain on the dash. Two body styles (459 Holiday hardtops and 56 sport coupes) were offered. All cars came with the audacious 4-4-2 red plastic inner fender wells, but were completely void of all 4-4-2 exterior body designation, including the traditional numbers across the grille.

Initially, Watson headed up the project for Hurst. He had called on John Demmer, whose tool and die company was the car's final assembly point, to rent additional space in their new building close to the Olds plant in Lansing. The cars were not built together in one lot, but instead were built at an average rate of 10 cars per day from mid April to late June 1968. Hurst's agreement specified he would deliver 10 finished cars per work day to Oldsmobile for delivery into its traditional distribution system.

Once the cars arrived at Demmer, one team taped the cars while another team masked the cars for the painting process.

A third team applied black paint from the body crest above the rear window down across the trunk. They added a black accent below the doors by using an inverted roof drip molding as a lower body template. Two accent stripes started at the front edge of each front fender across the top of the door ending with a turn up close to the rear side window. Two additional black stripes were painted from the outside of the grille up the center of the hood outlining the raised center section and meeting together along the back edge of the hood.

These seven 1968 H/Os are going through the final prep before being shipped from the rented Demmer facility in the spring of 1968. Hurst created temporary walls covered in plastic to separate the different departments for building cars. This was to protect the property of AMC, Chrysler, and General Motors which all did business with Hurst simultaneously. (Photo Courtesy Mark Fletcher Collection)

The Hurst assembly line process was quickly established at the Demmer facility because it was close to the Oldsmobile factory in Lansing. In 1968, the facility produced 515 H/Os. Here, 20 H/Os are going through the painting process. (Photo Courtesy Mark Fletcher Collection)

Silver with a contrasting black trunk and lower area designate the Hurst package from this angle in 1968. (Photo Courtesy Rich Truesdell)

A fourth team moved the cars from the paint area where they machine polished the new paint. Unlike the assembly-line process used for the Hurst taxi conversions at the Detroit building (see page 123), the cars were moved from station to station throughout the Demmer facility. Each station held up to four cars at a time. Delays at any one station slowed the total day's production.

Twice a week, Paul Hatton, an extremely talented pinstriper, free-hand painted a white pinstripe outlining each of the black painted accents. Hurst paid a flat $20 fee per car, as long as all the cars were completed by the following morning. In 10 weeks, Hatton made a tidy $10,000 moonlighting in the evenings. By comparison, these wages would have paid the sticker price for two of the special H/Os with change leftover.

The 1968 conversion process only required Hurst to perform one mechanical change. The factory automatic floor shifter and console were removed and replaced with a Hurst Dual Gate and a Pierce-supplied mini

HURST/OLDS: A silver milestone trimmed in black. *In mid-1968, Hurst was accorded a very unusual honor for a manufacturer of accessory products. One of Oldsmobiles most sensational new models was named the Hurst/Olds to designate its dual parenthood. The car began life as a top of the line 442, but the finished product is something else indeed. ■ The entire concept behind the H/O is to present a streetable vehicle that will appeal to the youth market as well as the young thinking executive. Thus, the best way to describe the new supercar is an "executive hot rod." Oldsmobile and Hurst engineers have put together a well balanced package of sports car performance and the luxury and convenience of an expensive sedan. ■ Power comes from a Toronado inspired 455 CID engine, sporting 390 horsepower. Special cylinder heads, a high performance camshaft and forced air induction coupled to a Hurst Dual-Gate equipped modified Turbo-Hydramatic transmission and high performance rear axle make up the go-power department. ■ The H/O gains its individuality from the custom silver finish, accented with black interior and exterior trim, and the identifying H/O emblem. ■ First it was the Hurst shifter on assembly line cars, then the Hurst name used by major auto manufacturers in national advertising programs and now . . . The fabulous Hurst Olds. ■ A great and unique honor for Hurst . . . the absolute pinnacle of motoring excellence, and performance . . .*

HURST OLDS

The 1968 Hurst catalog featured a page detailing the first Hurst Oldsmobile collaboration, of which 515 were built. (Photo Courtesy Mark Fletcher Collection)

The gold-and-black 1968 Hurst Olds convertible was a continuation of Hurst's traditional gold vehicles. A 1967 Hurst Pontiac Grand Prix convertible can be seen in the background of this photo taken at Hurst. (Photo Courtesy Pete Serio Collection)

console. Each car received four specially prepared black-and-red H/O emblems, which were attached to the trunk, low along each front fender, and the last in plain view of the passenger on the glove box door. The glove box emblem differed in that it stated "By 'Doc' Watson" directly under the red-and-black "H" for Hurst.

The First 500 H/Os

Oldsmobile's marketing department and Hurst Performance promoted the H/O. Hurst retained the third car produced, which was often loaned to magazines for press coverage. Ironically, the H/O production run was already sold

Hurst Family Matters

George had one sister, Delores Hurst Rudolph, living in New Jersey with her husband and five young children. To his nephew and nieces, George was a bit of an enigma.

"Uncle George was always dressed nice and came in and out of our lives in a whirlwind," his niece Beverly remembers. "In 1965, during the GTO Tiger promotion, Uncle George brought by a portable record player and a 45 record with the GTO song on it for us kids. Not realizing we weren't eligible to win, the five of us children listened to the song day and night each trying to accurately count the number of times that GTO was used in the song. Occasionally, fights broke out among us siblings over whose turn it was to use the record player.

"During a phone conversation, Mom told Uncle George how much turmoil 'that record player' had caused. Within a week, four additional record players and records arrived at our home to settle the matter."

Later, when the girls required braces that cost more than the family could afford, George stepped in to make sure his nieces received them. The only boy of the five was named after George. Today, nephew George has an uncanny resemblance to his famous uncle.

One day in July 1968, George called to let his sister know that he was coming to celebrate her birthday. He always did things in grand style, and on this occasion he was extremely generous. "Uncle George and Lila drove up in a brand-new black and silver H/O," nephew George recalls. "It was common for Uncle George to visit in the company of a pretty young lady. It was not uncommon for Uncle George to be driving a new, expensive car when he came to visit. We lived in a modest neighborhood, and in those days, a new car in the driveway brought most neighbors out of their homes to examine it. Soon we had a crowd admiring the car; then he handed Mom the keys and told her to take her new car for a test drive. All five kids piled in while Uncle George and Lila watched us

George Hurst with his sister Delores and her husband George Rudolph. (Photo Courtesy Beverly Anderson Collection)

out by the time the articles went to press and the public became aware of the cars' existence. Hurst recognized that the marketing of the car was more important to promote Hurst's customizing capabilities than to actually help Oldsmobile sell the cars. The cars were advertised as an exclusive gentleman's hot rod, and most were sold long before they were delivered to the dealership.

Oldsmobile planned to build only 500 cars, but there were more than 900 Oldsmobile dealers, so it became evident that supply would not meet demand. Production was limited to 500, mainly due to the model change scheduled for late July 1968. Story Olds, located in Oldsmobile's home town of Lansing, Michigan, had taken 15 individual orders for the new Hurst specialty car. When Oldsmobile informed the dealership that they would only be receiving one unit, the owner immediately called the factory and worked his way up the management chain until a commitment was made to extend the build to cover his open orders.

Auto racing legend Briggs Cunningham put in a special order, requesting a 1968 H/O be built with white interior due to the hot California sun. Oddly, this was not one of the 153 cars equipped with air conditioning. The Hurst/Olds Club of America rediscovered, documented, and authenticated this car. Two 1968 H/O convertibles were created for promotional purposes. Both started out as special-order black-on-black 4-4-2 convertibles with instructions to delete the traditional badging and correlating holes from the front fenders and trunk lid. Both were equipped with bucket seats, air conditioning, power antennas, and power tops. Both of these cars were built near the end of production in the first week of July. Hurst painted the sides and accents in traditional Hurst Gold and designated both cars for promotional purposes. They were most often seen at racing events with the 10-foot-tall gold shifter and Linda Vaughn entertaining the crowd. The first car received Hurst gold wheels identical to those used on

---

proudly drive through the surrounding neighborhood."

When they returned, George had another surprise. In the trunk was a gift and a card. In the birthday card George had hand written, "Happiness multiplies when divided with others." When his sister opened the gift, she found a new mink stole.

Although generous, neither the mink stole nor the car were practical for the family of seven. The H/O only seated five adults, and as the kids grew, the family outgrew the car. Both gifts were kept for many years, but finally, in the late 1970s, the family had racked up high miles on the car and it had been exposed to the harsh New Jersey winters. Hence, the H/O no longer provided reliable transportation for the family and was regrettably sold.

George Hurst was a very generous man, and in June of 1968, he gave his sister Dolores a 1968 H/O for her birthday. While not the most practical family car, the car provided performance and style. (Photo Courtesy Beverly Anderson Collection)

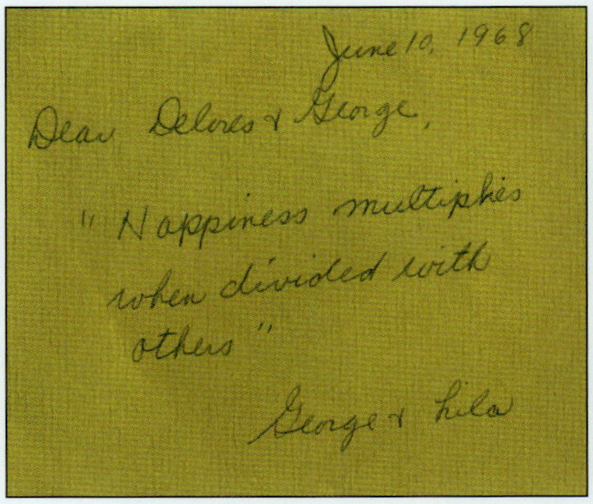

June 10, 1968

Dear Delores & George,

"Happiness multiplies when divided with others"

George & Lila

This handwritten note from George Hurst to his sister accompanied the birthday gift of a 1968 H/O. (Photo Courtesy Beverly Anderson Collection)

Lila gives George Hurst's sister a mink stole for her birthday, but Hurst also gave his sister some family hardware. Her new ride is the H/O that they're standing beside. (Photo Courtesy Beverly Anderson Collection)

the 1965 GTO Hurst promotional car, while the second sported the standard polished aluminum Hurst wheels.

The history of the first black-and-gold H/O convertible is well documented with photos showing the details of the unique gold wheels and the angled Hurst logo on the door. Once Hurst had received the new 1969 H/O, it sold the 1968 car to Atco Raceway in New Jersey. Atco used it as a track and parade car until it suffered its second engine failure with 111,000 miles on the odometer in the mid 1970s. The car was sold to a local Mobil service station owner who rebuilt the engine and raced it often. The car again changed hands in 1984, and the current owner has reportedly kept it in seclusion.

Late one night in 1968, a Hurst employee drove the second convertible off the road in a single-car accident. The car sustained cosmetic damage and was quickly repaired in the Hurst garage in Michigan. Upon further inspection, Hurst employees found that the frame had been bent, and Oldsmobile offered to replace the car with a new convertible. The second gold car was returned to Oldsmobile and was reportedly destroyed. A standard 4-4-2 convertible from a dealer's lot replaced the car and was delivered to Hurst. There it was painted to more closely resemble the production version, and became the third 1968 H/O convert. Although used by Hurst and photographed often in its black and silver finish, if found today this car would be very difficult to authenticate without credible provenance because it started life as a standard production 4-4-2 convertible.

John Demmer's son Ed received the first 1968 H/O as partial payment for the use of Demmer's facility. The car was the only 4-speed 1968 H/O to ever be built, and Demmer still owns it. The car has often been displayed at shows in the Lansing area and photographed with its interesting option package. While it has a Hurst Competition Plus shifter, it does not have the 4-4-2 gauge package. This unique H/O was last displayed sporting an Oldsmobile L69 Tri-Power assembly and aftermarket Centerline wheels. Unfortunately, the original H/O prototype Hurst used to win the Oldsmobile project was returned to Oldsmobile, and it unceremoniously disappeared. Most likely, it suffered the fate of many development mules and was sent to scrap. The fact that it was a production serial numbered 4-4-2 provides some hope that it survived and will someday reappear. The third H/O hardtop that rolled off the assembly line became the promotional car Hurst loaned to major publications for road testing. It was kept in Warminster and was George's favorite car to drive.

1969 Program

By late 1968, the staff at Hurst Performance was hard at work planning to launch the 1969 H/O. Vice President of Hurst Performance Research Dave Landreth and Marketing Director Jack Duffy guided the 1969 H/O program. By the time the program started, both Doc Watson and Hurst founder Bill Campbell had left the company. The overwhelming success of the first year's collaboration was carried over into the 1969 proposal. Discussions began in November of 1968, and a production 1969 Olds 4-4-2 was loaned to Hurst Performance. Dave Landreth and Dick Chrysler approached Chuck Miller to assist in the building of the prototype car.

By early December, the first prototype was completed and dressed in Cameo White. A wide Firefrost Gold racing stripe ran over the top, and gold accents on the top of each front fender swooped back across each door ending on each quarter panel below the side glass. Additionally, matching gold accents ran the entire length of the car below each side belt line. The rear spoiler was mounted high on the trunk, and two large spoiler support braces flanked the center stripe. This original version did not continue the gold stripe over the top of the rear spoiler or the front hood scoop. Hurst's original proposed hood-scoop design was awkward in appearance and non-functioning. Chrome Cragar 15-inch wheels with white-letter Goodyear tires, along with white Bullitt-style

Hurst proposed a massive three-piece spoiler that hung down low on each quarter panel. This 1969 H/O prototype car was owned by Marc Jungermann in Missouri. It has been restored by the new owner and displayed at MCACN in 2018 in its original prototype configuration. (Photo Courtesy Hurst/Olds Club of America)

This is the first prototype hood scoop shown to Oldsmobile in 1969. The Hurst-designed Forced Air graphic, similar in fashion to the Air Foil spoiler, was later used on the 1969 AMC SC/Rambler hood. (Photo Courtesy Hurst/Olds Club of America)

Hurst labeled the three-piece spoiler the Air Foil. This block lettering was later used on the 1969 SC/Rambler hood. (Photo Courtesy Hurst/Olds Club of America)

racing mirrors, finished the performance look of the proposal.

Oldsmobile did not accept the first proposal. While it was a solid foundation, Oldsmobile needed to see some changes. By early January, Hurst had developed a second version from the original proposal. Still finished in Cameo White with the same Firefrost Gold stripes and accents, it featured a unique split ram-air hood scoop with large, red, block lettering spelling out "Forced AIR" on the scoop, with an arrow showing the direction of the airflow. (This same lettering and arrow was later adapted to the 1969 Hurst S/C Rambler.) Out back was a massive three-piece duck-tail-type airfoil flowing three-quarters of the way down each rear quarter panel. Inside the car, the addition of the Hurst Dual Gate shifter on a mini console, and a wide gold band added to each headrest, were the only significant changes, but Hurst still didn't have approval for the final conversion package.

By late January, Oldsmobile management approved the third and final version of the prototype for production. The car now had the one-piece pedestal rear wing with the gold stripe in the center of the car. The hood scoop was similar to the hood scoop on the second proposal, but a continuation of the gold hood stripe was used instead of the arrow and letters from the previous proposal. The H/O also used Olds' newly released 1969 Rallye wheels with Firefrost Gold in the center and Goodyear white-lettered Polyglas tires.

The 455 Engine Swap

In the original documents exchanged between Hurst and the Oldsmobile Division, an approved and completed 1969 H/O build plan featured the spoilers, graphics, and mechanical changes that Hurst recommended to Oldsmobile. Interestingly, the build plan made no mention of Hurst performing the engine swap for the 1969 H/O project. As a result, this provided further evidence that, although unknown to senior GM management, the installation of the 455 V-8 in all 1968 and 1969 was done on the Oldsmobile production line.

Hurst Performance Vice President Dave Landreth and employee Dick Chrysler have both confirmed that Hurst did not swap the 455 into the car at the Demmer facility, and therefore the factory performed the engine conversions. This was in direct violation of General Motors' ban, which forbade installing engines larger than 400 ci in the intermediate-size cars (less than 117-inch wheelbases). And this ban remained in effect until the 1970 production model announcements.

Other GM divisions were also working around this ban. General Motors had a Central Office Production Order (COPO) process allowing fleet customers to order options or configurations that were not available to the general public. This program allowed some of the large Chevy dealers to covertly circumvent the corporate ban, and therefore these dealers were able to acquire large-displacement engines in Camaros, Chevelles, and similar models with special performance packages to sell to the performance car buyer. By 1969, Yenko, Nicky, Dana, Berger, and other dealers had created a cottage industry of selling big-block GM muscle cars that General Motors didn't build itself. In reality, General Motors was building them as long as they were delivered and marketed as aftermarket performance vehicles. It was many years before the true story was told of how these cars were actually built.

In reality, Oldsmobile installed the big-block engine in all 1969 H/Os on the Lansing assembly line. The cars

1969 Hurst Oldsmobile H/O 455

With Hurst hitting on all cylinders, with a variety of OEM programs, the 1969 Hurst/Olds program is considered to be the high-water mark of the Hurst Oldsmobile collaboration. A total of 911 coupes were reported to have been built along with as many as five convertibles. (Photos Courtesy Rich Truesdell)

Hurst used the same sport mirror on both the 1969 H/O and the SC/Rambler. Mercury also used this mirror on the 1968 Cougar XR7/G. (Photo Courtesy Mark Fletcher)

After installing the Dual Gate shifter, Hurst added gold-striped headrests to the interior of the 1969 H/O. (Photo Courtesy Mark Fletcher)

came equipped with the 455-ci V-8 and 10.25:1 compression, which was conservatively rated at 380 hp and a massive 500 ft-lbs of torque. Although each car was outfitted with the W-30 air cleaner base, the engines were not W-30s. Each car received a numbered transmission when assembled by Oldsmobile in Lansing. The stamped transmission code read OH-69-1XXX, with the last three digits specifying the build order of the transmission, from early to late.

The highest transmission number discovered to date ends in number 1922, which has lead to some speculation that at least 922 H/Os were built in 1969. The count is more likely 911, with 906 known coupes built and another suspected five convertibles assembled. The difference in quantity could also be explained by defective transmissions that may have been replaced in quality control prior to the cars being transported to the Hurst facility.

On the Assembly Line

Once again, Hurst personnel at the Demmer facility transformed the demure-appearing white Oldsmobiles into tire-burning street dominators. The first car rolled off Oldsmobile's assembly line in the third week of March, with the last production vehicles departing the fourth week of May. The facility was more centralized and larger, and that allowed for more cars to be simultaneously built.

George Hurst (left) stands with two H/O coupes and an original H/O convert at the Tavern on the Green in New York City during the winter of 1969. (Photo Courtesy Pete Serio Collection)

The all-white 4-4-2s were driven in the back door from the storage lot. At the first station, painted gold wheels replaced the original wheels. Once removed, each wheel had the center section repainted in gold and the chrome center trim pieces were replaced. Special Goodyear F60 X15-inch white-letter Polyglas tires were mounted and balanced and then set aside for the next exchange.

At the second station, Hurst technicians made interior conversions. Gold-striped Hurst headrests replaced the stock ones. Also at this station, a Hurst Dual Gate shifter and mini console replaced the factory units. Lastly, the H/O owner's manual insert was added to the glove box and the dash decal was applied.

Assembly-line workers rolled the cars from station to station, so the building didn't fill with exhaust gases. The line did a U-turn where the body and paint preparation began. A template was placed on the hood to cut away the Ram Air opening and drill the hood scoop attaching points. Workers installed a Ford air-cleaner lid with a flapper and vacuum solenoid to the factory base. Off to the side of the area, a production line painted the scoops, mirrors, and spoilers. Each was painted Cameo White with Firefrost Gold accents. Initially, the grille and headlight doors were removed and painted flat black. Dick Chrysler explained, "Over time, the procedure was changed to a masking process and the grille and headlight doors were painted on the car."

At the next station, the hood, roof, and trunk lid were masked for the addition of the over-roof stripe. Inverted roof drip rail moldings served as the template for masking of the lower body panels. Finally, all of the exposed areas were prepped for the addition of gold.

All chrome and stainless window trim remained on the car and were simply masked prior to the application of gold. Not all cars received the gold wheel treatment throughout production, and the reason for this inconsistency is not known for sure. One possibility is that this step may have slowed down the conversion process. Dick Chrysler spent two days per week in Lansing, and he recalls having to work at this station more than once during his visits because the wheel painting process was slowing vehicle production.

Cars were then pushed into the paint booth where the familiar Hurst Gold was applied to the exposed area. Each car remained in the paint booth less than 30 minutes, often with 20 cars being painted during a single day's production. The following day, these cars were unmasked. Then the hood scoops, mirrors, and rear wing were bolted into place. The external plastic chrome H/O

Hood scoops were big back in 1969, and this dual-snorkel Hurst addition clearly stated the H/O meant business. (Photo Courtesy Rich Truesdell)

Hurst added the Ram Air system when they installed the hood scoop in 1969. This H/O engine compartment is original and unrestored. (Photo Courtesy Rich Truesdell)

A Very Rare Convertible

The 1969 H/O convertible is extremely rare, and the precise number manufactured is unknown. These convertibles were often used for marketing and promotional events. At that time, production and sales were growing, and Hurst was present at more events than in previous years.

It is believed that Hurst built as many as five different 1969 H/O convertibles. Jack Duffy and later Richard Pierce drove one convertible, and this car currently resides in Northern California with gold carpets and a prototype automatic transmission shifter, which at first glance looks like a 4-speed stick. The current owner purchased this car in 1979. It was stored outside for many years until it was restored and offered for sale on eBay and at a California specialty car broker in 2010.

Only two other original H/O convertibles have been identified and authenticated. These currently have national club membership.

While many clone H/O convertibles have been built, knowledgeable enthusiasts are easily able to identify these copies. The easiest way to identify any H/O as original is the serial numbered transmission and factory body build tag found on the firewall.

Hurstette Nikki Phillips stands on the platform on the back of one of the 1969 H/O convertibles during this 1969 Christmas parade. (Mark Fletcher Collection)

This is one of five 1969 H/O convertibles made for Hurst's promotional department. This car is unusual, with the Hurst Autostick shifter and gold colored carpet. (Photo Courtesy Rich Truesdell)

This 1969 H/O convertible was owned for more than 25 years by a Hurst enthusiast who often states that he purchased the one-of-five convertible from a past Hurst employee in the 1970s. (Photo Courtesy Rich Truesdell)

Only Hurst employees drove H/O convertibles in 1969. Hurst built up to five different H/O convertibles that year. This car has undergone a full and accurate restoration and is in a private collection. (Photo Courtesy Rich Truesdell)

emblems were installed last. Most finished cars were stored outside the facility until the pinstriper arrived and put the final touches on each car. This makeshift production line doubled output and production from the previous year.

Hurst applied an H/O dash emblem to each of the 911 cars they produced in 1969. (Photo Courtesy Rich Truesdell)

A Unique Marketing Campaign

Oldsmobile had 400 dealers in the United States and Canada willing to sell the high-performance car, and with significant demand the expectation was to build 700 units. Even though some dealers didn't order one of these wild machines, other dealers placed multiple orders and they added up quickly. Soon Oldsmobile received more than 900 orders for the H/O. Any open allocations were quickly absorbed to fill the need of those dealers with more customers demanding the specialized performance model.

Many dealers ordered well-equipped cars with luxury options. It's common to find air conditioning, power windows, tilt wheel steering, or factory 8-track players on these cars. The A/C-equipped cars came with the 3.23:1 rear axle ratio, while the 3.42:1 was standard, and the 3.91:1 was optional on the non-air cars. All the luxury options created a very well appointed yet expensive car for its time. The Hurst conversion added $684 to the optioned-out Oldsmobile 4-4-2 list price.

On April 7, 1969, the 1969 H/O launch party was held at the famous Tavern on the Green in New York City. Planned in conjunction with the New York International Auto Show, George Hurst brought along two very well-equipped hardtops and one unique convertible, which had a white canvas top with the same stitched wide gold stripe.

George unveiled the company's unique marketing campaign for the car outlined in the official press release. Any original owner that registered a car with Hurst received an engraved plaque with the owner's name. Instructions on where to place this on the dash were included, and many cars still have this item today.

The appearance of the 1969 H/O model was much bolder than the previous year's offering. The dynamic look of the dual, large, open hood scoops, wide gold stripe, and oversize rear wing spoiler combined to make an aggressive styling package. For certain, the H/O didn't seamlessly blend into traffic. Instead, it projected a bold, muscular presence that rivaled any of the other special-build muscle cars of the day. Hurst's marketing department capitalized on the look and characterized the model as a snarling machine in their "Snarls softly and carries a big stick" print ads.

Hurst created a cartoon character advertisement to announce the 1969 H/O with the phrase "Snarls Softly and Carries a Big Stick." The scoops, stripes, and spoiler were a radical departure from the subtle colors and look of the 1968 Hurst Olds. (Photo Courtesy Mark Fletcher Collection)

1970 Program

Hurst enjoyed the overwhelming success of both the 1968 and the 1969 H/O programs, so he felt that a return to performance was inevitable for the 1970 H/O model. Oldsmobile had a plan of its own and felt it could retain the youth market without sharing the additional revenue with Hurst.

Bold colors and wild graphics had been a large influence in the phenomenal growth in the performance market in 1969. Most manufacturers introduced special editions. Pontiac took the wraps off the midyear GTO Judge and the inaugural Trans Am model. Chevrolet released the midyear white and orange Camaro Pace Car series. Ford had successfully introduced the Boss 302 and the mammoth big-block in the Boss 429 Mustang. Mercury launched the Eliminator in the brightest of colors. Even little American Motors had successfully distracted the market with the SC/Rambler.

After sizing up the muscle car landscape, the Olds marketing team felt they needed to compete with the Road Runner and Judge with a lower-cost, small-block, insurance-beating package.

Internal to Oldsmobile, there was a bit of a battle among various product development factions. For the past dozen years, engineering had developed performance packages and the marketing team wrapped them in an attractive package to promote the resulting cars. This program became a political hotbed, and the boys at Hurst made their proposal to friends in the engineering department.

Oldsmobile Chief Engineer John Beltz ordered an all-black 1970 H/O

Hurst's marketing department created a display as a color test prior to finalizing the packages, circa 1970. (Photo Courtesy Pete Serio Collection)

In 1970, most families drove a wagon. Hurst created the ultimate wagon combining an H/O and the family hauler. (Photo Courtesy Rich Truesdell)

Cutlass in October of 1969, and had Jim Wangers, now working for Hurst, transform the car into an exceptional muscle car. Designated as an H/O proposal car, it was a black SX coupe with the W-32 455 with 365 hp and a W-25 Ram Air hood option. Hurst added the Dual Gate shifter, H/O emblems on the trunk, and both rear quarter panels ahead of the rear wheels and the special electric sunroof.

The model concept was never pitched to Oldsmobile, as the Olds marketing department announced it would be producing its own specialty performance model for 1970 and did not need Hurst for this project. At the time, speculation abounded that the Hurst programs had been the cover for manufacturing to bypass the 400-ci cap for intermediate-body GM cars.

Hurst tried to create product demand by using the black SX as a parade and promotional car at national events. After the proposal was officially killed, Hurst sold the car to Key Olds in March 1970. Later, it was involved in a collision and stored for more than 25 years. Currently, the documented car has been rediscovered and is undergoing a full restoration.

For the 1970 model year, General Motors lifted its self-imposed ban on installing engines larger than 400 ci in A-body cars. General Motors had first partnered with Hurst to get around the 400-ci corporate edict, and therefore the partnership was forced to take a new direction. Now, any 1970 4-4-2 could be ordered with the factory 370-hp W-30 model 455-ci engine that was unique to the H/O the previous year. If Hurst created an additional big-block specialty car, it would only compete with the standard Oldsmobile offerings, but if Hurst developed a lower-cost and sporty small-block muscle car, it would be able to fill a new niche in the market. As a result, Hurst built the Rallye 350 as Oldsmobile's response to the low-cost, small-block wars.

The Rallye design had a screaming yellow monochromatic look featuring painted bumpers and bright accents. Originally envisioned with the high-horsepower W-31 350-ci V-8, only two such units were built as prototypes. By the time production commenced, the reliable 310-hp L-74 Olds 350 was the only available engine. Many dealers were forced to swap chrome bumpers in favor of the brash painted bumpers to satisfy customers' tastes.

The Rallye 350 was a sales disappointment, and a total of 3,547 Rallye 350 W-45 package cars were assembled in Lansing. About two-thirds were the top model Cutlass Holiday hardtop coupe with an additional 1,020 base F-85 Club coupes. An additional 160 F-85 Sport coupes with the B-pillar post and front-door window frames were built.

During the 1969 model year, Hurst

The Hurst and Yenko Alliance

Racer and supercar builder Don Yenko had been assembling the Yenko Deuce, based on the 350-ci, 360-hp Corvette LT-1 powertrain in the light and utilitarian Nova, and it was a strong seller for Yenko. In the spring of 1970, Don Yenko asked George if he could help convert some Yenko Novas at Hurst facilities. A financial and logistical arrangement was reached and Hurst built a total of 50 Nova Deuces for Yenko in five different colors.

Hugger Orange, Sunflower Yellow, and Citrus Green were colors unique to Hurst's build run, and therefore these colors alone identify Hurst-built cars. Additionally, 20 cars were built in non-exclusive Hurst colors, 10 units each in Fathom Blue and Cranberry Red. (Yenko had earlier built 25 of each of these colors on its own.)

For the 1970 model year, 175 Yenko Deuces were built as "insurance busters." Because the standard 350 was available in any Nova, most insurance companies never caught on to the special performance recipe that Yenko Performance had concocted. Similar to the H/O project, General Motors installed the high-performance drivetrain on the Chevrolet production line under the COPO program coded 9737.

The Yenko Deuce was equipped with either the 4-speed Muncie M-21 or the Turbo 400 automatic transmission, the heavy-duty F-41 suspension package, disc brakes, and a steep 4.10:1 final drive ratio. These cars were truly wolves in sheep's clothing. The cars started as bare-bones non-Super Stock cars with bench seats and rubber floor mats in the sparse interior.

To prep each car, Hurst installed either a Competition Plus manual stick or the usual Auto Stick shifter for automatic-equipped cars. The massive white or black Yenko graphics were installed along with the factory hood tach and Yenko Chevrolet front fender emblems. Hurst offered a rare optional hood scoop with built-in tach for the Yenko Deuce (similar to a setup found on the 1970 AMC Rebel Machine), but very few have been found so equipped. The "Deuce" moniker was derived from the original Chevy II designation that was used on the Nova through 1968.

Performance had completed more than 10,000 specialty car conversions. In fact, Hurst converted 7,500 Chrysler sedans for the New York taxi cab project, which required Hurst to substantially alter the rear floor to meet the passenger compartment space requirements (see page 123). The Hurst/Olds, SC/Rambler, SS AMX, and the 1969 Dart and Barracuda 440 conversions made up the remaining 2,500 units. But the work flow at Hurst was about to change.

For 1970, the company had no Oldsmobile project, the Chrysler taxi cab project was winding down, and sales of the Hurst Chrysler 300 were far below expectations. As a result, Dave Landreth was looking for another project to keep the Hurst team busy and drive revenue into the company.

1972 Indy 500 Pace Car

Indianapolis-area Dodge dealers sponsored the pace car program for the 1971 Indianapolis 500, so the group ordered 50 red Challenger convertibles to be used both on the track and around the city during the month-long festivities.

Two Challengers were equipped with the 4-barrel 383-ci engine to pace the actual race, while six other cars were fitted with the 2-barrel 383. In addition, six more of the E-Body Dodge cars had the high-performance 340-ci powertrain while the remaining 36 cars were equipped with the more sedate 318-ci engine.

Each car appeared identical with the standard flat hood and full wheel covers. The dealers equipped the pace cars in this fashion to control costs, and based on the historical sales data, this allowed the group to better sell the cars after the race.

Throughout the month of May, the cars performed their assigned duties admirably. But tragedy occurred with the pace car during the Indy 500. As tradition, the pace car led the field on the warmup laps as the open-wheel race cars lined up for the rolling start of the race.

Oldsmobile put the 1972 H/O prototype on center stage at the Southern California International Auto Show. (Photo Courtesy Pete Serio Collection)

The 1972 Hurst Olds was also the Indy 500 Pace Car. All of the performance parts were installed on the assembly line, including the Hurst Dual Gate shifter. Hurst applied the decal package, added H/O badges, and painted the wheels gold. Warren Gilliland owns this example. (Photo Courtesy Rich Truesdell)

For the 1972 H/O Indy 500 Pace Car, Hurst applied decals rather than painted graphics. Some of the "Official Pace Car" decals were defective, requiring Hurst to send a crew to the Indianapolis 500 to replace the decals with new ones supplied by 3M. (Photo Courtesy Rich Truesdell)

As standard procedure, the pace car leads the field at more than 100 mph and then exits the track at Turn 4, entering the pits when the green flag waves to start the race. As the green flag waved and the race started, pace car driver Eldon Palmer entered the pits at a high rate of speed and crashed into the photographer's grandstand. The accident injured 19 photographers and spectators who sat next to the pit road.

In preparation for the start, Palmer had marked his braking point along pit row so that he could safely stop the Challenger. During final preparations, the marker had been either removed or obscured and Palmer started braking too late, eventually losing control of the car and crashing into the photographer's stand. The incident was shown live on national television, and the negative publicity for Dodge was overwhelming. All new-car manufacturers

A fully restored 1972 H/O engine compartment, detailed down to the original chalk marks used by Oldsmobile during the assembly line process. There was no requirement for Hurst to even open the hood during the conversion process in 1972. (Photo Courtesy Rich Truesdell)

The profile of the 1972 H/O shows the more formal roofline as compared to previous year's fastback design. A Hurst-installed power sunroof became an option for the first time. (Photo Courtesy Rich Truesdell)

were then reluctant to sponsor the following year's Indianapolis 500 pace car program.

George once again recognized a prime business opportunity and a way for the Indianapolis 500 to move past the tragedy of the previous year. Tony Hulman and George Hurst had become friends over the previous decade, and although George was no longer president of Hurst Performance, he was an active board member of Indianapolis Motor Speedway. George saw the promotional opportunity of supporting his friend, and stepped in to create 76 official H/O cars to be used during the festivities and the historic race.

Having reached an Indy 500 Pace Car deal with the Speedway, Hurst was able to get Oldsmobile's marketing department to resurrect the H/O program for 1972. The 72 H/O models featured a convertible and a traditional hardtop with an optional Hurst-installed sunroof. During the holiday season, Dave Landreth and Don Morton asked Chuck Miller to once again develop a white and gold prototype coupe. Oldsmobile chose a Cutlass SX with the W-45 455 V-8 as the platform. Miller created a design that had extended sail panels under a padded vinyl top with an aftermarket sunroof. The two wide gold stripes were painted in a lace pattern that was distinctive for custom paint jobs of the time. Hurst presented the paint scheme to Oldsmobile's marketing department, but it was deemed too garish and a simpler package was approved. This proposal car was returned to Oldsmobile, and most likely met the traditional demise of non-serialized promotional cars.

Powered by the W-45 engine, all of the 72 H/Os were factory-prepared 4-4-2 coupes equipped with Turbo 400 automatic transmissions, dual exhaust, and rear bumper exhaust tip reliefs. A heavy-duty F-41 suspension with seven-inch Rallye SS II wheels and power steering combined to provide precise handling. Wisco, a specialty company, installed both the padded vinyl tops and the sunroof for Hurst.

By this time, Dick Chrysler had left Hurst and had lived in California for two years. After Dave Landreth had successfully proposed the 1972 H/O car to Olds, he tracked down Dick Chrysler in California and convinced him to rejoin the Hurst team. Almost immediately into the pace car program, Dave Landreth and Don Morton also moved from Hurst to Wisco. With the experience of two previous Olds projects, Dick Chrysler moved into the vice president's position and managed the 1972 H/O production.

For the first time, Oldsmobile installed Hurst Dual Gate shifters in the factory console at the Lansing assembly line, just as Pontiac had done on the GTO line for five years. Hurst's agreement with Indianapolis Motor Speedway was reached in February and, as such, Hurst was in a race against the clock to complete the conversions on time for the Indy 500 events at the beginning of May. The company had guaranteed Indianapolis Speedway owner Tony Hulman that

If you sat in the car, there was no mistake that this was the Hurst Indy 500 Pace Car. Hurst's conversion projected a unique identity and these styling touches were part of the package. Hurst applied the 1972 Hurst Olds Pace Car badge on the dashboard. (Photo Courtesy Rich Truesdell)

Oldsmobile installed the Hurst Dual Gate shifter on the regular production line in 1972. (Photo Courtesy Rich Truesdell)

it would provide 76 cars to Indianapolis Speedway for the Indy 500 parade, the Indy 500 race, and all associated events.

The specifications were to convert 4-4-2 convertibles and Cutlass SX coupes into H/O pace cars. Once again, the cars were brought from Lansing to nearby rented space at Demmer for assembly. The cars entered through the back of the building. Similar to past projects, the cars moved from station to station along the assembly line.

At the first station, the Hurst painted gold wheels replaced the standard Rally SSII wheels. The car was hand-pushed around the corner to the decal application station. Each car was carefully wiped down, and the Hurst Firefrost Gold stripes were added to the top of the W-25 Ram Air hood with matching dual stripes added to the trunk lid. The gold side decals were sometimes difficult to apply correctly because the trailing edge of the front fender and the door had to be correctly aligned. The grille and headlight doors were detailed in Satin Black and the H/O emblems were installed on both front fenders and the trunk. At the final station, the owner's manual supplement was added to the owner's packet and placed in the glove box. Also, the H/O dash emblem was fitted to the glove box door.

Since Oldsmobile had performed all mechanical upgrades, the process of creating this H/O model was much less complicated than in years past. Additional time was saved with the application of decals instead of the time-consuming mask-and-paint process. Hurst saved conversion time because the factory had installed the Ram Air, and the car was not fitted with a trunk spoiler or aftermarket mirrors, so more vehicles were completed each day than in previous years. As a result, Hurst produced a total of 629 H/Os, which included 130 convertibles, 220 hardtops with sunroof, and 279 hardtops without sunroofs for the 1972 model year.

Six H/O Vista Cruiser station wagons were built specifically for the Indianapolis 500 race. Each was labeled for a particular group such as the unique label medical director, track, or press emblazoned across the front fender. They were all similarly equipped with 455-ci, W-25

One of the six 1972 Indy 500 H/O station wagons, this is designated for the medical staff at the track. This car has been professionally restored, so it appears as it was for the Indianapolis 500 in May 1972. (Photo Courtesy Mark Fletcher)

The 1973 black H/O proposal car shows the padded top, gold side stripes, and trunk edge. The 1973 model was a big departure from the previous year because it featured the new pillared Colonnade styling. (Photo Courtesy Hurst/Olds Club of America)

For 1973, one of the two Hurst proposal or prototype cars for Oldsmobile featured black with gold trim, standard rally wheels, and power sunroof. (Photo Courtesy Hurst/Olds Club of America)

Ram Air hood, Turbo 400 transmissions with column shift, and bench front seat with the optional third seat in back. Tilt wheel, air conditioning, power steering, and power disc brakes were added. Gold-painted Rallye SS II wheels and a unique Hurst-added padded vinyl top covering the rear two-thirds of the massive long roof enhanced the appearance. Two documented wagons exist today and are frequently seen at major Oldsmobile events.

For the first time, Hurst applied decals rather than painted graphics, but this presented its own challenge. The quality of the original decals did not live up to expectation. The decals started peeling off the Official Pace Car cars before the Indianapolis 500 in May. Dick Chrysler and his crew of Hurst employees throughout Indianapolis tracked down and replaced both the "Pace Car" and date decals on some 70 individual H/O convertibles and the 6 Hurst-prepared Vista Cruisers during the weeks prior to the 1972 festivities.

The successful pace car program was instrumental in reviving the H/O relationship, thus allowing Hurst to become the premier Indianapolis Speedway partner in the ensuing years.

Performance on the Decline

In 1973, General Motors made a bold move by introducing the new Colonnade styling. The new body style featured pillared hardtops, which was a distinct departure from the previous pillarless design. While it was marketed as European in style, European cars at the time didn't reflect this styling. It was a drastic change in design direction for the intermediate-size models, which were a large portion of sales across the Chevrolet, Buick, Oldsmobile, and Pontiac brands.

The redesign was purely cosmetic, eliminating convertible and hardtop offerings for the intermediate-size Oldsmobile lineup. The mechanical components remained the same, and therefore both the 455 and 350 V-8s were installed in Cutlass sedans. However, these engines had lowered compression ratios and restrictive pollution-control equipment.

Then came the second shock to the system: the first OPEC oil embargo. Almost overnight the price of a gallon of gasoline went from less than $.35 to almost $.80. The resulting gas crunch resulted in long lines at the pump. In response, U.S. manufacturers released subcompacts, such as the AMC Gremlin, the Chevy Vega, and the Ford Pinto. However, the buying public embraced

The white 1973 proposal car featured a gold stripe at the top of each quarter panel and no horizontal trunk stripe. These graphic features were not incorporated into the production units. (Photo Courtesy Hurst/Olds Club of America)

Oldsmobile contemplated the differences between the two prototypes offered by Hurst in 1973. The production cars were available as either solid black or white Cutlass S coupes. (Photo Courtesy Hurst/Olds Club of America)

The white 1973 H/O prototype had gold painted Polycast wheels for a more European look. With rising insurance rates and an anti-performance climate in the country, the 455 had a lowered compression and produced only 250 hp. (Photo Courtesy Hurst/Olds Club of America)

the foreign-built cars produced by Volkswagen, Toyota, and Datsun (later renamed Nissan) instead. And there was Honda, which introduced the slightly larger Accord to U.S. buyers in 1976, clearly the right car for the times.

High-performance muscle cars, a legacy of the 1960s, were no longer practical for many to drive. The combination of lower compression ratios and high insurance rates led to their decline early in the decade and eventual demise by the end of it. The gas crunch was simply the final nail in the coffin. Almost overnight those high-performance muscle cars went from objects of desire to very inexpensive used cars.

With this depressed sales environment as a backdrop, Oldsmobile management looked for ways to improve sales. Again, Oldsmobile turned to Hurst to create what we today call a halo vehicle. These are cars that draw new buyers to manufacturers' showrooms, but also sustain its performance legacy.

Don Morton and Dick Chrysler took Hurst-developed concepts to the brass at Oldsmobile on November 15, 1972, in preparation for building two 1973 model proposals based on the new Colonnade-style, two-door models. Oldsmobile's director of marketing John Fleming, Chuck Yerbic, Pete Gerosa, and D. Venti attended the meeting. From that meeting, Morton and Chrysler gained a solid understanding of what Oldsmobile wanted for the 1973 program.

Hurst awaited the arrival of the two special-ordered Cutlass S models equipped with the top-level, factory-installed performance suspension and most powerful engine options. In the meantime, Oldsmobile loaned Hurst a new 1973 4-4-2, so new hood louvers, a Hurst shifter, and a unique padded vinyl top with quarter window treatment could be developed.

Oldsmobile sent Hurst two special-order mule cars that arrived in Ferndale, Michigan, in early December. The team immediately started to prepare the two proposal cars for mid-January unveiling to the Oldsmobile management team. The black car was designated for a raw performance look, and was considered the more conservative of the two. It had gold stripes painted on the side and down the center of the hood, a Hurst-installed power sunroof, and a black swivel bucket seat interior. It sported a half-landau padded top with fixed rear side windows, which was characteristic of the Colonnade-style two-door models. The windows were reduced in size, resembling triangular port holes, and were embellished with large H/O decals in the glass.

A wide gold band crossed the lower edge of the trunk lid, equal in height to the taillights. Each car's taillights featured smoked lenses, and the housings were blacked out similar to the treatment used on the 1969 SC/Rambler. The black car carried a newly-designed direct-line shifter installed in the factory console. The ratchet-style shifter had a squeeze-style release handle. Original-equipment Oldsmobile Rallye wheels with 15-inch white-letter tires helped reinforce the sporty touring car look.

The white car was similar in design and options to the black proposal car, although gold accent stripes were added starting at a point directly behind the back edge of the door and ran to the top edge of each quarter panel ending right

The production 1973 H/O was very distinctive from all angles. In the final analysis, the Hurst Dual Gate shifter won out over the proposed new Hurst straight-line shifter. (Photo Courtesy Mark Fletcher)

above the taillights. The major difference was a manual sunroof, which Hurst proposed, adding to the European flavor and cutting costs. This car also sported the popular Chevrolet Monte Carlo Polycast wheel option, highlighted in gold by Hurst.

Hurst proposed three package options, which would be charged to the dealers as a second invoice. The base H/O package would cost each dealer $630, while the manual-crank sunroof option added an additional $365, with the power sunroof package costing $420. This would add approximately $1,000 to dealer cost, and $1,500 to the new owner once traditional dealer mark-up was realized.

On January 18, 1973, Hurst proposed to Oldsmobile's marketing and design teams a plan for producing 1,000 cars to start 60 days later. Hurst's expectation was to complete 15 cars per day over a 14-week period, concluding the project in mid June.

On January 23, another meeting was held to discuss the possible options and pricing. Both retractable sunroof options were eliminated due to cost, and the smoked taillights were eliminated due to possible difficulties with federal lighting regulations. The Hurst Dual Gate shifter won out over the proposed new Hurst straight-line shifter. In order to control costs, Oldsmobile chose to install the Dual Gate shifter on the assembly line and to paint its own factory 15 x 7-inch Rallye wheels in-house.

Once again, Demmer provided space in Lansing for the production Hurst cars. Hurst contracted with Dave Landreth's new company, Wisco, to provide the labor force needed for the 1973 production. Approximately 75 cars per week were scheduled to be delivered.

The cars were available as either solid black or white Cutlass S coupes with the 250-hp W-25 455-ci engine mated to the durable Turbo 400 3-speed automatic transmission. Oldsmobile deleted all of the external emblems, making sure to include the Rallye suspension and wheels, heavy-duty cooling package, and dual exhaust with chrome tips. A white or black swivel bucket seat interior could be specified, and the factory had installed Hurst Dual Gate shifters. Many cars were also equipped with air conditioning, tilt wheel, power windows, and other factory options providing comfort over acceleration.

The Hurst modifications included the addition of hood louvers along with the application of hood, side, and trunk-lid decal stripes. The modified side windows used a fiberglass plug, which was then covered by the heavily padded half-vinyl top in either black or white. The interior required a revised panel, H/O emblems, and additional owner information added to the owner's manual package.

Fewer Hurst modifications were performed on each vehicle than in previous years. However, labor and production problems plagued the build process. By mid May, public relations manager David Grob wrote an internal Hurst memo that described the delays and obstacles to be overcome. For example, the hood louvers proved to be problematic because of inconsistent stud locations on the vendor supplied hood scoops. To align the hood with the louvers, sometimes holes had to be elongated.

Initially, the rear side window covered up the LOF safety glass logo and required the addition of a decal until Oldsmobile changed the LOF location in production. Many cars leaked because window seals had not been re-glued after installation of the padded top. Once this problem was recognized, Oldsmobile responded by requiring a water soak test before each vehicle was delivered to verify that windows were indeed sealed.

Hurst billed the selling dealer for each conversion. This process allowed for Hurst-specific options to be installed and invoiced during the conversion

Linda Vaughn poses with a production 1974 H/O pace car. The W-30 designated the 455-ci engine option. The pace cars had a special handling package, which featured heavy-duty shocks, higher rate springs, heavier sway bars, and Delta 88 parts improving the braking performance on the car. (Photo Courtesy Pete Serio Collection)

This is believed to be the second, or back-up, pace car for the actual Indy 500 race. The lack of a large front spoiler is evidence of this. Joe Spagnoli of Illinois currently owns the car. (Photo Courtesy Rich Truesdell)

process. The options offered included a pop-up glass sunroof, Hurst air shocks, a digital tachometer, an alarm system, wheel locks, or a seldom seen Hurst digital computer, which carried a hefty $369 list price.

By the end of May, a revised production schedule required a six-day work week to make production goals. An average of 30 vehicles per day, or twice the anticipated daily rate, was required to meet the 1,000-unit goal. But the Hurst company rose to the challenge, building a grand total of 1,097 H/Os for 1973, with about 60 percent being white/gold and 40 percent being black/gold.

One of the white cars with the pop-up sunroof was retained by Hurst for promotional purposes and was soon sporting a set of Cragar five-spoke wheels.

In the fall of 1973, during discussions for the 1974 H/O, Dick Chrysler was driving the car home late one night, and as he negotiated a chicane in the road a little more aggressively than normal, one of the front wheels hit a Michigan pot hole and the wheel fractured. The car ended up skidding off the road into a culvert and flipped into a barrel roll, ending up back on the road and right side up. The car took the brunt of the accident, leaving Dick with only minor abrasions; unfortunately, the car was totaled.

1974 Program

The 1974 H/O was similar in appearance to the previous year's design. However, it had a padded half-vinyl top with the addition of a wide black or stainless steel band bridging the top, visually separating the front and back halves of the roof. The back half was covered in black or white vinyl, which either matched or contrasted the car's paint color. The side stripe was also different, in that it went the complete length of the car with an upturn on the back edge of each rear quarter panel that came back in the form of a "C" toward the back edge of each door. Additionally, the broad gold hood stripe continued across the trunk lid, replacing the previous year's horizontal trunk stripe.

The swivel buckets remained, and the Hurst Dual Gate shifter was located in the factory console. Similar to previous years, the interior featured the Rallye sport steering wheel, deluxe gauge package, and a menu of Oldsmobile comfort options. The black or stainless roof band created a striking appearance, and sales almost doubled.

Of the 1,800 H/O Cutlasses produced in 1974, the W-30, 455-ci Rocket V-8s producing 230 net horsepower were installed in 380 of them. The 350-ci Rocket V-8 with 180 hp was installed in the other 1,420 Hurst/Olds cars. The 350 V-8 was the only engine available for cars destined for California.

Once again, Oldsmobile had the distinguished honor of providing the pace car for the Indianapolis 500, and the 1974 H/O was chosen as the model for the "Greatest Spectacle in Racing." A special four-door H/O was assembled in 1974 specifically for Indianapolis track owner Tony Hulman for this event. It was identically equipped as the two-door models, with the exception of the stainless roof band and vinyl top treatment. It

One of two specially prepared Hurst pace cars used during the 1974 Indianapolis 500. Both cars survived and are in the protective hands of collectors. (Photo Courtesy Rich Truesdell)

was equipped with the 350 V-8 engine, a black swivel bucket interior, and a standard steering column-mounted shifter. Tony Hulman and his family owned the car for several decades. It is now in the care of Calvin Badgley of the Hurst/Olds Society.

The 1974 H/O pace car prototype was submitted with removable rear window and single-piece top section, similar to the 1978 and later Corvettes. Master craftsman Walt Phillips created the top conversions on two cars at his Brighton, Michigan, facility. By removing both panels, the H/O effectively became a convertible with a built-in roll bar that beauty queens and dignitaries could hold on to.

As proposed to Oldsmobile, the pace car sported a huge chin spoiler attached to the bottom of the front bumper covering both front turn signals. By the time the cars were displayed at Indianapolis in May the chin spoiler was eliminated. The pace car provided impeccable performance during the Indianapolis 500 race.

Both of the two pace cars have been rediscovered and are now in the care of enthusiast owners. Randy Bush owns pace car number one with the one-piece removable top. It is equipped with the factory-prepared, 500-hp, 455-ci engine created specifically to make sure the pace car topped 130 mph. Both cars had the specially built engines with the 1971 W-30 intake manifold and a chromed dual-snorkel air-cleaner assembly. The car prominently displays the W-30 designation on the front fenders and in the grille.

Equipped with oversize Delta 88 power disc brakes, a special high-performance suspension, and 15x8-inch all-chrome Rallye wheels, it was ready for track duty. After its Indianapolis 500 responsibilities, it was raced at Pikes Peak in Colorado. It was also used during 1974 and 1975 as an official USAC circuit track car before being returned to Oldsmobile. Oldsmobile sold this car to North Carolina Oldsmobile dealer Rooster Bush (Randy's Dad) in 1976 without a VIN or title. Although the car has been displayed and shown often over the last 35 years, it is unrestored and has less than 10,000 original miles.

Illinois Hurst collector Joe Spagnoli owns pace car number two. It was originally sold in 1975 to Jerry Remlinger, the former owner of an Oldsmobile dealership in Massilion, Ohio, without either a VIN or title.

The car changed hands to its current owner in 2006 at a Florida collector car auction. It is in original unrestored condition, except for the reapplication of the original hand-painted signage, and currently has less than 15,000 original miles. While detailing the car, Spagnoli discovered that the removable hardtop portions are fiberglass over wood, with spring-loaded pins and hold-down clips. He drives this historic car often, sharing it at many of the East Coast H/O events. (Co-author Fletcher was fortunate enough to lap Indianapolis Motor Speedway seated on the back area during the 2009 national H/O Society meet.)

In a departure from its efforts with the Oldsmobile intermediates, for 1974 Hurst also built 42 special Oldsmobile Delta 88 convertibles for dignitary use at the 58th annual Indianapolis 500 race. Each was finished in white with a white

Hurst Collector Joe Spagnoli brings the 1974 pace car to many collector car events. (Photo Courtesy Rich Truesdell)

The two Hurst pace cars were specially prepared in order to stay in front of the pack during the start of the race. (Photo Courtesy Rich Truesdell)

The W-30 designation indicated a powerful 455 under the hood, and 1,193 H/Os were built with this engine in 1974. But horsepower dropped once again, and this particular iteration of the 455 V-8 only produced 230 hp. (Photo Courtesy Rich Truesdell)

The Hurst Oldsmobile Club of America holds a National, bringing together some rare and seldom seen H/Os. (Photo Courtesy Mark Fletcher)

The Hurst Dual Gate shifter was incorporated into the standard Oldsmobile console using a specific top plate. For 1974, Hurst built 2,535 H/Os. (Photo Courtesy Rich Truesdell)

convertible top, bench seat interior, and column-shift 3-speed automatic without the addition of any Hurst performance components. Hurst was responsible for adding the decal graphics package to what was otherwise considered a common factory-produced vehicle. The Hurst trim added a wide gold stripe on the hood and trunk, with a "C" design side stripe matching the H/O Cutlass graphics.

These cars can be found with either black or white interiors, standard or wire wheel hub caps, with most featuring a complete list of power options. Other than one documented car factory-equipped with the 455 V-8, these cars all had a factory 350 V-8 engine, automatic transmission, and air conditioning. Interestingly, none of the documented cars had the standard body-side moldings because these interfered with the placement of the Official Indianapolis Pace Car decals.

The H/O vehicles gathered at the Indianapolis Speedway starting line prior to the 1974 race day. Tony Hulman's specially built four-door Cutlass with the H/O treatment, the two H/O Cutlass pace cars with removable roof panels, 42 H/O Delta 88 convertibles, six Oldsmobile Custom Cruiser station wagons equipped with the 455 V-8 and Hurst appearance package, and 46 Cameo White with white top H/O Cutlass two-doors were there.

It was a banner year for the H/O program, but not much was done at Hurst. After the previous year's difficulty meeting the production schedule, Hurst decided to move the conversion process to a larger facility located in Brighton, Michigan. The larger building was needed to establish a production-line process and provide additional storage for cars as they were staged.

Once again, Dick Chrysler worked with Oldsmobile from the initial concept to final production. Production started in mid March, with the first cars arriving at Oldsmobile showrooms by early April. The Hurst team set up an assembly line similar to previous years, but was able to accommodate a larger workforce. Once inside, each car had the hood scoop hole cut and drilled so that the louvers could be installed. A new template was utilized to allign the location for cutting and drilling the hood's edges.

Both side decal stripes were applied, along with the trunk and hood stripes, prior to starting the roof conversion. The next station masked the car's body with paper to protect the sides and trunk and removed the window surround moldings. The cars were manually pushed between stations in order to keep the emissions from polluting the inside air.

Next, the appropriate color of vinyl top was glued down and trimmed before the roof band and window trim was reinstalled. Emblems, hood ornament, and owner manuals finished off the process along with the installation of any optional Hurst components. Once finished and driven outside, the cars proceeded through a spray booth that soaked them to verify that all windows were sealed. After completion, the cars were shipped either by rail or truck back to Lansing for distribution to the ordering dealership.

Hurst maintained its production schedule, converting 26 cars on average per day, by using improved procedures and working hard over 14 weeks. Additionally, other parts of the building were

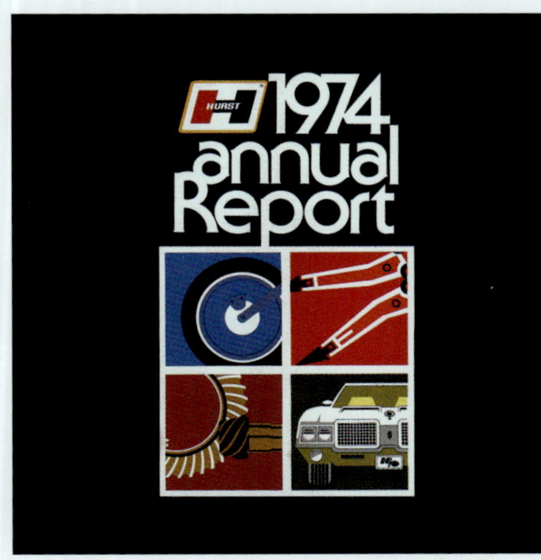

An annual report shows the many products that Hurst offered during the Sunbeam years. (Photo Courtesy Mark Fletcher Collection)

For 1974, Hurst built 42 Oldsmobile Delta 88 convertibles for use by dignitaries at the Indianapolis 500. (Photo Courtesy Mark Fletcher)

The H/O was once again the official pace car of the Indianapolis 500 in 1974. As an interesting sidenote, Hurst built a four-door Hurst Olds in 1974 for Indianapolis track owner Tony Hulman. Calvin Bagley of the Hurst Olds Society now owns the car. (Photo Courtesy Mark Fletcher)

used to prepare the 42 Delta 88 convertibles and the 6 Custom Cruiser station wagons to be used by dignitaries, the press, track medical staff, and the track-day care personnel. In all, 1974 H/O production totaled 1,851 units in four different model configurations.

1975 Program

William Kay, President and CEO of Hurst, based in Warminster, didn't fully support the Hurst Performance efforts in Michigan. He threatened to close the Brighton building and let the lease lapse if they did not secure another contract with Oldsmobile for 1975. Undaunted, Dick Chrysler continued in negotiations with Oldsmobile while working out of shared space at Walt Phillips' shop. Phillips had been instrumental during the 1970 Hurst Chrysler 300 project building the fiberglass pieces in his shop.

Oldsmobile changed the Cutlass roofline for 1975, eliminating the fastback rear window and creating a more upright, formal appearance. This change coincided with the introduction of Hurst's new T-tops, dubbed the "Hurst Hatch," bringing attention to the new look.

Phillips made the 1975 H/O prototype, and production units were again offered in either black or white with gold trim. The manufacturing was moved back into Hurst's vacant building in Brighton. Hurst cut out sections of the roof above the driver and front passenger seat to install the T-tops and added braces to reduce body flex. Then the two removable tinted-glass panels were installed. They were initially created without locks, and theft quickly became a major issue.

During this model year, Hurst made minimal modifications to the car other than T-top conversions. Hurst plugged the side windows and added the half-padded vinyl top and optional Hurst Hatch T-top conversion. The T-tops were a rather expensive option at $335 per vehicle. The actual number of cars ordered with this option is not known, but it is estimated that more than 50 percent of the 1975 H/Os received this conversion.

The body-side, hood, and trunk decal stripe kits were simpler in design, and primarily thick outlines revealed the body color in the center of the stripe. The traditional H/O emblems were applied both outside the car and to the passenger's side of the dashboard. In addition to the H/O owner manual insert, a second manual explaining the storage and care for the new Hurst Hatch was included with cars so equipped. Two storage bags were put into the trunk to protect the panels when removed from the car.

Once completed, the cars underwent the Oldsmobile-required wet-soak test in which water leaks were identified and addressed prior to shipment back to Oldsmobile. Water leaks were troublesome, and Hurst employees spent many hours reworking and improving the seal between the body and the T-top frame.

By 1975 the emphasis moved from performance to luxury, as evidenced by this 1975 Hurst Olds. This car features T-Tops, swivel bucket seats with reversible cushions, and has no opera windows. (Photo Courtesy Richard Truesdell)

Hurst eliminated the small opera windows for 1975. Available in either white or black, a gold outlined side stripe created a more subtle appearance than previous years. Hurst Hatch T-tops were a popular option. (Photo Courtesy Mark Fletcher)

Over the years, Oldsmobile had to deal with T-top leak warranty claims because of flex in the body from normal use. Top panels cracked due to body flex, and some owners reported hatch panels flying off when the cars were driven.

Drivetrain options were identical to 1974, and 1,342 W-25s were manufactured with the 350 V-8 and 1,193 of production W-30s were equipped with the 455 V-8 for the 1975 model year. The color split was almost even with 1,242 painted black and 1,293 painted white. The swivel bucket interior was again a staple of the Hurst package. For 1975, it had reversible inserts that allowed for either vinyl or cloth to enhance the look of the interior, setting the Hurst cars apart from the non-Hurst Cutlass models. The early production start in February allowed an additional six weeks and as a result a total of 2,535 units were produced.

1976, 1977, 1978 Proposals

Hurst created two 1976 H/O proposal cars in white with T-tops, based on the Cutlass S. The blacked-out headlight surrounds and dual grilles gave it a forceful and dominant look in an era when performance cars had become almost extinct. Dual, wide gold stripes outlined in black started from the top of each grille and continued down the trunk. A padded top covered the side windows similar to the 1975 top.

The H/O emblems were installed on each padded sail panel and the lower right corner of the trunk. Other factory options included swivel bucket seats, dual sport mirrors, and a tilt wheel. Contrary to what some have claimed, the car did not have a rear spoiler when it was proposed to Oldsmobile. Component choices were limited to the traditional Hurst Dual Gate shifter and factory-installed Rallye wheels with white-letter tires. The 1976 H/O program was well received, but Oldsmobile abruptly ended it when Dick Chrysler announced his departure from Hurst to start his own company, Cars and Concepts.

Based on production Oldsmobile-supplied vehicles, Hurst employees drove and later sold these cars. One of the proposal cars has been found and is still unrestored.

Hurst created at least two 1977 proposal cars using the exact same recipe as in 1976. Painted black with saddle tan bucket seat interior, it featured red pinstriping starting below each section of the split grille and outlining ghost stripes over the hood. An additional 4-inch-wide lower body stripe started on each front fender crossing the wheel wells at the midpoint. This gold stripe crossed each rear quarter, with Hurst/Olds spelled out in block letters and pinstriped around the edges in bright red.

Similar to the 1976 proposal, the 1977 model featured a padded top with a 2-inch band along the front edge covering both quarter windows. The car was equipped with Hurst-installed T-tops, as Hurst was doing approximately 70

Linda Vaughn's own 1978 Hurst Olds was often seen at the racetrack. (Photo Courtesy Hurst/Olds Club of America)

Oldsmobile offered two color combinations for the 1979 H/O program, either white or black, with the front part of the roof and hood in gold. T-tops were a popular option. (Photo Courtesy Mark Fletcher)

percent of the factory-ordered T-top installations at this time. This car did feature the understated trunk-mounted rear spoiler with an H/O emblem displayed prominently on the right edge. The car was well-equipped, with the contrasting saddle tan interior trim with high-back swivel bucket seats. It was also equipped with power windows, tilt sport steering wheel, console with Dual Gate shifter, and factory air conditioning. The factory Rallye wheels were painted with the traditional gold accent.

One of the two cars has been found and restored by a Hurst/Oldsmobile Society member. It has occasionally been seen at national H/O events.

There was also a 1978 Hurst proposal based on the new downsized Cutlass. It was all black with the traditional half-length padded vinyl top covering most of the rear quarter windows and each side having the H/O emblem. Additional equipment included the 350 V-8, 3-speed automatic transmission with a console-mounted Hurst shifter, T-top, power windows, and bucket seats, which no longer swiveled. The car wore side stripes similar to the 1977 proposal car with a prominent W-30 designation on the lower side of the unique front spoiler. A factory F-41 heavy-duty suspension package featured optional five-spoke cast wheels with Goodyear GT radial white-letter tires. Both grille sections were blacked out, although both the factory lower body aluminum trim and Cutlass hood emblem remained intact.

1979 Program

The 1979 H/O was completely assembled at the Olds factory in Lansing, Michigan, with the familiar two color options. Ordered in either white or black, Oldsmobile added the gold two-tone paint starting on the grille panel and incorporating the flat surface of the hood to include the top of each front fender. This blended into the front half of the roof section including both A-pillars. The top edge of each fender had a separate dual-lined gold pinstripe flowing back into the C-pillars and across the top. There was no vinyl top option available for 1979.

T-tops were optional yet very popular; more than half the owners purchased them. Each car was equipped with bucket seats and console; the General Motors heavy swiveling bucket was discontinued in 1978 in favor of the new thinner design. At the time, General Motors manufactured hoods from aluminum. This hampered any scoop or louver installation because any alterations required Oldsmobile to perform additional crash testing, as cutting a hole in the hood possibly weakened its structural integrity.

Oldsmobile retained the same awkward, thick, five-spoke wheel design, and it was painted Hurst Gold, with the exception of the raised outline around the five spokes and the outer lip. Dual

This dark blue 1981 Cutlass was the basis of the 1982 H/O proposal car. Hurst kept the car after Oldsmobile rejected the proposal. It was later sold to an employee and is thought to have survived. These cars were fitted with an Oldsmobile 307-ci V-8 producing about 180 hp, which was a far cry from the 1970 H/O 455-ci V-8 that produced about 430 hp. (Photo Courtesy Marty Danko)

Linda driving the Mini H/O at the races in 1979. (Photo Courtesy Marty Danko)

sport mirrors and exterior H/O emblems adorned the outside of the car. A V-8 in W-30 trim resided under the hood, and this was in a V-6 world. W-30 designated the 350 V-8 with mandatory F-41 heavy-duty suspension, and dual exhaust as part of the Oldsmobile option package. Other factory Cutlass options were also available, including the popular electric moon roof.

The W-30 designation had previously been reserved for the most powerful engine Oldsmobile had to offer. For 1979, it represented horsepower rather than cubic inches. The car almost didn't come to be, as Oldsmobile wanted to produce it without a Hurst shifter.

Hurst President E. Toomey refused to allow Oldsmobile to use the Hurst name unless the Dual Gate shifter was installed. In a last minute agreement, Hurst had the task of quickly producing unique brackets to hold the Dual Gate shifter in the factory console. With this accomplished, production started in early January. Only 2,499 units, which included 1,165 white and 1,334 black cars, were built for an obvious reason.

The Oldsmobile 350 V-8 was not EPA certified in the Cutlass body and Federal law required individual certification on any model with more than 2,500 units produced. To keep from incurring the added expense of recertification, Oldsmobile made sure to not exceed the specified number. Oldsmobile paid Hurst $200 per vehicle, plus the cost of the shifter, decals, and emblems. By now, the H/O option was a whopping $2,054. Many of the more well-appointed cars had a sticker price in excess of $10,000. Despite the added cost, the cars sold well, in part due to the three-year absence of H/O offerings.

Linda Vaughn was given a black and gold car for her personal use. There are many pictures of her sitting on the roof waving to race-day crowds with her legs draping over the passenger seat. She kept this car for many years until finally parting with it in 2007. It carried California personalized plates of LV79HO when it was sold, and it now belongs to an H/O collector.

Hurst was going through its own turmoil in the late 1970s. Most of the past management had left Hurst, taking with them the long-term relationships with the Detroit automotive community. Although ownership had changed and profits were dwindling, the Brighton location was busy doing T-top conversions for all of the Detroit car manufacturers. In fact, Hurst performed all of Pontiac's T-top conversions to the Grand Prix. Almost 25 percent of new-car models offering T-tops were delivered with the option.

1982 Proposal

Since 1976, Cars and Concepts (owned by former Divisional Vice President Dick Chrysler) was a significant competitor. Quality issues plagued the Hurst production team with higher-than-expected warranty claims and lower-than-expected manufacturer and customer satisfaction. Soon, contracts were either split with, or lost to, the growing competition.

Dick Chrysler purchased the failing Hurst division from Allegheny in 1981 and immediately created a 1982 proposal. Based on a 1981 model of the popular Cutlass, it was dark blue over silver with red pinstripes. It had a navy blue cloth bucket seat interior with console and Hurst shifter. Powered by a high-output version of the 5.0-liter (305-ci) V-8, it was mated to a Turbo 350 3-speed performance-tuned transmission. The proposal was not accepted, and therefore the car never entered production. Interestingly, the general manager at the Hurst plant in Warminster used the prototype car as his daily driver, and it was later sold to an employee. The subsequent owners are unknown, but many believe it remains somewhere close to the Warminster facility.

1983 Program

With Dick Chrysler's purchase of the Hurst Michigan operation, a 1983 proposal was submitted. He had quickly improved the build quality of the T-top conversions and set out to rebuild the damaged relationships with the Detroit manufacturers resulting from the leaking T-tops. Hurst Performance became a division of Cars and Concepts, and soon profitability was restored. To develop a unique identity with an alternative color scheme for Cars and Concepts, Hurst resurrected the historic black with silver combination to commemorate the 15th anniversary of the first 1968 H/O.

Similar to the 1979 model, the 1983 cars were primarily assembled at the Lansing Oldsmobile factory. A rear-end gear ratio of 3.73:1 helped boost acceleration. The cars were assembled with Oldsmobile's 307-ci V-8 rated at an anemic 180 hp. Oldsmobile transported them by rail to the Cars and Concepts facility in Brighton, Michigan. Once unloaded, the crew installed the new Lightning Rod shifter.

This new shifter emulated the triple arm shifters being used in racing applications. In reality, it was a modified dual-gate pattern with the ability to manually pull back each of the arms, manually shifting the Turbo 350 transmission from first to second, and second to high gear. When it was time to race, the driver placed the closest arm in drive leaving the two right arms forward and disengaged.

Every passenger recognized the eye-catching shifter topped by three

Hurst was a primary sponsor of *Silver Bullitt* in 1983. At this stage, the car is ready to have the decals and graphics applied prior to the racing season. The Hurst semi-trailer was used to transport the race car, the crew, and spare parts to the track. (Photo Courtesy Marty Danko)

Warren Johnson and Marty Danko both campaigned drag cars for Hurst during the 1983 NHRA season. As a Hurst employee under Allegheny ownership, Marty received the use of the second car which he raced with his own engine and crew. (Photo Courtesy Marty Danko)

The Hurst Lightning Rod Shifter was standard on the H/O for 1983 and 1984. The red warning tag was meant to keep the driver from jamming the linkage by engaging all the levers at one time. (Photo Courtesy Rich Truesdell)

bright red shifter balls. Despite its high-performance look, it suffered from certain problems. Often drivers pulled all of the levers back toward them until they jammed.

The production line also added the H/O decals separating the upper black and lower silver two-tone paint scheme. The red highlighted stripes and badging created a striking package with the contrasting bright red cloth-trimmed bucket seat interior. Two body modifications were added that included a non-functioning cowl hood scoop and a rear trunk spoiler. If the car was designated to get a T-top, it was also installed prior to returning the car to the Oldsmobile distribution system.

Cars and Concepts produced a total of 3,000 black and silver cars. One unique white car with gold stripe was created for promotional use and has often been associated with Linda Vaughn. It was reported that the car had a modified non-production (and therefore non-EPA certified) 350 V-8 engine. The car was never given a production VIN and Oldsmobile later destroyed it.

The final production total for the fifteenth-anniversary H/O was 3,001.

1984 Program

The success of the 1983 anniversary model provided the foundation for the 1984 version. Nothing was changed from that recipe. The two-tone colors were reversed, and the primary color became silver with black accents. The stripe kit consisting of silver outlined in black and red remained the same. Only the fifteenth-anniversary decals were absent from the 1984 version.

A total of 3,500 units were built starting in November and ending in mid June 1984. Documentation shows that Hurst retained three cars for promotional purposes. Oldsmobile retained 46 units for field sales and marketing purposes and 220 units were shipped to Canada, while in May 1984, Oldsmobile scrapped car number-two for some reason.

The Hurst/Olds Society retains the complete list of VINs and original

The 1984 Hurst Olds was available with optional Hurst Hatch T-tops. Although they were a popular option, they were prone to leaking and easy to steal. After T-top leaking had been identified as the problem, Oldsmobile required Hurst to "wet test" every car before it was released to the dealership to verify the seals were tight. (Photo Courtesy Mark Fletcher)

This special Oldsmobile FE3-X prototype was created in conjunction with Hurst Performance in 1985. (Photo Courtesy Mark Fletcher)

Hurst developed the "Darth Vader" Oldsmobile FE3-X proposal car as a possible 1985 H/O. The car is now owned by Angelo Valenti. (Photo Courtesy Mark Fletcher)

The 1984 H/O program was nearly identical to the 1983 Hurst program. The colors were simply reversed from a black car with silver trim (1983) to a silver car with black trim (1984). (Photo Courtesy Rich Truesdell)

owners for the 1984 production run. Owners can request their specific vehicle information with proof of ownership and a nominal fee.

The Oldsmobile Cutlass was an extremely successful car for Oldsmobile in the 1980s, and in many years of the decade it was the best-selling car in the U.S. It shared a dubious distinction with its GM cousins, the Chevrolet Monte Carlo, Pontiac Grand Prix, and Buick Regal. All built on the same GM A-body platform, these two-door versions consistently topped the "most stolen car" lists each year throughout the 1980s.

Most major components were interchangeable among years and models, and it is common to see Hurst-specific items on non-Hurst cars. Knowing the VIN details that specify the Hurst option for 1983 and 1984 is important prior to investing in models from these years.

During the 2009 Hurst/Olds Club national convention, professional thieves stole four show-quality H/Os from the hotel complex. The thieves targeted one 1979, two 1983s, and one 1984 H/O model. The 1979 car was later recovered disguised in primer, stripped of most of its Hurst-specific components.

Marketing of the final H/O was primarily handled by Oldsmobile. Dick Chrysler was eager to bring the Hurst/Olds name back to the races and created two full-tube-frame drag cars. Veteran racer Warren Johnson was asked to campaign a 1983–1984 H/O with a 650-ci engine. The drag car was featured on the cover of the May 1983 issue of *Hot Rod* with Linda Vaughn in a red jumpsuit.

Warminster employee Marty Danko also successfully raced a 1984 H/O provided by Hurst under the *Silver Bullet* moniker. Marty explained that the chassis was a back-up car for Warren that Hurst let him race until he left the company in 1986. Marty built his own engine for the car and was supported by Hurst for the 1984–1986 race seasons. The budget for his travel and expenses were supported by the Hurst marketing department.

1988 Aero Program

In 1988, former Hurst employee Jack "Doc" Watson developed and sold an aftermarket lower body fairing kit with H/O emblems. Approximately 100 were constructed and sold, primarily to Hurst/Olds club members to be used on 1988 and older Cutlass two-door models. Once installed, the cars were referred to as Aero cars. None of the Aero cars were a result of the previous collaboration between Oldsmobile and Hurst Performance.

Conclusion

In 2004, General Motors stopped producing the Oldsmobile line. Oldsmobile was started in 1899 by visionary founder Ransom Eli Olds, who was one of the first to develop a mass-produced automobile. Over the next 105 years Oldsmobile produced many trend-setting models and the cars they collaborated on share this legacy.

Today, the Lansing, Michigan, facilities sit idle after having more than 14 million vehicles roll off the production line. It serves as a memorial to the great cars bearing the name Oldsmobile. Through a sporadic 17-year production run of nine different factory-authorized H/O models, more than 17,000 cars were assembled. Among all collectible Oldsmobiles, the cars from the Hurst collaboration are among the most prized.

The Hurst Equipped emblem refers to the Hurst Lightning Rod Shifters, which were used in the prototype. Note the massive hinged rear spoiler. (Photo Courtesy Mark Fletcher)

A low stance and custom body styling add to the sinister look of the Hurst proposal car. The car is now owned by Angelo Valenti. (Photo Courtesy Mark Fletcher)

In 1988, the Hurst Aero kit was sold by "Doc" Watson and installed on regular production Oldsmobile Cutlass Supremes. (Photo Courtesy Rich Truesdell)

Mopars with a Twist of Hurst

A Match Made in Performance Heaven

In the 1960s, Super Stock racing was the most competitive form of stock-based drag racing. High-performance customers looked at Super Stock class as a proving ground for the quickest cars. It was the class to been seen in and the class to win. Mopar needed a high-performance partner to dominate the class, so Chrysler and Hurst teamed to produce the fastest production muscle cars of all time—the 1968 Super Stock Hemi Darts, which covered the quarter-mile in 10 seconds.

Hurst built 82 Hemi-powered Darts for Chrysler in 1968. These lightweight drag cars terrorized the competition at the strip. Today, a restored example can top $250,000. This model is a recreation in honor of the original created by SS/AFX in Arizona. (Photo Courtesy Rich Truesdell)

CHAPTER 7

Competition Heats Up

In the early 1960s, Detroit introduced compact vehicle platforms to stem the tide of the import invasion spearheaded by Volkswagen. In order to compete (with the exception of the Chevrolet Corvair), Detroit took a conventional approach, scaling down the size of its mainstay, front-engined, rear-wheel-drive cars into a package with more compact dimensions.

Ford led the way with the Falcon, which was matched by Chrysler with the Plymouth Valiant. But almost by accident, when Chrysler downsized its 1962 full-size models, it became a powerhouse in drag racing by combining the lightweight B-Body with a modern version of the Hemi, introduced for the 1964 racing season.

At about the same time, Pontiac was working to be competitive in what became the NHRA Factory Experimental (AFX) class. In late 1962 it built what became known as the Super Duty Tempest. With General Motors withdrawing from factory-sponsored racing efforts, the 14 Super Duty Tempests, Pontiac's version of the GM compact platform introduced in 1961, were powered by a 421-ci engine from its Catalina full-size model. Campaigned by the likes of Wild Bill Shrewsberry and Stan Antlocer (whose car was auctioned off on eBay in October 2008 for $226,521), the Super Duty Tempests were the template for the AFX cars that followed. In 1964, Ford countered by fielding 100 midsize Fairlane two-door sedans equipped with the venerable 427 side-oiler big-block and was dubbed the Thunderbolt. Ford contracted Dearborn Steel Tubing to make the race conversions, and the company transformed the docile Ford compact into a fierce fire-breathing competitor.

The recipe required major alteration to the engine bay, making room for the wide big-block mill that replaced the standard 221-260-289 small-block V-8. The Thunderbolt benefited from replacing the front sheet metal components with lightweight fiberglass. Side glass replaced with Lexan windows with pull-up straps replaced the manual window mechanisms. Both front bucket seats were borrowed from the Econoline van parts bin, trimming precious pounds. To handle the added torque, the Thunderbolts were equipped with a heavy-duty 3-speed automatic transmission lifted from the Lincoln Continental that rotated a 9-inch rear with a 4.44:1 final drive ratio.

Ford Thunderbolts were formidable competitors, capturing the Top Stock crown and the 1964 NHRA Manufacturer's Cup for Ford. These cars had a small Hurst connection, as supplier of their shifters to Dearborn Steel Tubing as part of the conversion process. In 1964, Chrysler introduced the Super Stock Hemi 426 Dodges and Plymouths. These were the natural evolution from the competitive 413 Max Wedge cars that benefited from the 1962 downsize. Almost overnight, Chrysler's Hemi-powered B-Bodies set the pace in the NHRA's increasingly popular AFX Class, which attracted support, some of it clandestine, from Detroit's Big Three.

Tarozzi and the Test Mule

Cultural changes played a part as drag racing became a major spectator sport in the 1960s. As U.S. involvement in Vietnam grew, many soldiers sent their pay home to buy high-powered compacts and intermediates, as muscle cars went from niche to mainstream. And as many returned home after serving in the military, drag racing became a place for a young independent to square off with the established names of racing.

Bob Tarozzi was a young engineer for Chrysler who was recently transferred to the racing development department. In the fall of 1967, this engineering team met with Dick Maxwell, head of Chrysler's domestic product planning. Tarozzi was assigned the task of evaluating and improving the suspension on the A-Body compact cars, the Plymouth Barracuda and Valiant, and the Dodge Dart, all three of which were substantially revised for the 1967 model year. Tarozzi worked under direction of Tom Hoover

As hard as it is to believe, the original Tarozzi Barracuda test mule survived, shown here in 2008 at the All Hemi Reunion at Quaker City Raceway, New Salem, Ohio, where it was part of the largest single gathering of Hemi-powered drag race cars. (Photo Courtesy Greg Fernald)

and was teamed with fellow engineer Larry Knowlton for this project.

More than four decades later, Tarozzi explained, "We were first assigned the task of developing a set of A-Body contenders in November 1967. The expected delivery to our growing fleet of racers was promised for March 1968. The project was behind before we got started. For this reason, we chose to construct the project by pulling from our existing parts bins and past experiences."

Tarozzi and Knowlton started working on a leftover 1967 Barracuda equipped with a factory 383 in Chrysler's Woodward facility. They updated the grille and trim to represent a 1968 model. Bob knew that the A-Body rear axle could not be strengthened to withstand the punishment from the torque generated by Chrysler's Hemi and Wedge big-blocks. Therefore, the larger B-Body rear axle was adapted to the A-Body car by relocating the spring perches and opening up the restrictive rear wheel well found on the Dodge Dart. The Barracuda required only minor body modifications to adapt the wider-than-normal rear assemblies.

Tarozzi retained the Chrysler corporate A833 4-speed transmission mated to the bulletproof Dana 60 rear with 4.88:1 cogs. With a minimal amount of engineering effort, this off-the-shelf drivetrain solution could be easily adapted to the narrower Barracuda and Dart body shells. "Corporate development of the drag racing products were an afterthought," recalls Tarozzi. "There was a growing animosity within the Chrysler ranks with the full knowledge that the NASCAR program received the bulk of the racing department funding."

Tarozzi kept the rear suspension conventional with specially rated heavy-duty springs provided by an outside Canadian vendor that allowed for better weight transfer during hard launches. He designed new offset shackles moving the springs 3/4 inch inward for larger tire clearance. The conventional large, rubber rear-end snubber, normally attached to the front of the center section functionally limiting axle windup, was conspicuously absent from this car.

The front suspension consisted of a combination of lightweight six-cylinder springs and torsion bars in combination with heavy-duty Hemi components. The B-Body rear axles required a 4.5-inch five-lug bolt pattern in place of the standard 4-inch units. Front brake rotors found on the larger export model suspension (Mexican production) were used to standardize the wheel bolt pattern front and rear. Most of these components were installed by Chrysler while the cars came down the Hamtramck, Michigan, assembly line.

A specially designed K-member, Mopar's engine crossmember, allowed the engine to be lowered by more than 1 inch in the cramped engine bay. This lowered K-member noticeably altered the steering geometry of the Barracuda

Mr. Norm's Grand Spaulding Dodge contracted Hurst to stuff the 440 Magnum engine into engine bay of the diminutive A-Body Dodge Dart. The 1968 GSS Dart is equipped with a 375-hp 440-ci engine rather than a 383 as the badges indicate. The heavy 440 and the lack of power steering meant it was handful to drive, but in a straight-up street race, few other cars could match it.

New York Taxi Project

Over the years, Hurst had developed a successful and trusted partnership with Chrysler, starting in 1961 with the addition of the Hurst shifter as an over-the-counter option at Dodge dealers across the nation. Hurst had remained actively involved with Dick Maxwell and the racing development team in the following four years, primarily through the successful *Hemi Under Glass* Barracuda program showcasing the Plymouth Barracuda at racetracks across the nation.

For 1968, Chrysler depended on Hurst's offsite production capabilities for three major projects. The first Hurst project involved assisting Chrysler in displacing the Checker Taxi as New York City's only official cab. Checker had capitalized on the larger design of therear passenger compartment and had been successful in getting the New York Taxi Authority to include leg room as factor in the selection process. Competitors, Chrysler included, felt that the requirement was unfair, but the Taxi Authority did not budge. Chrysler's product development team determined that the shared chassis configuration of the Dodge Coronet and Plymouth Belvedere, in addition to the larger Fury, could all be altered to meet New York City's requirement.

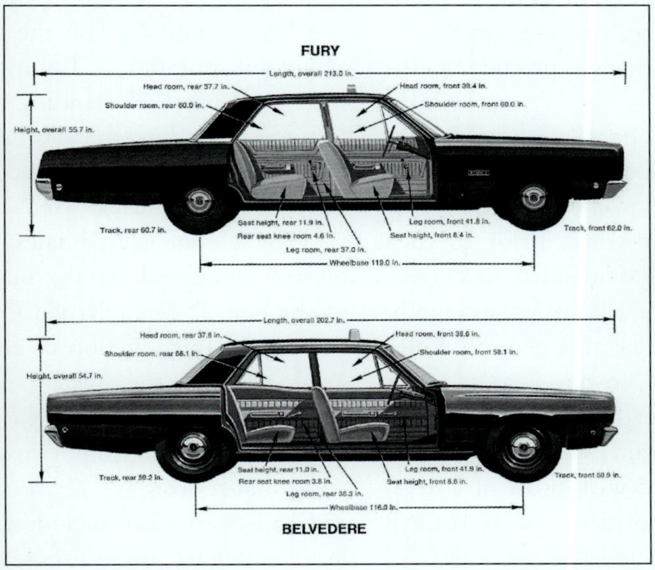

Hurst replaced the floors for Chrysler so it could meet the New York taxi requirement for back-seat passenger room in 1968 and 1969. (Photo Courtesy Mark Fletcher Collection)

Hurst was contracted to alter 25,000 vehicles over two years for this project. Hurst Performance's Dave Landreth oversaw the project for Hurst and developed an ad hoc assembly line. Dave recalls, "Paul Phelps found and purchased a used automatic car wash setup that we installed in the facility we leased in Madison Heights. Chrysler delivered the cars by carrier where they were immediately put onto the assembly line as we didn't have the room to store more than 20 to 30 vehicles before or after the conversion.

"We removed the front and rear seats and placed them on the roof and trunk of the car. We cut out the rear floor by placing a pattern on the floor and using a cut-off wheel around it. Every 10 or so minutes a bell rang and the car wash mechanism was turned on until each car progressed to the next station. A new, lower, rear floor section was welded in place at the second station. Soon, the bell again rang signifying the progression to the next station where the door-opening pinch welds were bent back. This helped increase the door opening to the required New York City specifications. The last station replaced the rear floor covering, seats, and finish trim. The car was then driven off the line and returned to the Chrysler distribution system for delivery."

Chrysler paid Hurst Performance $43.50 per converted taxi at a 50 percent profit, which increased Hurst's profitability by half a million dollars over the two years of the program.

Hurst was paid $43.50 for each Chrysler product that it converted to meet the New York City taxi ingress and egress specifications. (Photo Courtesy Mark Fletcher Collection)

One of the SS/AFX Hemi Barracudas launches for a nostalgic quarter-mile trip at the 2010 Mopars at the Strip in Las Vegas. (Photo Courtesy Rich Truesdell)

test mule. Bob Tarozzi brought this to Tom Hoover's attention during testing, but the deficiency was overlooked due to no "off-the-shelf" part being available and a demandingly short timeline.

The Hemi Barracuda test mule was set for its maiden shakedown in the last two weeks of January 1968. The car was transported during a frozen Detroit winter to the warm Irwindale drag strip in sunny Southern California. Bob Tarrozzi explains, "In our first outing, the rear suspension worked as proposed with the heavy-duty springs allowing for rear axle wind-up. This directly stored kinetic energy and transferred it back into traction during each launch.

"On the other hand, the front suspension immediately showed its weakness in that the vehicle hopped each time the front wheels returned to the track. With each hop a change in steering direction occurred, making the car difficult to control under full acceleration as it went down the track." At the track, a combination of alterations to the upper control arms and steering arms were tried, and these changes provided better stability.

During the final week of testing at Irwindale, Dick Maxwell invited the automotive press to witness the Barracuda's time trials. Prior to their arrival, Maxwell demanded that Tarozzi remove the rear license plate sign he had customized for this project, which simply stated "No-one Cares." This reflected the fact that the drag racing development team was understaffed and underfunded with most of Chrysler's money supporting the NASCAR racing program.

With development nearing completion, attention was turned to determining how to build the required 50 each of the two models in order to meet NHRA homologation requirements in time for the 1968 spring season.

Mr. Norm's 1968 Dart GSS

The second leg of the Chrysler-Hurst collaboration had Hurst building the Dart GSS (GSS standing for Grand Spaulding Dodge, the legendary Chicago Dodge dealership owned by Norm Kraus, better known as Mr. Norm).

The Dodge Dart's sales had been severely impacted by the introduction of the new 1967 Chevrolet Camaro, as well as the introduction of an optional 390-ci engine in the substantially revised 1967 Mustang. *Motor Trend* magazine had identified this competitive class of performance iron as "The Pony Cars," and had overlooked including the Dart in this category, its stylish new hardtop and convertible models boasting all-new styling for 1967. For the 1968 model year, Ford upped the ante with its January release of the new Cobra Jet engines displacing 428 ci and rated at a conservative 335 hp.

For 1968, Dodge countered with the top-line 383-ci engine rated at 330 hp for the Dart and Barracuda, but suffered in direct comparison to the competition. Mr. Norm placed a contract with Hurst Performance to modify 50 Dodge Dart GTS models after demonstrating that the 440-ci big-block could be shoehorned into the A-Body engine bay with a few select modifications.

Chrysler delivered the 383-equipped Darts to Hurst for a heart transplant, with Hurst removing the factory 383 engine and replacing it with the 375-hp version of the 440 engine. Although the first car built was a 4-speed with the Hurst Competition Plus shifter, the following 49 cars were equipped with the 3-speed TorqueFlite automatic transmission retaining the factory console shifter.

Hurst attached an additional "S" highlighted with red in place of the middle "T" in the GTS designation, creating the specialized GSS badges.

Hurst built two special Mopars to convince the Dodge boys to create a car to compete with the H/O. The Dodge Swinging Bee Dart and Merada Charger failed to enter into production. The whereabouts of either of these prototypes today is unknown. (Photo Courtesy Hurst/Olds Club of America)

Norm Kraus of Mr. Norm's Grand Spaulding Dodge contracted Hurst to convert the 383-equipped Dodge Darts to 440-powered Darts. Fitted with 375-hp 440 engines, the GSS Darts were blindingly fast, and faster than most muscle cars of the day. Here, Norm Kraus (left), the Dodge Rebellion Girl (center), and Gary Dyer (right, Mr. Norm's driver) are shown at the Chicago Auto Show in the late 1960s. (Photo Courtesy Mr. Norm's Grand Spaulding Dodge)

The Hemi Dart interior was all business, utilizing the lighter A-100 van seats on special aluminum support pieces. (Photo Courtesy Rich Truesdell)

The factory 383 front fender badges were left on the car, to possibly catch the unsuspecting street racer off-guard by concealing the monster lurking underneath the hood.

Each car was equipped with manual front disc brakes and manual steering due to restricted space in the engine compartment. *Hot Rod* reported quarter-mile times at 13.3 seconds and 107 mph right off the showroom floor.

Grand Spaulding Dodge exclusively sold the cars and only about a dozen exist today. They are well-known within Mopar collectors and highly valued.

Hemi Darts and Barracudas

While Bob Tarozzi was testing the prototype Barracuda Hemi car in California, Dick Maxwell met with the Hurst team's Jack Watson, Dave Landreth, and Jack Duffy, to ask them to be ready to build 100 cars in 100 days. Landreth set up room at the Madison Heights location to create the first few samples and then moved production to the Ferndale warehouse where they were converting taxi cabs.

Both models were produced on the Hamtramck assembly line, the Darts as 383 GTS business coupes, the Barracudas as factory 383 fastbacks, similarly equipped. Each car went down the assembly line with very specific instructions. The serial numbers all started with LO23 for the Darts and BO29 for the Barracudas. All components for regular production models were installed

The Holley carbs are perched on 426 race Hemi. (Photo Courtesy Rich Truesdell)

Cragar wheels add a period-correct look to this early Mopar. (Photo Courtesy Rich Truesdell)

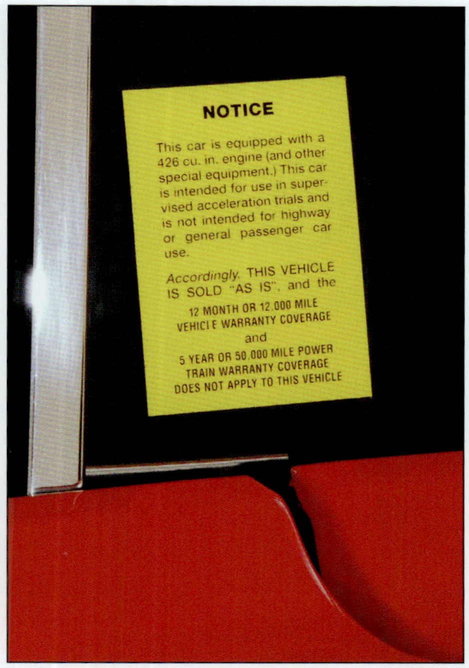

The sticker affixed to each Hemi Dart reminded the recipient that the car was not created for regular street usage and that there was no factory warranty. (Photo Courtesy Rich Truesdell)

on the line. The standard 383 suspension, manual disc-brake system, front crossmember, and rear end created the rolling chassis. Chrysler also designed and assembled a special steering column manufactured with a 2-inch-shorter sleeve, moving the shaft bearing closer to the firewall, freeing valuable space needed for the exhaust headers.

The body was fully assembled, with the exception of the hood hinges and latching mechanism, hood, battery tray, front bumper, and horns. Deleted items included the heater, radio, fuel lines, sound deadeners, undercoating, carpet backing, rear window mechanisms, back seat, spare tire and jack, and driver-side mirror. Two Bostrom lightweight bucket seats (similar to the ones installed in the Dodge A100 vans) were mounted on specially fabricated aluminum seat brackets. An export-only mirror delete plate was part of the standard driver-door assembly installed at the factory.

The cars left the factory on 14 x 5-inch-wide rear wheels with the standard A-Body five-lug-by-4-inch bolt pattern. Although these cars traveled the full distance of the Hamtramck assembly line, they were physically pushed off the end of the line and delivered to Hurst minus engine, transmission, driveshaft, exhaust, and paint.

Cars unceremoniously traveled the 8 miles to the Ferndale facility on the back of a private contractor's tow truck. The incomplete and primered bodies looked like they were being towed to a wrecking yard to be destroyed. Instead, they were individually delivered to the facility where the additional Chrysler-specified ingredients completed the recipe and began the lifecycle of these historic cars.

On the Assembly Line

Hurst's production process was far from sophisticated. Each car was manually pushed into the building where the rear axle was quickly removed and the back of the body was put onto a stand. Every evening, three men arrived at the Hurst facility and worked through the night altering the factory-fresh panels. One template outlined the area to remove from each of the Dart's rear quarter panels with an air-powered sheet-metal nibbler.

The VIN tag identifies this car as a recreation built by SS/AFX in New River, Arizona. (Photo Courtesy Rich Truesdell)

Chrysler Announces Its Super Stock Program

Chrysler announced the Super Stock program to its dealer network with the following letter dated February 20, 1968:

To: All Plymouth Dealers

Subject: 1968 Hemi Barracuda Super Stock

The Chrysler-Plymouth Division offers for the 1968 models a 426 Hemi-Powered Barracuda Fastback for use in supervised acceleration trials. These cars will weigh approximately 3,000 pounds and have been designed to meet the 1968 specifications of the major sanctioning drag strip organizations.

The Hemi-Powered Barracudas will be available through production in limited quantities in March. To order this vehicle, use the Barracuda Order Form and specify Body Code BO29 and Transmission Code, either 4 Speed Manual, Code 393, or Automatic, Code 395. No other specifications are necessary.

Description of Components

426 cu. in. 8-cylinder engine with dual 4-barrel carburetors–12.5:1 compression ratio.
Cross Ram Intake manifold.
1 11/16" x 1 11/16" Holley carburetors.
Competition Hooker headers, exhaust pipes, and mufflers.
High capacity oil pump.
Roller timing chain (reduced timing chain stretch for more consistent engine performance).
Mechanical valve gear.
Dual breaker distributor.
Transistor ignition.
Metal core type ignition wires.
Unsilenced air cleaners.
Deep groove fan drive pulleys.
Heavy duty radiator.
Aluminum seven-blade fan equipped with Viscous drive.
Special offset 15" rear wheels.
Chrysler-built 8¾" large stem pinion gear set, and heavy-duty axle shafts with automatic transmission (4.86 axle ratio).
Dana-built 9" heavy-duty axle with manual transmission (4.88 axle ratio).
Sure-Grip differential.
135 Amp. Hr. battery (located in rear compartment).
Heavy-duty high control rear suspension.
Front disc brakes 4½" Bolt Circle.
Fiberglass front fenders.
Fiberglass hood with scoop.
Light weight steel doors.
Light weight front bumper.
Light weight side window glass.
High capacity fuel lines.
Business coupe interior (2 bucket seats - no rear seat).

For Manual Transmission Only

Special heavy-duty 10" clutch and flywheel.
Safety steel clutch housing.
Competition "Slick Shift" 4-speed transmission.
Hurst remote mounted floor-shift unit with reverse lockout.
For Automatic Transmission Only
High stall speed torque converter (large drive lugs and 7/16" diameter attaching screws).
Heavy-duty manual shift TorqueFlite transmission.
Hurst floor-mounted shift unit.

Please Note

The following items are deleted on this body type:

Heater, Body Sealer and Sound Deadeners, Silence Pads, Outside Mirrors, Right Side Seat Belt and Body Color Paint.

NO OPTIONAL EQUIPMENT OF ANY KIND CAN BE ORDERED

The policy of Chrysler Corporation is one of continual improvement in design and manufacture, wherever possible, to insure a still finer car. Hence, specifications, equipment and prices are subject to change without notice.

These vehicles are intended to use in supervised acceleration trials and other competitive events, therefore, they will be sold without warrant. Special stickers will be provided for plant installation (attached to left "A" post) which will read as follows: "This vehicle was not manufactured for use on public streets, roads or highways and does not conform to Motor Vehicle Safety Standards.

All customer orders must be accompanied by a signed disclaimer (sample attached) indicating that the purchaser understands that this vehicle is sold without warranty and does not conform to Federal Vehicle Safety Standards.

Any prospective customer who desires to purchase one of these maximum performance vehicles should be made aware of the following characteristics which make them unsuitable for general use.

A high idle speed is required to ensure adequate lubrication, minimize roughness, and to keep the engine from stalling.

The modified intake manifold causes a rich surging condition, misfiring and unstable engine operation in cold weather, which makes ordinary street driving extremely difficult and it is not recommended for this use.

Higher than normal oil consumption will be encountered because of increased lubrication to the valvetrain and cylinder walls.

The carburetors are calibrated for maximum power and a high numerical axle ratio is used for acceleration. As a result, the gas mileage is considerably less than for a conventional car.

Engine noise would be objectionable due to increased piston clearance and mechanical valve tappet clearance.

The ignition system is designed for optimum engine output and must be kept in top condition. This makes it necessary to inspect, adjust and replace the spark plugs and ignition points more frequently than would be necessary on a standard engine.

On cars equipped with automatic transmission, band adjustment must be made frequently.

Due to performance characteristics, maintenance and operating expense will be high since premium fuel is required and frequent oil changes are a MUST.

Does not conform to Motor Vehicle Safety Standards.

Warranty and Policy Coverage

Any customer purchasing this model vehicle should be advised that due to the expected use, the vehicle is sold "as is" and the 24-month or 24,000-mile vehicle warranty coverage, the five-year or 50,000-mile Power Train Warranty coverage, or any other warranty coverage (including, but not limited to the implied warranties of fitness for purpose intended or merchantability) will not apply to the vehicle. The manufacturer assumes no responsibility for the manner in which such vehicles operate.

Any repairs or adjustments which you believe warranty factory participation should be brought to the attention of your Regional Service Office where such requests will be handled on individual merits.

Attached is a form letter (to be prepared on your letterhead) which should be thoroughly understood and signed by each prospective purchaser and attached to your order for each Hemi Barracuda Super Stock. The purpose of the letter is to explain the normal operation characteristics of these vehicles and clarify that the warranty coverage's do not apply. Be sure a letter in this form, signed by your customer, is included with your order so there will be no delay.

A second template designated the location of the three vertical cuts; the metal was beat back and braised into a new rear wheel lip. The Barracuda's open-wheel design did not require Hurst to perform this extensive alteration, so no template was used, although some of the racers requested enlarged wheel wells for bigger rear racing tires. Hurst made a triangular cut at the lower portion in front of the rear wheels to accommodate these special requests.

With the Dart's rear body modifications complete, B-Body rear axles were installed with the new Super Stock springs and 3/4-inch offset brackets. The 15 x 6-inch rear wheels with 1.5-inch positive offset and 7.75 x 15 tires were also installed. Based on the factory transmission preparation, the automatic-equipped cars were equipped with Chrysler's battle-proven 8¾-inch rear end outfitted with a 4.86:1 gear ratio. The cars with a 4-speed transmission were mated to the bullet-proof Dana 60 rear with 4.88:1 cogs.

Next, the Hemi K-member replaced the standard unit and was installed with 1-inch-tall spacers between the unibody and the K-member. This, in essence, increased the engine compartment height, allowing for additional room for the cross-ram engine. Each front shock tower was indented with a large hammer between the top of the shock and where the mammoth valve covers resided in the engine bay. This crude modification was made not to clear the heads and exhaust headers, but to allow access for the removal of the valve covers without requiring the lifting of the engine.

The master cylinder was removed so that an offset plate provided by Chrysler could relocate the unit 3/4 inch outward, providing more space for the mill to be attached. Because the brake master cylinder required removal to service the engine, flexible brake hoses were attached in order to maintain the integrity of the braking system. Larger export-only disc brake rotor assemblies with five-on-4.5-inch bolt pattern were installed with correlating D70 tires on 14 x 5.5-inch steel wheels. An oversize 3/8-inch

1968 Dodge Dart GSS Grand Spaulding

In 1968 Hurst worked with Norm Kraus' Grand Spaulding Dodge in Chicago on the Dodge Dart GSS. This fully restored version is a wolf in sheep's clothing as it is equipped with 383 fender badges but has a 440 shoehorned under the hood. (Photos Courtesy Rich Truesdell)

fuel line was added in order to feed the combined 1,540 cfm flowing through two Holley carbs.

Chrysler Marine and Industrial division provided the 426-ci iron Hemi engines. Each was hand built, starting with October 1966 cast blocks. The compression ratio increased from the standard 10.5:1 to 12.5:1 by the use of custom Dykes ring pistons. The engine's bore mechanical lifters combined with a mild Street Hemi cam profile. A roller timing chain and a high-capacity oil pump with a deep-sump 7-quart oil pan kept the engine turning freely. Transistorized ignition with a dual-point distributor were standard racing fare.

Chrysler also provided a Winters Foundry magnesium cross-ram intake manifold with two Holley 770-cfm 4150 model 4-barrel carburetors. The engine was underrated at 425 hp and it didn't take long until the NHRA officials factored them at 500 hp. Even the corrected calculation was 10 percent more conservative than reality.

On the Hamtramck factory production line, engine and transmissions were bolted together and installed from below the car while perched atop the crossmember. The width of the Hemi engine demanded that Hurst drop the engine into the restricted A-Body engine bay from above. They were then required to marry the transmission from beneath while attaching Haynes racing clutch components and blow-proof scatter shields on the manual-equipped cars. Appropriate heavy-duty driveshafts finished connecting the power to the street.

The Hurst shifters were one of the last items installed. The 4-speed cars received Competition Plus shifters with increased-diameter shift rods and a bracket that moved the handle both up and back toward the driver. The automatic-equipped cars received Hurst Dual Gate floor shifters with a Hurst mini floor console. Hooker exhaust headers with 2-inch primaries were adapted to a restrictive collector and routed straight into Hooker glass-pack-style mufflers with the pipes being finished off with a pair of standard turndowns, all to meet the NHRA class specifications. The 135-amp industrial battery was mounted in the truck using a Ford battery tray, and the battery assembly added 85 pounds of weight bias to the rear of the car.

The original steel doors and front fenders added on the assembly line were replaced with lightweight, acid-dipped components. Chemcor Corning glass, which was half the thickness and weight of the original glass, was installed. All window crank mechanisms were removed and replaced by webbed straps that snapped on the door, requiring the window to either be all the way up or down. The fiberglass front fenders and pin-on hoods were initially manufactured by B&N Fiberglass in Ohio. The fast pace of production proved to be too challenging for the small company and a second manufacturer in Canada was added.

Hurst purchased the Mr. Gasket hood pin kits from Gratiot Auto Supply and installed four per car. The front bumpers were made of steel in a gauge thinner than standard and were not acid-dipped as suggested. Those components removed during the conversion were returned to Chrysler for reintroduction to the factory assembly line. It was later reported that some of the original doors

At the All Hemi Reunion held at the Quaker City Raceway in Salem, Ohio, the greatest collection of authentic Hemi-powered race cars was assembled, including the Sox & Martin Plymouth Barracuda and GTX, brought to the event on a Sox & Martin Dodge hauler. The 1969 Barracuda Super Stock and the 1969 Plymouth GTX Super Stock race cars are both equipped with a 426 Hemi. Ronnie Sox drove the Sox & Martin Barracuda, which was one of the most dominating cars in drag race history.

The dual-quad Hemi had a 12.5:1 compression ratio and produced an advertised 425 hp, but the NHRA rated it at 500 hp. Most in the know, estimated the true horsepower to be in excess of the 550 mark. (Photo Courtesy Rich Truesdell)

The Hurst Pro-Matic shifter was installed in a variety of muscle cars. It was one of best automatic transmission shifters of its era and featured a full forward and reverse ratchet action.

and fenders ended up being scrapped due to the difficulty of entering them back into the system.

Dealer Delivery

Once the transformation was completed by Hurst, the cars were shipped back to Chrysler and forwarded onto the delivering dealers with a minimum of quality-control inspection. During production front ends were not aligned, and many bolt-on parts were not torqued to Chrysler specs. Reports of broken 5/16-inch intake bolts making their way into and destroying a few engines came back to Chrysler and Hurst. Each car carried a sticker stating it was not legal for street use. In addition, these cars did not carry a factory warranty.

Hurst production began in early February with the first car reported to be delivered on February 18, 1968, to Grand Spaulding Dodge, which had come from Chicago to Hurst's production facility to personally pick up its car. The end product hardly looked finished as it sat in light gray primer, dark gray fiberglass front-end components, and undersize taxi cab wheels and tires. Many racers also made the trek to Hurst to pick up their cars quicker than they could be shipped through the system.

Chrysler's dealer delivery process required that the converted cars could only be loaded at the farthest back position of the bottom level of the trucks. This was to protect the 9-quart oil pans from hitting the cross braces on the car carriers. Due to delays with the fiberglass components, many cars were delivered without a hood. At one point, even the front fender had to be shipped separately to be installed by the customer.

Cars for Racers

Many of the recipients were experienced dealer-sponsored racers in line for an updated car, at $5,200 each. With the

A factory promotional photo of the Hurst Chrysler 300. (Photo Courtesy Hurst/Olds Club of America)

The luxurious interior did not include the Hurst Dual Gate shifter because Chrysler was experiencing high warranty claims for the TorqueFlite transmission. Chrysler executives thought that a manual-controlled automatic shifter would add to these dependability issues. (Photo Courtesy Hurst/Olds Club of America)

expansion of the program by 50 additional cars, some racers were piloting a Mopar for the first time. Some racers complained that a few cars had been delivered with blown engines due to some unauthorized drag testing while in transit. Chrysler also shipped new steering arms to help correct the bump steering problems discovered during initial testing. These Hurst quality concerns accompanied the fact that some racers were in need of additional information on how to best set up these purpose-built machines.

In April 1968, Chrysler hosted a special Chrysler racers school. Dick Landy, Shirley and H.L. Shahan, and others instructed racers how to prepare their cars. Chrysler's Dick Maxwell spoke on tuning the Hemi engine, Bob Tarozzi discussed TorqueFlite transmissions and stall converters, and Jack Watson from Hurst spoke on how to adjust linkage based on his acquired knowledge as Hurst's "Shifty Doctor." This seminar was conducted as the racers were making final preparations to their cars and prior to NHRA's official sanctioning of the A-Body Hemi in June of 1968.

Production Totals

In the end, Hurst built 82 Darts and 70 Barracudas. Combined with the Dart built by Dick Landy, the Barracuda assembled by Sox and Martin, and the original Chrysler Barracuda mule, total production was 155 units. The final product weighed 3,020 pounds, which equated to a 6-pound-per-horsepower production car. Shirley Shahan drove the *Drag-On-Lady* automatic Dart in SS/BA Class with a best ET of 10.79 and 123 mph at Pomona Raceway. Hurst-prepared Mopars went on to dominate the NHRA SS/B and SS/BA classes, and AHRA Super Stock class across the nation through 1968 and 1969. These cars remained contenders for many years, and are still raced competitively today.

The 300H

In addition to the Super Stock program, Hurst had another conversion project with Chrysler Corporation, but this was a high-performance full-size street car. Over the years, Hurst had developed a strong relationship with Chrysler, and so Dave Landreth and Don Morton proposed a Hurst Chrysler 300H model.

The original concept was based on a Spinnaker White 1970 Chrysler 300 two-door hardtop equipped with bucket seats, 440-ci TNT engine, Hurst straight-line ratchet shifter, Ram Air hood, and built-in rear trunk spoiler and quarter end caps. Retaining the now famous white with gold trim, Hurst built just 501 units, 500 coupes and a single convertible, which Hurst used in 1970 as Linda's track car.

Linda Vaughn (left) and Nikki Phillips (right) are perched on the only Hurst Chrysler 300 convertible made. Hurst used it for promotional functions in 1970. The 1970 Hurst Chrysler 300 convertible has been found and restored. (Photo Courtesy Pete Serio Collection)

The major change from proposal to production was the exclusion of any Hurst shifter. In 1970, Chrysler was suffering from a high failure rate with the TorqueFlite transmission and chose to produce most cars with the leather split-bench seat interior and the standard Chrysler automatic shift lever on the steering column. Fewer than 10 percent were built with leather bucket seats and floor console shift, but even these units were not delivered with a Hurst shifter.

The cars were assembled at the Ferndale facility in Michigan. Production changes consisted of removing the stock hood, trunk, and quarter panel end caps, and replacing them with the fiberglass units. Hurst Gold was painted on the cars as an accent color, and Hurst emblems were added both inside and out. After the conversion, the cars were returned to the Hamtramck facility to be shipped to the dealers.

The Hurst magic was absent without any performance improvements to the car. The Hurst Chrysler 300 was equipped with the 375-hp, 440-ci engine and the 3-speed TorqueFlite transmission mated to a 3.23:1 rear axle. The car was a look into the future of cosmetically enhanced specialty car programs of the 1970s—scoops, stripes, and spoilers without any real performance enhancements. Although both distinctive and attractive in appearance, they were extremely expensive, with a sticker price of more than $4,500.

The 300H languished on Chrysler lots with many dealers resorting to heavily discounting the cars below cost to finally sell them. There have been reports that two units were produced equipped with the 426 Hemi engine, although neither one of these cars has been discovered or documented during the past four decades.

The Hurst Marketing Machine

Making History

Bob Riggle and Linda Vaughn pose with *Frantic Fish* in front of the Sears automotive service center after putting on a show for U.S. servicemen. (Photo Courtesy Bob Riggle Collection)

Hurst had served our country for more than a dozen years when he was stationed at Johnstown naval base in Warminster. Trained as an aircraft machinist, he was already making extra money by working on the cars of friends and customers.

George learned to be a self-promoter early on in his business life. Never the shy one in a group, when he spoke others stopped to listen. As dominant a personality as he was, he still had a way of making others feel valuable. Many have said that the world was a better place because of George Hurst and he had an impact on many who knew him.

CHAPTER 8

Hurst Ads

As a young man in the Navy, George was an avid reader of *Hot Rod* magazine. When it came time to advertise his growing engine conversion business, the choice of where to place his ad dollars was obvious. There were few hot rod magazines published in the 1960s that didn't have one, two, and sometimes three different Hurst ads in a single issue. Don Lane, one of Hurst's first full-time employees, remembers putting together the ads at home on his own time and mailing them to *Hot Rod*'s editor in 1956.

George was creative and liked to write his own ads. Early on, he found himself in legal trouble when he used the trademarked VW logo in one of his first ads for the massive Hurst Volkswagen Microbus bumper guards. His primary customer for this product was a prominent Volkswagen dealer in New York, and through this connection Volkswagen of America quickly saw the ad.

Hurst was sent a stern letter from the VW legal staff demanding that he stop using the VW logo in all ads going forward, and recall and destroy any and all copies of the brochure. Not long after, VW started adding bumper override bars to all of the VW buses imported into the United States. Overnight, this eliminated the need for the Hurst bumper guards and almost bankrupted the new Hurst-Campbell partnership in 1959.

When more orders were needed, George himself hit the road and promoted his products to speed shops and performance centers, just as he did in 1959 in his drafty 1956 Chevy convertible. Later, it was common for George to pick up the phone and speak directly with the speed shop owners and employees about sales numbers and promotional programs.

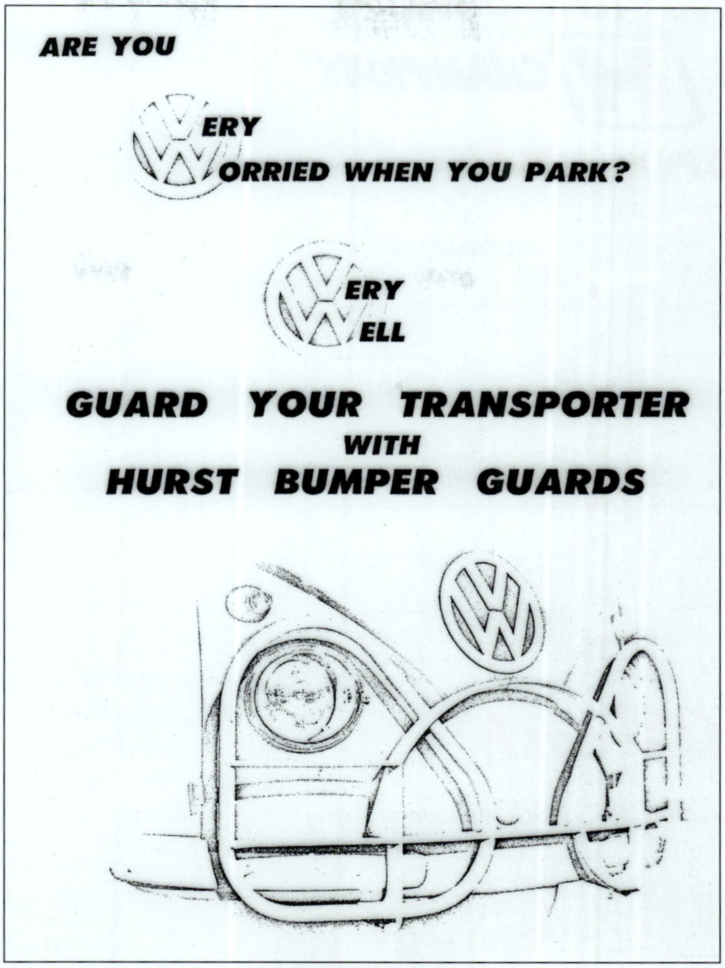

George wrote and helped create this ad to help market and sell the bumper guard. While the product provided vastly improved occupant protection, the import market was not Hurst's core business. Beyond that, the ad infringed on the VW logo which was used without permission, and as a result, Volkswagen of North America demanded Hurst destroy all the ads and literature of the product. (Photo Courtesy Dennis Kirban)

This Hurst Aid truck was used throughout the 1970s as a rolling mechanics shop. (Photo Courtesy Marty Danko)

Hurst often hired a large bus to take the Hurst "Associates" and their family members to nearby Atco raceway. The only trade-off was that all employees had to wear Hurst shirts and hats and act as representatives of the company.

A Passion for Racing

Hurst created the Hurst Aid station where employees like Jack "Doc" Watson, Dick Chrysler, Bob Riggle, Paul Phelps, and many others repaired race cars that were unable to pass tech inspection. Hurst set up a rolling machine shop to install shifters and make minor repairs, including welding, if required.

Soon, the Hurst Aid station became a staple at most East Coast raceways, with racetrack owners giving favors to Hurst in exchange for its presence. When the Hurst Aid team was there, the number of participants, and therefore spectators, increased.

Hurst gravitated toward major racing events where he established relationships with most of the legends in

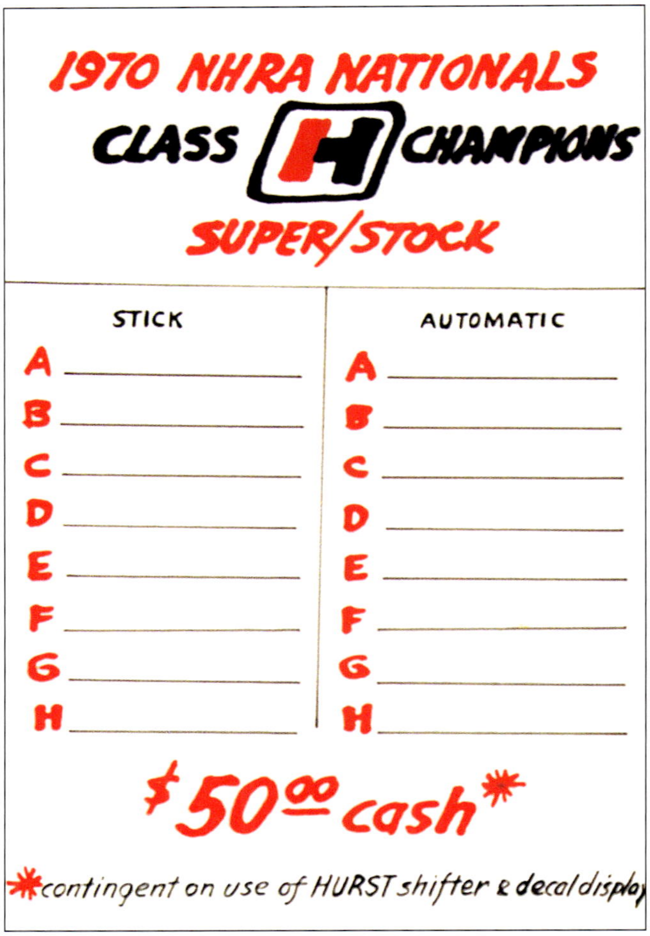

1970 NHRA NATIONALS

CLASS CHAMPIONS

SUPER/STOCK

STICK	AUTOMATIC
A ____	A ____
B ____	B ____
C ____	C ____
D ____	D ____
E ____	E ____
F ____	F ____
G ____	G ____
H ____	H ____

$50.00 cash*

*contingent on use of HURST shifter & decal display

Hurst offered contingency money to those winners who displayed Hurst decals on their cars. (Photo Courtesy Pete Serio Collection)

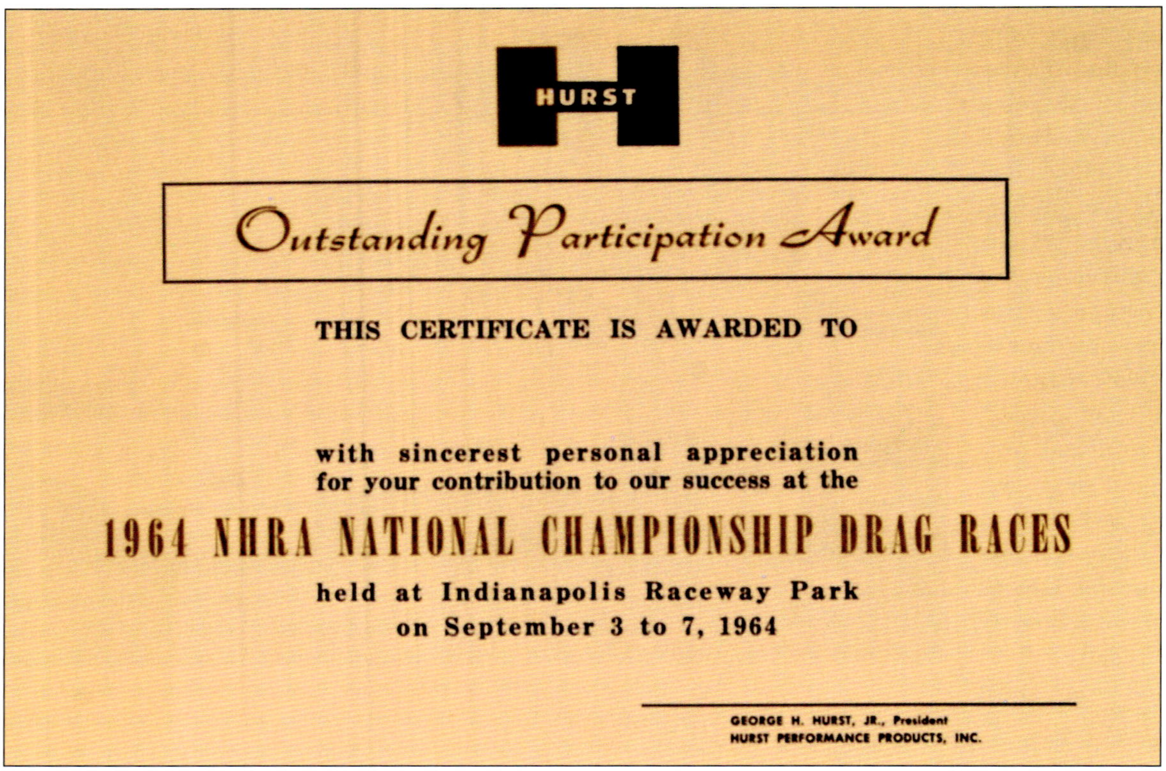

HURST

Outstanding Participation Award

THIS CERTIFICATE IS AWARDED TO

with sincerest personal appreciation for your contribution to our success at the

1964 NHRA NATIONAL CHAMPIONSHIP DRAG RACES

held at Indianapolis Raceway Park on September 3 to 7, 1964

GEORGE H. HURST, JR., President
HURST PERFORMANCE PRODUCTS, INC.

This was the participation award given to each driver in the NHRA National Championship held at Indianapolis Motor Speedway in the fall of 1964. Hurst was always generous with the prizes he awarded because Hurst firmly believed satisfied and loyal racers became satisfied and loyal customers. (Photo Courtesy Pete Serio Collection)

drag racing history. Don Garlits was a frequent visitor to the Glenside and Warminster facilities. On one occasion, he completely tore down his dragster and reassembled it in the matter of a few hours at the Hurst building.

A little known fact is that George contracted with Elmore Leonard to write catchy *Hot Rod* magazine ads for Hurst from 1962 to 1965. Elmore went on to become a famous author of almost 50 published books, including *Get Shorty*, which became a hit film.

Following Elmore was Bob Held who became the Hurst Art Director based in Warminster. Bob was an exceptional artist and had a long and varied career within Hurst writing creative ads, marketing materials, catalogs, and promotional banners used at the races.

Hurst awarded a complete set of uniforms to the winning crew at the 1964 NHRA Indianapolis Nationals. (Photo Courtesy Pete Serio Collection)

Although *Hemi Under Glass* was a popular advertising vehicle, Hurst was paid to have the car perform at the racetracks. Each weekend brought a fee between $500 and $1,000 to Bob Riggle and his crew. From these proceeds, Riggle paid Hurst about 25 percent and the rest paid expenses and wages for the two-man crew. It didn't take long for this rolling billboard to pay back Hurst the initial investment required to build it.

Chrysler supplied all repair and update parts for the program, and soon *Hemi Under Glass* had more requests for appearances than it could meet. In 1966, the Hurst *Hairy Olds* was created as a second showpiece for the Hurst team, and for two years it, too, drew crowds to the track. Each raceway promoted the appearance of either of these two cars. Hurst required each track to utilize both print and radio ads emblazoned with the Hurst name and logo. Through this symbiotic relationship, Hurst received free advertising, plus compensation to fund the program and racetrack owners got their name connected to the popular Hurst brand.

George enhanced his personal relationships with the NHRA staff by giving away new cars, stereos, watches, and cash to the national racing champions each year. The goal was to make Hurst the most visible marketing presence at every sanctioned racing event.

George was extremely fond of the Indy 500 race and all of the festivities leading up to the race. He and track owner Tony Hullman were close friends, and Hurst developed a personal connection with the event. Once the races were started, the track became two separate cities of spectators divided by the race itself. Tony and George devised a plan to build a pedestrian bridge over the track permitting spectators access to the pits during the race. George paid for the improvement with the requirement that each side of the walkway bear the Hurst name in 10-foot-high red and black letters.

1967 Pontiac Grand Prix Convertible

In 1967 this 428-powered Grand Prix was one of a reported three convertibles purchased by Hurst Campbell, Inc. as verified by its ProtectoPlate and by Pontiac Historic Services. Later it was purchased by George Hurst's personal secretary. (Photos Courtesy Mike Pemberton)

The Hurst name was emblazoned on almost every item imaginable. The most memorable were the Hurst Gold cars, which were mostly Pontiacs in the early years. It was a common site to see at least two at every major race that Hurst attended. One convertible was always mandatory, most often seen driving down the tarmac with an 8-foot-high gold shifter and a Hurst Girl hanging on for dear life. These platforms were designed to attach over the top well and be supported by brackets attached to the rear bumper. At least one platform was adjustable and could be attached to any convertible, requiring less than one hour's work.

The First Hurst Girl

Unknown to most hot rodders, Janene Walsh was the first Hurst Girl hired by George in the fall of 1964. Her first ride was on top of the back seat of the blue 1964 Pontiac Bonneville convertible.

Soon, she and George came up with the idea of having a mobile winner's stand with a giant Hurst shifter. A platform was created and attached over the trunk of a 1964 Dodge convertible for her to stand on while waving to the crowd as the car slowly drove down the 1,320 feet in front of the grandstands. Interestingly, the large Hurst letters along the side of the shifter were not present when it was first introduced.

GeeTO Tiger Giveaway

Janene Walsh sometimes wore the GTO Tiger outfit that Hurst and Wangers used to promote a Hurst GTO giveaway contest. During this promotion, the Tiger walked in front of the crowd and challenged a driver from the crowd to race one of two Royal Bobcat Pontiac–prepared GTOs.

George Hurst awards the keys for a new Dodge to Dave Strickler for his win driving a 409 Chevy at the 1963 NHRA Indianapolis Nationals. (Photo Courtesy Pete Serio Collection)

The contest was established to promote both Pontiac's new GTO and Hurst. The top prize was a special 389 Tri-Power–equipped Hurst Gold 1965 GTO with black vinyl top, with a gold-plated Hurst shifter and Hurst Dazzler wheels, along with Safe-T-Track, power windows, a white interior, console, and factory reverb AM/FM stereo. The car was specially prepared by Royal Pontiac with the High Performance Bobcat treatment.

The GeeTO Tiger was heavily promoted for months in 1965 with full-page ads and editorial coverage in most automotive magazines. To enter the contest, you had to listen to the new Colpix hit song "GeeTO Tiger" and count the number of times you heard the word "tiger." Additionally, a 25-word-or-less essay was required, stating why you would like to own the car. Both Hurst and Pontiac promoted the record and the contest in their ads, culminating in more than 450,000 "GeeTO Tiger" albums being distributed.

Alex Lampone, a 19 year old from West Allis, Wisconsin, saw an ad in *Hot Rod* magazine and entered the contest on July 27, 1965, four days prior to the July 31 deadline. He answered with the correct count of 42 times, and submitted the following words: "Prowling around in a custom Tiger like the GeeTO, I'd be as sure as a Hurst shift to make a hit with all the 'cats." These words made a hit with the judges—NHRA director Wally Parks, *Car Craft* magazine's Dick Day, and George Hurst—and he won the contest.

As a result of this contest entry, young Alex's life dramatically changed. In early September, George Hurst personally hosted him at the NHRA National Drags in Indianapolis. The GeeTO Tiger keys were formally presented to him by George Hurst, Jim Wangers, Jack "Doc" Watson, and Pat Flannery.

Lampone kept the unique car for only a few years, and then sold it to Pete Yeko who lived in the same town. Yeko successfully raced the car while keeping it in as close to original condition as possible. In 1975, he sold the car to Pontiac collector Jim Urban in nearby Appleton, Wisconsin. The car was still as-delivered to Lampone, except the engine was growing tired. Urban rebuilt the engine and sold the car to Jerry Treleven, also of Appleton, who recognized the unique history of the car. He repainted the car in the early 1980s, and after keeping the car for 30 years, he sold it at the Mecum auction in 2005 with 59,000 original miles. The car was auctioned again in May 2010, where it was purchased for $250,000.

During the four-month promotion, the tiger-suited driver was actually either one of Royal Pontiac's mechanics, Jim Wangers, or even George Hurst himself. Who was hidden in the tiger suit became the question of the day. Jim Wangers never let a chance go by to create more hype, so he soon created a second contest to guess who the driver really was. At the last race in Indianapolis, the costumed tiger's head was very ceremoniously removed to reveal George Hurst as the tiger.

Miss Golden Shifter Program

George Hurst was a savvy promoter, marketer, and showman. He also developed a keen sense for effective marketing techniques for the company's customer base. In the male-dominated sport of racing and in the hot rod scene, young, pretty women helped promote products, and certainly these young beauties handed out trophies at racing events. Hurst wanted his own beauty queens to represent the company and promote its products. Eventually, the Hurst Shifter Girls became staples at race tracks around the country in the 1960s and 1970s.

Pat Flannery

Pat Flannery first met George Hurst while she was working at a Ford dealer in Mefford, Ohio. She was one of a handful of women within the male-dominated automotive industry working in the customer relations department. The Ford sales team was very "old boys school" during the 1960s and Pat knew just how to navigate the shark-infested waters. Soon, she and George were discussing how she could join the Hurst team as the new Hurst Miss Golden Shifter. She began her reign at the May 1965 Indianapolis 500 race where most of the Hurst team was also present.

Throughout 1965, she continued to travel with Hurst to all the races. George also hired different girls for particular races. On one such occasion, George was at the wheel with Pat and four unidentified girls aboard the platform on the back of the Pontiac convertible. Each girl other than Pat was in a different armed forces-style uniform.

During her one-year reign, Pat was on hand for the Summers Brothers' land speed record run at the Bonneville Salt Flats. Hurst was a majority sponsor, sharing in the effort with both Firestone and Mobil. Christened *Goldenrod*, the cylindrical machine was powered by four 426 Hemi engines, each with mechanical fuel injection. After *Goldenrod* recorded a wheel-driven record of 409.277 mph, Pat reached into her purse and pulled

George Hurst and John DeLorean

George was a good friend of Pontiac's John Z. DeLorean. In 1966, DeLorean introduced the Pontiac overhead-cam six-cylinder engine with 10.5:1 compression ratio, and a 4-barrel Quadrajet carb on a special intake manifold boasting 207 hp, and installed it in the midsize Tempest lineup. He wanted to show the public how European the design was, and how competitive its engine was to the British Jaguar XKE unit.

To illustrate this point, Hurst purchased a used 1963 Jaguar S-1 coupe and set out to test the theory. Hurst employees Jack Watson, Dave Landreth, Paul Phelps, and Bob "Animal" Lathrum removed the stock drivetrain and installed the new Pontiac OHC six and Muncie 4-speed in place of the British drivetrain. The car was painted Hurst Gold and then loaned to several magazines, requesting that they evaluate the car without having disclosed the actual drivetrain changes.

The car appeared in a major feature in the July 1966 issue of *Car and Driver*. The engine fooled the drivers with the exception of the significant improvement in the ease of shifting with the Muncie box when equipped with the Hurst short-throw shifter. Initially, the car had a lower top-end speed by 5 mph compared to the stock Jaguar engine, so the Hurst team installed a set of triple Weber carburetors, a custom-built header, and aftermarket camshafts, bringing it to an estimated 315 hp.

The Jaguar was later sold to Ford engineer Don Coleman, who removed the Pontiac engine and installed a high-performance version of the Ford 300-ci straight-6.

out bright red lipstick and proceeded to write the official time on the tail section to commemorate the event. The *Goldenrod* record stood unbroken for the next 27 years.

After relinquishing her Hurst Girl title, Pat Flannery began contributing to Hurst newsletters. George had always felt that the young men serving our country in foreign lands were missing out on the racing hobby back home. He started to publish the *Defender Newsletter* that was shipped to servicemen around the world.

Soon, the Hurst marketing team began publishing *The Hurst Hustler Club* magazine for civilian racing enthusiasts and the *Hurst Campbell Banner* reporting company information for all Hurst employees.

Pat retained this position for a year then returned to her business career as a customer relations manager for Savin Business products.

Linda Vaughn

When Pat announced her move into the Hurst offices to work on the publications, George ran an ad in *Hot Rod* magazine looking for the next Miss Hurst Golden Shifter. He received many applications, but one individual stood out from the sea of young beauties. Linda Vaughn grew up in Dalton, Georgia. Linda often visited the local racetrack with her family, and as a young child she realized she had gasoline and racing in her veins. As a young woman, she competed for and was crowned Miss Atlanta International Raceway (AIR) in 1961.

During her one-year reign, the curvaceous and outgoing beauty attracted the attention of men in the sport. She was soon offered a full-time position from Pure Oil as Miss Firebird Fuel, traveling from track to track across the south.

Three years later, when Pure Oil was about to merge with Union Oil, Linda applyed to be the new Miss Hurst Golden Shifter. George quickly hired her. Public relations director Jack Duffy now had three crowd pleasers to schedule at the multiple Hurst-hosted race events around the country: *Hemi Under Glass*, *Hairy Olds*, and Miss Hurst Golden Shifter Linda Vaughn.

Linda was far more than an average beauty queen—she loved racing, and

Hurst congratulates Gas Ronda's win at Riverside and announces the NHRA national prize of a new 1964 Barracuda with a Hurst 4-speed shifter in this low-resolution archival *Hot Rod* magazine ad. (Photo Courtesy Mark Fletcher Collection)

Hurst created the GeeTO Tiger contest. A special 389 Tri Power–equipped 1965 GTO was the grand prize. But this was no ordinary GTO; Hurst lavishly customized it and Royal Pontiac provided the high-performance tuning. It carried Hurst gold paint, a black vinyl top with a gold-plated Hurst shifter, and Hurst Dazzler wheels, along with Safe-T-Track, power windows, a white interior, console, and factory reverb AM/FM stereo. (This is a low-resolution archival ad.)

immediately immersed herself in the community and culture that made up racing. In January 1966, she started the Motor Trend 500 at the Riverside International Raceway, then the Daytona 500 the following month. Throughout her career with Hurst, Linda's mother often made the outfits she wore at events. Gold, tight, and revealing was the recipe for an effective costume, and Linda was able to wear the sexiest of outfits with poise and confidence, often reminding the press during interviews that it was all part of the show.

The racing schedule was brutal. Most races lasted all weekend, with only enough time to pack everything back up on Sunday evening before moving on. The following week's race could be as close as 300 miles, but often was 800 to 1,000 miles away. With few multi-lane interstates, highways went right through most cities and towns, so traveling more than 400 miles per day was difficult.

Hurst produced the stand-up Linda Vaughn display in 1971 in conjunction with the Pontiac Hurst SSJ promotion. (Photo Courtesy Pete Serio Collection)

Linda either rode with the crew to the next race, returned to the Warminster offices, or flew across country to another major event. This grueling schedule became an ongoing weekly cadence. It was not unusual for Linda to make 150 appearances per year, often traveling with a van load of suitcases to enable her to have up to four different costume changes per day.

Linda's obvious physical attributes were matched by her larger-than-life personality. She was not content to appear in the winner's circle just in time to award the trophy and customary kiss to the triumphant competitor. Linda was at the races from beginning to end, her sweet southern hospitality an important part of the promotional effort. Soon, she knew more than just the faces and names of the professionals in racing, and she became an extended part of racing clans such as the Andrettis, Garlitses, Pettys, and Granatellis.

She was constantly in the pits walking among the professional and amateur racers, graciously posing for photos whenever she was asked. All the while, she let everyone know she was there to represent the Hurst company. Many racers patiently waited in line for their turn down the track, only to have the door quickly opened by Linda, where she would exclaim a big thank you for displaying the Hurst sticker on the outside of the car.

A Special Race Event: Linda was soon the favorite of young servicemen, and Hurst set up the Hurst Armed Forces Club traveling to Hawaii and Puerto Rico to bring a pure American performance to troops stationed away from home. In the following years, Linda and others from Hurst toured Vietnam twice, bringing a taste of home to the jungle.

On Christmas 1966, drag races were held at Hawaii Raceway Park where more than 12,000 spectators were in attendance. Hurst had both *Hemi Under Glass* and Linda Vaughn to help entertain the crowds. Between heats, Bob Riggle often stood the golden *Hemi Under Glass* on its rear wheels covering the complete quarter-mile distance before bringing the front tires back to the pavement. A scantily-clad Linda rode on the back of a convertible, waving and bowing to the crowd while standing on a platform hanging onto the giant Hurst shifter.

After the races, the Hurst team proceeded to Wheeler Air Force Base and the Marine Corps base at Kaneohe Bay, where they performed for the troops under threatening skies. Next, the Frantic Fish show was interrupted at the United States Coast Guard Air station at Barber's Point with a torrential rain storm. Not to be excluded from the festivities, the Coast Guard quickly emptied a hangar where Bob Riggle brought the crowds to their feet with the wheelstanding display of *Hemi Under Glass.* Between these three days of festivities, Linda Vaughn, George Hurst, Bob Riggle, and other Hurst team members toured the base hospitals and took time to meet with and talk to injured soldiers.

Win a Date Promotion: In 1967, the Hurst Defender "Win a Date with Linda" program was launched. The new 1967 Pontiac firebird was a full six months behind the introduction of its sister car, the Chevrolet Camaro. Pontiac's Jim Wangers wanted to make sure the introduction garnered a sizable amount of attention. Hurst and Pontiac created a contest where servicemen in combat could compete for a date with Linda Vaughn at the 1967 Daytona 500. The date was to include an official Daytona dinner with racers and track officials.

The randomly drawn date turned out to be married ADJ3 Leonard Hobbs of Fort Worth, Texas. He was flown from the jungle of Vietnam and joined his wife at the track in Daytona. His wife was a good sport, and Linda had a date with both of them. Years later, it was revealed that Linda and the Hurst team had a concern for Linda if they were to bring a young single serviceman out of the war in Vietnam and allow them to be un-chaperoned. It was convenient that the winner was married, although some felt it was a requirement to win the contest.

The Hurstettes: Public relations director Jack Duffy managed the Hurst promotional schedule, including Linda Vaughn's appearances and official activities. Soon the requested demand for Linda's presence outpaced her ability to keep up. She simply could not be at opposite sides of the country on the same weekend. George Hurst chose to expand the Hurst Shifter Girl program with the addition of the Hurstettes. Linda trained and managed the other young ladies to assist her in the Hurst promotional duties.

Although many photos show Linda and the Hurstettes together, this was primarily during the largest racing events of the year. During the rest of the time, the girls divided and conquered. Hurstettes attended performance store openings, promotional events, and regional races. Since most of Hurst's activities occurred during evening and weekend hours, this arrangement worked well, other than travel time for the major events. Most of the girls had additional jobs in order to make ends meet.

Linda's Later Career: By 1981, when ownership of Hurst once again changed hands, Linda found herself without a job, so she became the face of Detroit-based Gratiot Auto Supply performing in television spots, print media, and promotional events. Linda was also involved with the big screen where she participated in two classic car movies, *Gumball Rally* in 1976 and *Stroker Ace* with Burt Reynolds in 1983.

Linda Vaughn was soon traveling the world representing Hurst. She and Bob Riggle sign autographs in Hawaii circa 1966. (Photo Courtesy Bob Riggle)

Hurst supported the armed services whenever possible. Here the Hurst team has lined up its specialized vehicles during an airbase open house. (Photo Courtesy of Pete Serio Collection)

The 1967 Firebird was a midyear introduction. In order to help Pontiac support the new model, Hurst created a contest to win a date with Linda Vaughn and this Firebird convertible. The only catch was that you had to give both of the prizes back to Hurst. (Photo Courtesy Mark Fletcher Collection)

Hurst Girl Legacy

George Hurst made the final decision in the selection of any new Hurst Girl. It is estimated that there were most likely 30 to 40 different Hurst girls over the years. Some of these Hurstettes garnered their own fan base with devoted followers even 40 years later.

Janene Walsh was the first "Miss Hurst Shifter" in 1964.

Pat Flannery expanded the role from trophy girl to Hurst representative.

Linda Vaughn developed the role into an ambassador position for Hurst Performance. She is the recognized face of Hurst and has remained so more than any executive in the life of the company. She was selected as the Specialty Equipment Market Association (SEMA) Person of the Year in 1979 and inducted into the SEMA Hall of Fame in 1985. She has also been elected into the drag racing hall of fame.

June Cochran was a former Playboy Playmate of the Year in 1963 and was an instrumental Hurst representative at the major racing events in the late 1960s and early 1970s.

Nikki Phillips, Miss Hurst 4 Speed, was a tall, slender, Australian young lady who remains a favorite Hurstette to this day. She was often photographed with Linda and June at Indianapolis Speedway events.

Marsha Bennett was a Miss Hurst Dual/Shifter and a semifinalist during the 1970 Miss USA contest. She was one of the most popular Hurst girls. Her full-time profession was as an airline flight attendant.

Lynn Reck, Ellsie Colter, Sheli Harmon, and Tami Pitman are just a few of the many other Hurst girls from the era.

Once Sunbeam took control of Hurst in the mid 1970s, cutbacks to the Hurst Girl program were instituted. Soon, Linda was once again the sole Hurst representative under the Hurst umbrella.

Linda married racer Billy Tidwell in 1972 and no doubt many racers and fans adored her. One young racer was overheard saying, "At least when she was single, we had a chance."

The Hurst and Hertz names were often confused. Two Hurst girls sit in the Hurst golf cart at one of the races. The Hurst Girls, and in particular Linda Vaughn, were the face of the company at the racetrack. No other aftermarket company at the time promoted its products in the same way as Hurst. (Photo Courtesy Pete Serio Collection)

Hurst Performance Company

Missed Shifts and Rebirth

Both George Hurst and Bill Campbell had settled into their partnership and respective areas of expertise, George as the visionary and promoter, Bill as the engineer refining both process and product. This partnership created its own checks and balances, which provided stability during the company's fast-paced growth of the 1960s. The vast contrast of their dynamic personalities complemented each other, although not always fostering a harmonious environment.

The Rescue Tool is predominantly displayed along with other Hurst products, circa 1973. (Photo Courtesy Pete Serio Collection)

CHAPTER 9

Hurst introduced the automated Light Tender in the early 1970s. Today, most cars come standard with time delay headlight shut-offs. (Photo Courtesy Pete Serio Collection)

Hurst was ahead of its time with the Fuel Monitor, which provided an audible tone to warn when the tank was nearing empty. (Photo Courtesy Pete Serio Collection)

Two additional personalities helped to support Hurst Performance's fast-paced growth. Larry Greenwald was an early Hurst garage customer who became a silent partner and the primary financial backer. Additionally, Louis Palitz was an accountant who kept the money flowing and drove the financial end of the business.

In late 1964, George Hurst was interviewed for an article in the Detroit publication *Wards Quarterly*. Published in January 1965, George spoke of his determination to improve the safety for commuters and racers. George was both serious and generous as it related to this endeavor. As his company grew, so did his involvement in free safety repairs, and driver and pit crew training at the racetrack. In this interview, Hurst-Campbell was identified as a company that had grown from certain bankruptcy in 1959 to a value of more than $5 million just six years later, with annual sales of more than $20 million.

By the summer of 1968, Jack "Doc" Watson had relocated from Dearborn Heights to the home office in Warminster. His time there was short-lived and he left the company prior to the public stock offering on July 3, 1968.

Hurst Innovations

George was a visionary who saw life through a unique set of lenses. He had experienced both failure and success prior to reaching middle age, but through it all he remained optimistic. George was never complacent and consistently pursued his next big victory. Whether it was developing and promoting a new product, growing Hurst Performance, or courting a pretty young lady, George approached it all with passion. In his fast-paced world, everything new carried more value than anything he currently held.

Conversely, Bill Campbell was the *yin* to George's *yang*, and adapted a necessary balance within the company he shared with Hurst. As vice president of Hurst Performance, he was content to take a second seat to George. He

Hurst privately labeled the packaging for JCPenney, but Hurst insisted the product retained the Hurst name on all of the shifters and boots it sold. (Photo Courtesy Pete Serio collection)

JCPenney
auto center
AFX PRICE LIST

J.C.Penney

PART NUMBER	RETAIL PRICE	LOT NUMBER
AFX BOOT		**4535**
114 8291	4.95	
AFX T-HANDLE		**4537**
153 8288	5.95	
3 SPEED AFX CONVERSION SHIFTER		**4514**
501 0001	25.70	
501 8069	25.70	
501 8070	25.70	
501 8071	25.70	
3 SPEED AFX COMPETITION SHIFTER		**4520**
502 8164	36.95	
502 8165	36.95	
502 8166	36.95	
502 8167	36.95	
502 8168	36.95	
502 8169	36.95	
502 8170	36.95	
502 8171	36.95	
502 8172	36.95	
502 8439	36.95	
4 SPEED AFX COMPETITION SHIFTER		**4530**
503 0001	47.95	
503 0002	47.95	
503 0003	47.95	
503 0004	47.95	
503 8122	47.95	
503 8123	47.95	
503 8125	47.95	
503 8127	47.95	
503 8490	47.95	
503 8491	47.95	
503 8492	47.95	
503 8493	47.95	
503 8494	47.95	
503 8495	47.95	
503 8552	47.95	
503 8553	47.95	
503 8554	47.95	
503 8555	47.95	
503 8556	47.95	
AFX - VW SHIFTER		**4520**
504 0002	17.95	
AFX TRACTION BAR		**1000**
505 0003	19.49	
AFX AUTOMATIC SHIFTER		**0001**
506 0002	25.70	

AFX BOOT • AFX T-HANDLE
AFX 3 SPEED CONVERSION SHIFTER • AFX VW SHIFTER
AFX AUTOMATIC SHIFTER • AFX 3 SPEED COMPETITION SHIFTER
AFX 4 SPEED COMPETITION SHIFTER • AFX TRACTION BAR

JCPenney created its own A F/X performance brand using Hurst products. (Photo Courtesy Pete Serio Collection)

consistently strived to sustain the company's momentum without exposing it to risk. For many years, this led to a successful partnership where Bill took great new product concepts, improved them, and applied the best manufacturing processes and innovations.

This is the 1970s Hurst/Schieffer Performance team decal. (Photo Courtesy Pete Serio Collection)

The Hurst Shifter

A good example of Bill's prowess occurred early in the development of the Hurst shifter. Bill patented the process that created stronger shifter rods by applying longitudinal hydraulic pressure to the rods while they were being bent to fit the application. These strengthened rods prevented distortion during hard shifting. The racing community soon identified the superior (and more costly) Hurst product as a necessity at the track. Hurst emphasized this advantage by offering and promoting a lifetime warranty.

In 1964, Hurst produced more than 100,000 shifters. Of these, 40 percent were factory-installed by Pontiac and Plymouth with the balance sold to the public, mostly through auto parts stores and performance shops.

Some Hurst wheels were available either anodized or ready to paint to match your car. (Photo Courtesy Dennis Kirban Collection via Mark Fletcher)

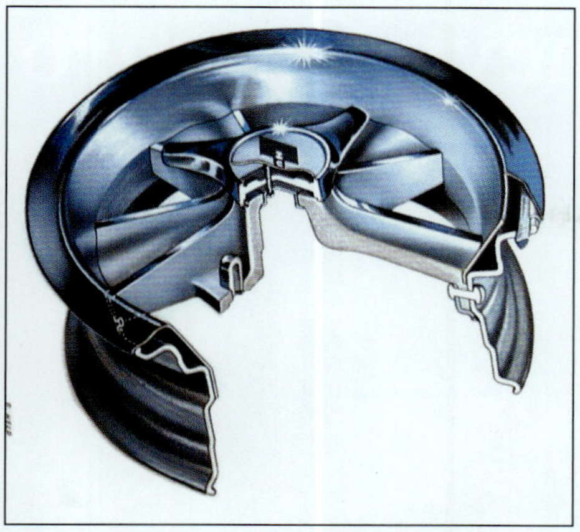

Hurst artist Bob Held created this artistic cutaway showing the unique design of the two-piece wheels. (Photo Courtesy Dennis Kirban Collection)

Dazzler Aluminum Wheels

Among the performance products developed at this time were the beautiful Hurst "Dazzler" aluminum wheels. Bill Campbell had previously worked for the Heinz Wheel Company and had seen firsthand what happened to aftermarket wheels under strenuous conditions. Brightly polished cast-aluminum wheels were growing in popularity, but were inherently weak due to the design and components used.

Hurst introduced an attractive and durable forged-aluminum wheel riveted to a sturdy steel rim. The centers were forged by Harvey with Kelsey-Hayes steel outer rims. The wheels have a chromed steel trim ring extending between each of the five spokes which, when combined with the highly polished aluminum spokes, creates the appearance of an all-chromed wheel. The center cap is chromed cast metal with a relieved stylized "H" filled with a gold and black decal.

Promoted as the safest aftermarket wheel, Bill Campbell built a 2,000-pound concrete test guillotine system that was dropped onto a production Hurst wheel to demonstrate its designed strength as compared to other aftermarket wheels. While over-engineered, they were equally overpriced compared to the competition. Although the wheels could make any used car look modern, they were nearly four times the price of popular cast aluminum wheels. Only the wealthiest of performance car owners could afford the wheels, and production was discontinued by early 1968 due to low sales.

Today, these original Hurst wheels are highly prized, especially by muscle car enthusiasts, as a period-correct

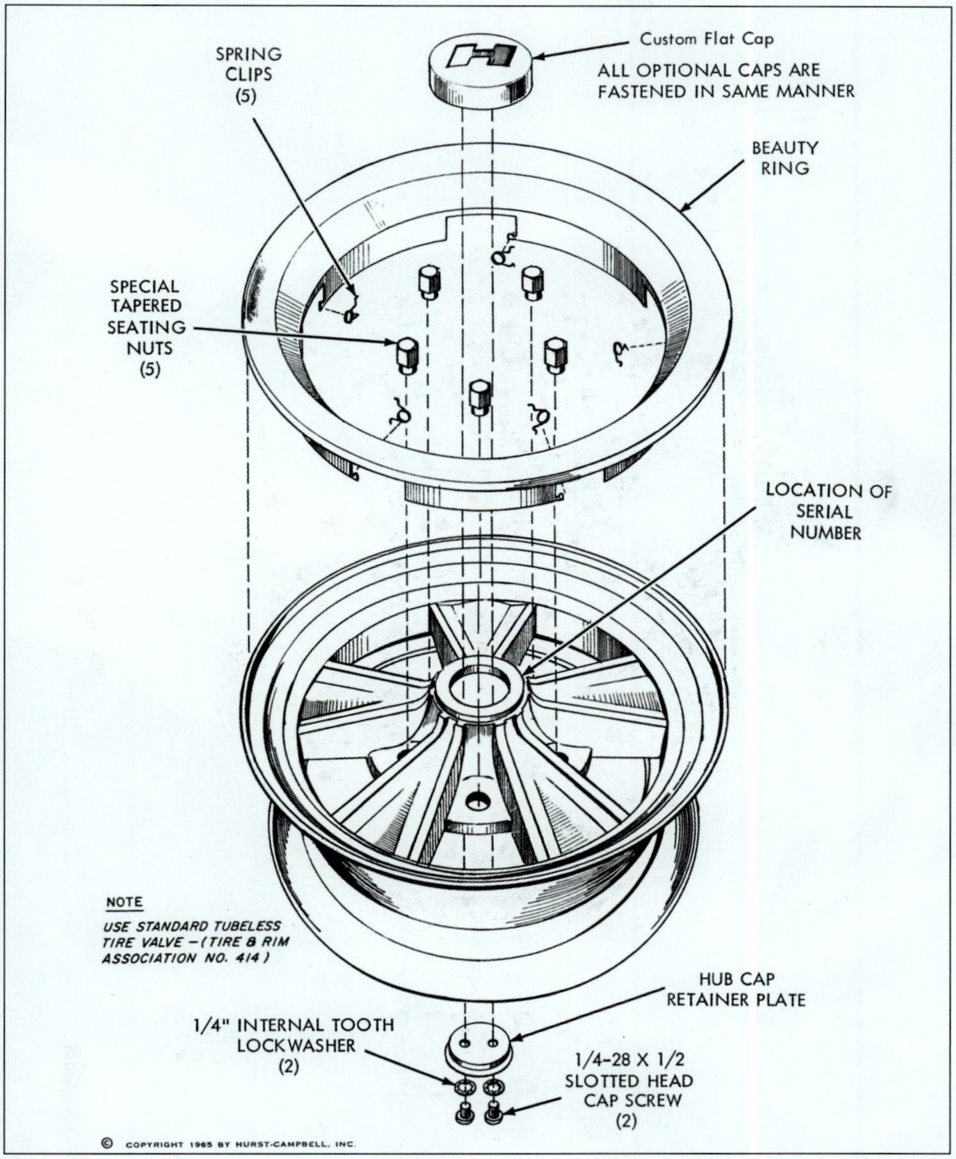

Hurst's wheel instruction shows how to use the unique chromed trim ring and special tapered seating lug nuts. (Photo Courtesy Dennis Kirban)

1970 Hurst Chevy Camaro Z/28 Sunshine

Special

With the threat of convertibles being legislated out of existence, Hurst turned to convertible conversions, to give motorists an open-air driving experience. This is the Hurst Sunshine Special, a 1970½ Chevrolet Camaro Z/28 sporting a Hurst-installed cloth sunroof. (Photos Courtesy Rich Truesdell)

accessory. In essence, there are matching number sets of wheels, as each wheel was individually serialized with sequential numbers. Today, collectors value matched sets, which command a premium over unmatched serial number sets. The wheels were shipped two at a time in a mini steel drum embellished with Hurst black and gold logo. These shipping containers are also extremely valuable by Hurst collectors and, like the wheels, are now being reproduced.

FORGED ALUMINUM

WHEELS

U.S. PATENT NO. 3,346,301

FOR SAFETY AND BEAUTY

APPLICATIONS

MAKE AND MODEL OF CAR	YEAR	FOOT NOTES	BOLT CIRCLE	NUT PACK NO.	OLD NUMBERS		NEW NUMBERS	
					POLISHED	PAINTED	POLISHED	PAINTED
BUICK Special	'64-'67		4¾"	5856	6F29W	6F20	5935	5936
CHEVROLET	'57-'68	4	4¾"	5855	6B29W	6B20	5927	5928
CHEVY II V-8	'64-'66		4¾"	5856	6F29W	6F20	5935	5936
CHEVY II 6 & V-8	'67		4¾"	5856	6F29W	6F20	5935	5936
CHEVELLE	'64-'68		4¾"	5856	6F29W	6F20	5935	5936
CAMARO Except disc brakes	'67-'68		4¾"	5856	6B29W	6B20	5927	5928
CORVAIR (14" Tire)	'65-'67		4¾"	5856	6F29W	6F20	5935	5936
CHRYSLER Except Wagons	'57-'67	1-3	4½"	5853-5854	6C19W	6C10	5931	5932
DESOTO Except Wagons	'57-'61	1-3	4½"	5853-5854	6C19W	6C10	5931	5932
DODGE Except Wagons	'57-'67	1-3	4½"	5853-5854	6C19W	6C10	5931	5932
PLYMOUTH Exc disc brakes & Wagons	'57-'68	1-3	4½"	5853-5854	6C19W	6C10	5931	5932
PLYMOUTH Disc brakes	'66-'67	3	4½"	5853-5854	6C19W	6C10	5931	5932
FORD Except Wagons	'57-'64		4½"	5853	6C19W	6C10	5931	5932
FORD Except Wagons	'65-'66		4½"	5853	6B19W	6B10	5925	5926
MUSTANG Drum brakes	'64-'67		4½"	5853-5854	6C19W	6C10	5931	5932
MUSTANG Disc brakes	'65-'67		4½"	5853	6B19W	6B10	5925	5926
FAIRLANE	'67		4½"	5853	6C19W	6C10	5931	5932
FAIRLANE	'63-'65		4½"	5853	6C19W	6C10	5931	5932
FALCON V-8	'65-'67		4½"	5853	6C19W	6C10	5931	5932
THUNDERBIRD	'58-'60		4½"	5853	6B19W	6B10	5925	5926
MERCURY	'61-'64	2	4½"	5853	6C19W	6C10	5931	5932
COUGAR	'67		4½"	5853	6B19W	6B10	5925	5926
COMET V-8	'64-'67		4½"	5853	6C19W	6C10	5931	5932
METEOR	'62-'63		4½"	5853	6C19W	6C10	5931	5932
MARLIN & JAVELIN Exc. disc brakes	'66-'68		4½"	5853	6B19W	6B10	5925	5926
REBEL Except disc brakes	'66-'67		4½"	5853	6B19W	6B10	5925	5926
OLDS Except J-88	'59-'63	3	5.0	5853-5854	6B39W	6B30	5929	5930
OLDS Except J-88 & DELMONT	'64-'67		5.0	5853	6B39W	6B30	5929	5930
OLDS J-88, VISTA-CRUISER & DELMONT	'64-'67		4¾"	5856	6F29W	6F20	5935	5936
OLDS F-85 & 442 Except disc brakes	'64-'68		4¾"	5856	6F29W	6F20	5935	5936
PONTIAC	'57-'63	3	5.0	5853-5854	6C39W	6C30	5933	5934
PONTIAC	'64-'67		5.0	5853	6C39W	6C30	5933	5934
TEMPEST & GTO Except disc brakes	'64-'68		4¾"	5856	6F29W	6F20	5935	5936
FIREBIRD Except disc brakes	'67-'68		4¾"	5856	6B29W	6B20	5927	5928

ALSO PAINTABLE

THE PAINTABLE WHEEL COMES TO YOU WITH A UNIQUE FINISH THAT CAN BE MOUNTED AS IS OR ANY GOOD FINISH PAINT CAN BE APPLIED OVER IT AS THIS BLACK FINISH IS ALSO AN EXCELLENT PRIME.

JUST PAINT THE CENTER WITH TOUCH-UP SPRAY TO MATCH THE CAR FINISH. NO MASKING NECESSARY! TWO THIN COATS ARE BEST -- ALLOW TIME FOR EACH APPLICATION TO CURE -- (FOLLOW PAINT MANUFACTURERS INSTRUCTIONS ON SPRAY CAN). WHEN SPRAYING, MOVE AROUND WHEEL SO THAT ALL AREAS ARE SPRAYED UNIFORMLY.

AFTER PAINT IS COMPLETELY CURED, TIRE CAN BE MOUNTED CAREFULLY TO AVOID DAMAGING FINISH. AFTER TIRE HAS BEEN MOUNTED, THE FLAT CAP AND BEAUTY RING CAN BE INSTALLED. THE WHEEL IS THEN READY FOR MOUNTING ON CAR.

1. EXCEPT '57-'60 CHRYSLER PRODUCTS THAT USE CAP SCREWS TO FASTEN WHEELS.
2. FITS MONTEREY, MONTCLAIR, PARK LANE.
3. REQUIRE BOTH RIGHT- AND LEFT-HAND THREAD NUTS.
4. EXCEPT CARS WITH 396 AND 427 C.I.D. ENGINES.

HURST WHEELS may fit other cars than those specified. However, the user should check for proper offset and clearance. Too great a deviation from these standards in any wheel may cause too much strain on wheel bearings and ball joints.

34 THE PICK OF THE PROS HURST PERFORMANCE PRODUCTS

By 1968, Hurst had expanded its wheel application to include most domestic manufacturers. This page also shows the process used to paint the wheels prior to installing tires. (Photo Courtesy Mark Fletcher Collection)

Hurst Rescue Tool

Bill and George had been developing another safety innovation throughout their partnership. The Hurst Rescue Tool was finally patented in 1965 after more than seven years of development. The device was originally a two-piece system using a 32-inch hydraulic spreader powered by an attached hydraulic power supply. The spreaders opened like scissors, forcing crushed metal away from victims trapped in damaged vehicles. The phrase "Jaws of Life" came from the idea that the tool kept the individuals out of the jaws of death. George never liked this name and insisted on the "Hurst Rescue Tool" name.

Conceived in 1958 after Bill Campbell and George read about the death of a trapped truck driver, the first prototype was demonstrated to the highway traffic community in 1962. Weighing almost 200 pounds, it was difficult to maneuver for even two average-strength men. The primary obstacle in bringing the product to market was the weight of the tool combined with its hydraulics and power supply.

The 1965 patent identified the separation of the power supply from the hydraulic spreader unit, although at that time more development was still required.

Hurst Dazzler wheels are most often found on early Pontiac GTOs. The weight of the wheel added to its strength, but also kept General Motors from carrying it as a production line option. (Photo Courtesy Rich Truesdell)

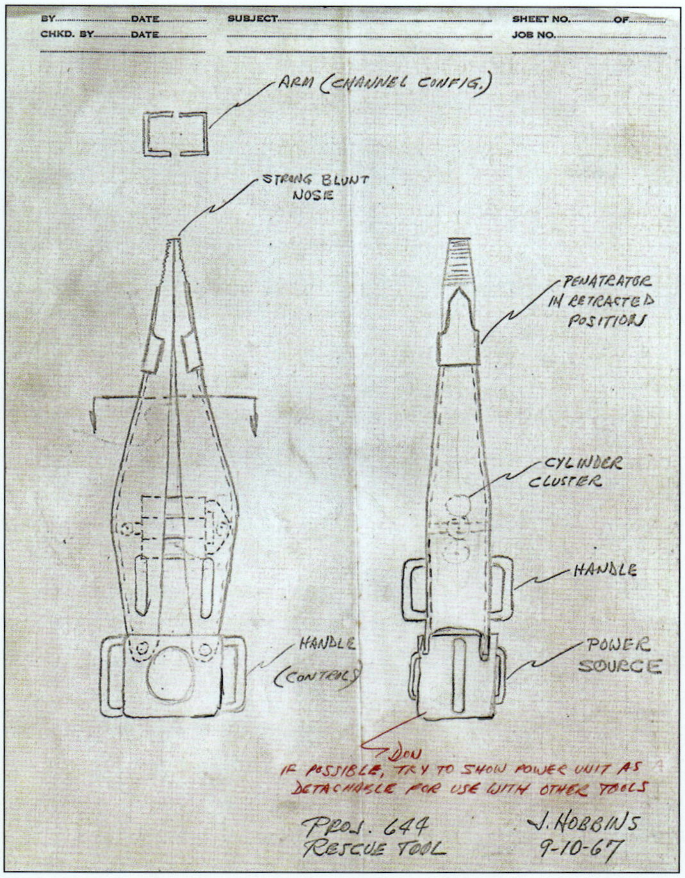

Throughout his career, George Hurst was dedicated to the personal safety of others, and the consummate innovator developed the Hurst Rescue Tool. He recognized a need for a tool that cut sheet metal and chassis structures so a person could quickly be removed from a vehicle after an accident. (Photo Courtesy Don Lane)

Safe Brakes and Clutches

During these growth years, Hurst led the automotive aftermarket as the fastest growing company in the industry. In 10 short years, it was safe to say Hurst had become a household name in America.

Hurst continued to rapidly grow, acquiring Airheart Brakes in 1966 and Scheifer Clutches in 1968. Both acquisitions can be attributed to George's pursuit of safety-related devices. Racing put a severe strain on the quality of a component, and it was common for poor-quality clutches to come apart at speed, becoming a freewheeling circular saw cutting through the car. Many racers and spectators were injured or worse due to these types of failures. Hurst invested in Scheifer because of its outstanding safety record and in anticipation of further improving their products and related components.

Airheart brakes were aftermarket disc brake conversions in a world

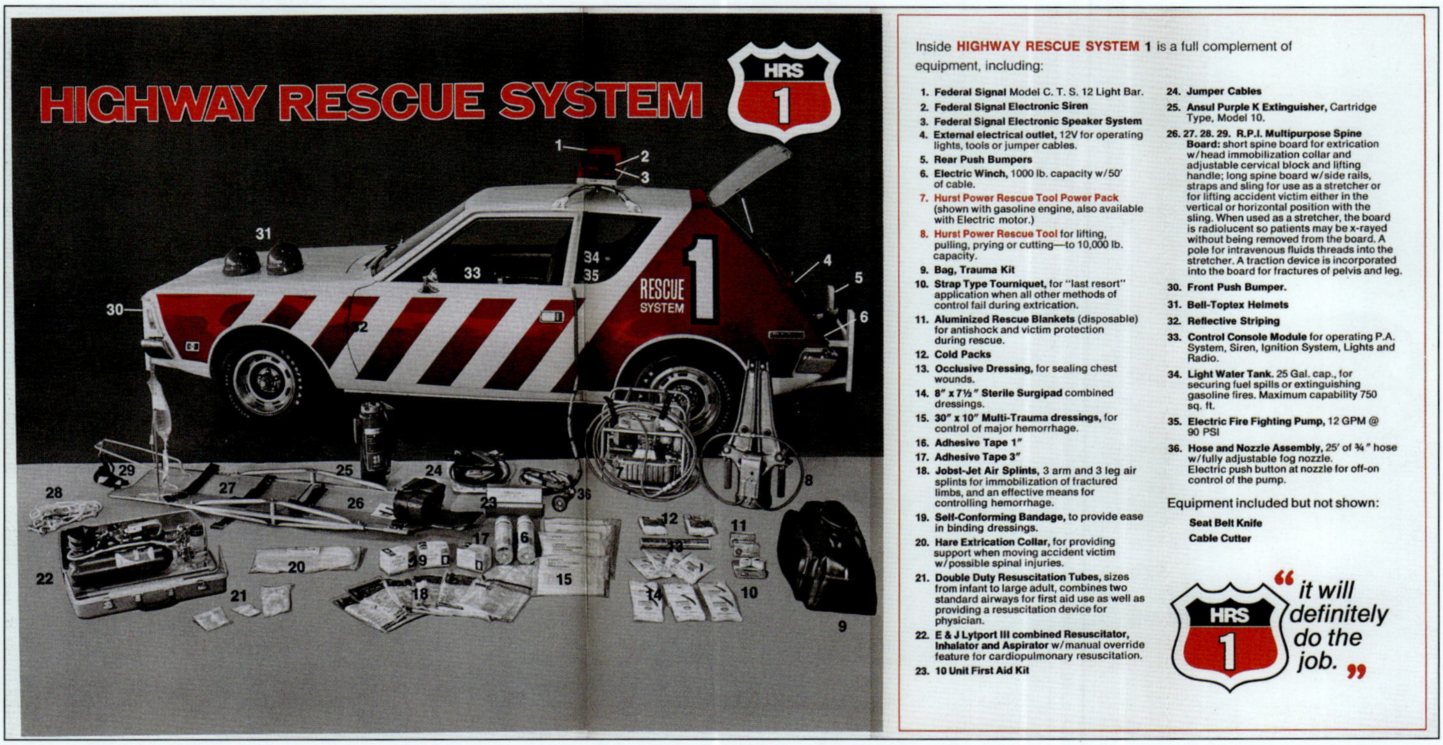

The Hurst Rescue Tool went through many renditions prior to its release in 1972. This version has a note to separate the power unit from the jaws. The rescue tool brochure gave a complete list of the items included with the Highway Rescue System. (Photo Courtesy Pete Serio Collection)

dominated by drum brakes. These conversions were excellent in quality, but both expensive and difficult to install. Based in California, Airheart brakes were used in industrial applications and on public transportation, the most prominent of which was the new Bay Area Rapid Transit (BART) system in the San Francisco area launched in 1970.

Through this acquired company, George was eager to continue the early development of anti-lock braking systems, a dream he never saw come to reality while he was at Hurst's helm.

Hurst Goes Public

Hurst's decision to offer its stock to the public was based on the company's rapid growth, including the first year of the special H/O production. The company was hitting on all cylinders, sales and profits had repeatedly surpassed the company's projections, the company had a steady stream of production in the pipeline for the catalog, and car conversions were going strong. Money was needed for new equipment and for research and development. Specifically, Hurst was looking to lead the industry in creating an inexpensive anti-lock brake system that George believed should be included on every car manufactured by Detroit.

Hurst Performance had four partners at the time of the stock offering: George Hurst, Bill Campbell, and Larry Greenwald each held a 25.9-percent ownership in the company, with Louis Palitz retaining an 11.3-percent interest. This left 10.4 percent of the company available in the form of 250,000 shares for public offering. Each of the three primary partners owned 594,037 shares of the company out of a total of almost 2.3 million common shares.

The stock offering changed the company forever, and unfortunately the passion of the company diverted from growth to wealth in a single day. As with many companies today, the leadership was more focused on making decisions based on the reactions of Wall Street and the investment community, a clear departure from past practice. George was later quoted as saying that he became a millionaire over lunch the day the stock went public. When that fundamental shift took place, the core passion and focus were lost, and this had an impact on all the key figures who owned the vast majority of the stock.

At this point, the Hurst Performance Company was valued at more than $18 million, a full 3.5 times its stated value three years earlier in 1965.

Hurst stock was initially valued at $8 per share, but employees were offered a chance to purchase stock at $6 per share and many savvy employees took advantage of this offer. There were reports that some employees took out loans and even second mortgages on their homes in order to buy stock in the company.

One-Off Vehicles

Both George Hurst and the new owners at Sunbeam were disappointed

The Hurst Rescue Tool tore the roof and doors off of this Ford Falcon during a product demonstration. It eventually became trademarked as the Jaws of Life, and is now a standard safety tool used by fire and rescue departments. (Photo Courtesy Pete Serio Collection)

Hurst shifter packages featured a red, white, and blue color scheme around the Bicentennial in 1976. (Photo Courtesy Pete Serio Collection)

Hurst had a diversity of products in the early 1970s and displayed them at most racing events. (Photo Courtesy Pete Serio)

in Oldsmobile's decision to not contract with Hurst for the 1970 model year. Dave Landrith was quickly tasked with helping to secure a new contract to keep the Detroit operations flowing.

Dart GTS and Dodge Merada Charger

With the success of the 1968 H/O, and the Hemi and 440 Dart and Barracuda programs, the Hurst Performance team of Dave Landreth and Bob Tarrozi went calling on R. B. McCurry, then head of the Dodge Division, looking for another car program partner for 1970. Hurst purchased two production cars and created a prototype of each model to present to the Chrysler marketing team in March 1969.

The first proposal was a bright yellow and black bumble-bee-striped 383-powered Dart GTS two-door hardtop with a few Hurst items borrowed from the 1969 Hurst production runs. The vacuum-operated Ram Air flapper built into the hood utilized a Ford door and actuator, as did the SC/Rambler. The Hurst emblems were the "H" from an H/O with the addition of a bumble-bee cartoon character with a V-8 and headers on its back wearing a racing helmet and goggles. The name "Swinging Bee" was in bold black letters above the caricature.

The Dart was to be available with either a Hurst 4-speed shifter or an optional Hurst Dual Gate shifter in the factory console. The top of the console received a bright-colored cover to match the Sunrise Yellow exterior. The exterior

Hurst's Stock Offering

Following is a brief summary of the financial proposals filed with, and actions by, the S.E.C.:

(Issue No. 68-130)

FOR RELEASE July 3, 1968

HURST PERFORMANCE PROPOSES OFFERING. Hurst Performance Inc., 50 West St. Road. Warminster, Pa. 18974, filed a registration statement (File 2-29485) with the SEC on June 28 seeking registration of 250,000 shares of common stock. The shares are to be offered for public sale through underwriters headed by Butcher & Sherrerd, 1500 Walnut St., Philadelphia. Pa. 19102; the offering price ($8 per share maximum*) and underwriting terms are to be supplied by amendment.

The company manufactures and sells products of its own design for the automotive industry. Of the net proceeds of its stock sale, the company will use $1,000,000 for the purchase of new equipment over the next two years, primarily for improving and increasing manufacturing capability in the company's principal plant, $500,000 for research and development over the next two years in the field of disc brakes and anti-skid devices; until the amounts allocated to the foregoing purposes are expended for such purposes, such funds as well as the unallocated balance of this offering, will be used as working capital and temporarily to reduce short term bank loans. In addition to indebtedness, the company has outstanding 957,350 common shares, of which George H. Hurst, president, William G. Campbell, senior vice president, and Lawrence H. Greenwald, board chairman, own 25.97 percent each and Louis R. Palitz, director, 11.3 percent.

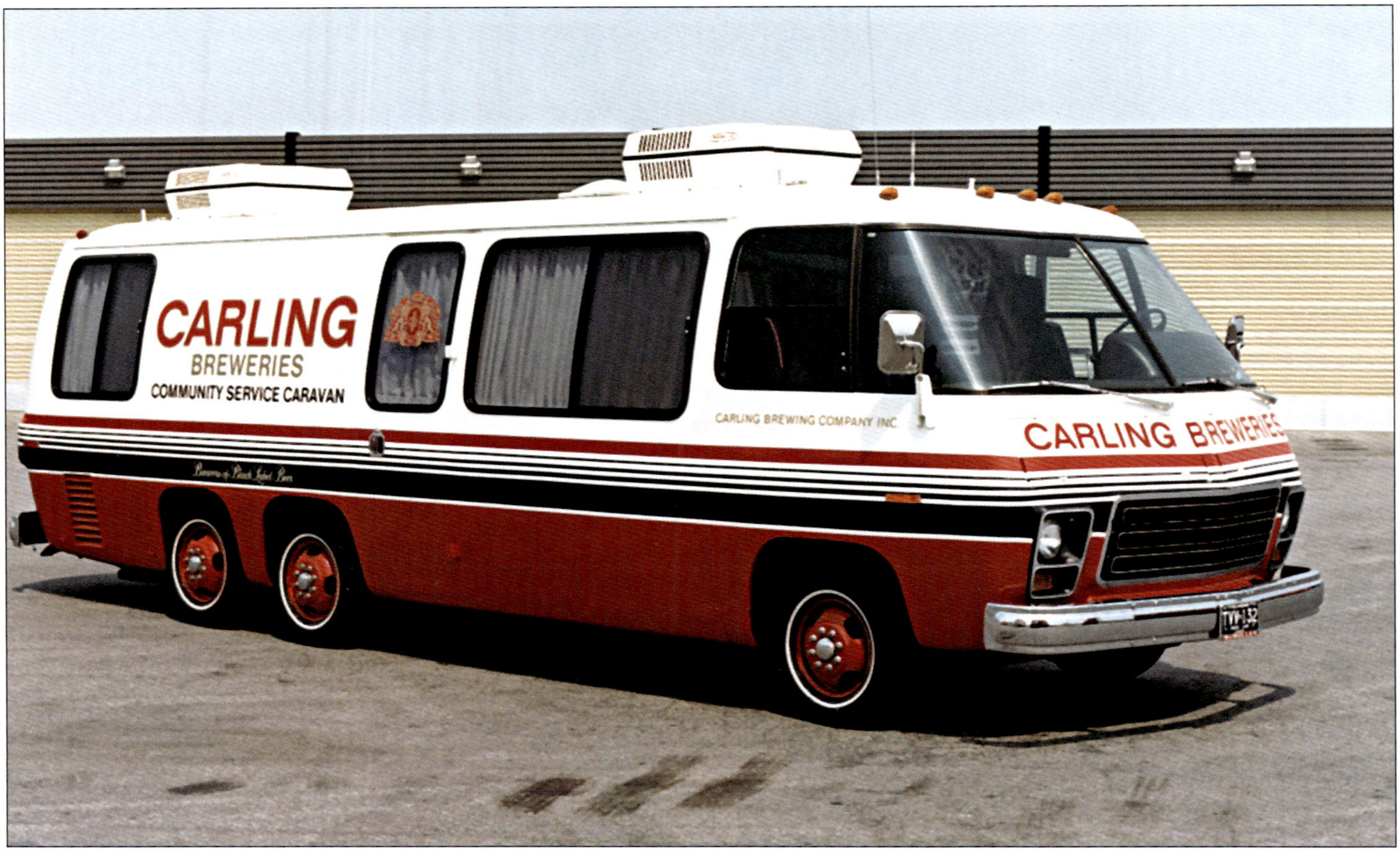

Hurst performed the conversion of this Toronado-based motor home for Carling Breweries in the mid 1970s. (Photo Courtesy Hurst/Olds Club of America)

of the "Bee" had a subtle fiberglass hood scoop molded onto the factory steel hood and a small spoiler along the back edge of the trunk. Both proposals had black interiors and sported bullet-style body-color mirrors as found on the SC/Rambler and Hurst/Olds.

Later, Hurst presented the Dodge Merada Charger to compete with the Hurst Pontiac Grand Prix SSJ (and most likely the H/O) as a new category of executive performance cars created over the previous two years. Equipped as a Charger RT with the 440 V-8, heavy-duty suspension, and either a 4-speed manual or 3-speed automatic transmission. It was finished in a dark "Sunset Orange" with pewter side accents.

This car had two unique design components that quickly identified it as different from a stock Charger. One was the enlarged lower grille opening, which created an open-mouth effect suspended below the front bumper. The second was a hood scoop that was flush with the hood while closed, but opened up like a clamshell under full acceleration and the subsequent lower engine vacuum.

Although Hurst promoted its prowess in creating exciting cars, it may have inadvertently been feeding product ideas to the Dodge boys. Neither Hurst proposal was accepted by Dodge, but both may have influenced the marketing of special Dodge models spanning the next two years.

The 1970 model year saw the introduction of the Dart Swinger with a wide bumblebee stripe and dual-scoop Ram Air hood. The 1970 Road Runner and 1971 Charger featured an air grabber hood scoop that lay flush when closed and opened like a clamshell under acceleration. Both prototypes were very similar to the Hurst Merada design, and both were sold by Hurst to private parties around 1971; their current whereabouts are unknown.

Z-28 Sunshine Special

Hurst created and proposed the 1970 Chevrolet Z-28 Sunshine Special. Based on the new 1970 Camaro second-generation body design with the high-horsepower LT1 (360 hp) Z-28 small-block package. The most distinctive component of the car was the addition of a sliding canvas sunroof and the "Hurst Sunshine Special" emblems adorning the dash and the Hurst "H" on both front fenders. Chevrolet didn't offer a convertible second-generation Camaro, so Hurst saw an opportunity and offered a sliding sunroof as an alternative to the convertible. The Hurst Hatch T-top was still years away from becoming a popular aftermarket option, and Hurst searched for a way to capitalize on the impending demise of the convertible.

The bright yellow Z-28 actually belonged to a special Hurst customer, Dick Jesse, who had been a Pontiac Funny Car driver and owned Detroit-based Merollis Chevrolet. He asked Hurst to create a special car based on the factory Z-28 package. Hurst added the roof, a custom steering wheel with Hurst-emblazoned center, and a Hurst auto stick that made the TurboHydramatic resemble a manual 4-speed gearbox. They also reworked the transmission, adding a high-performance shift kit.

Hurst presented the Z28 Sunshine Special to management at GM. While the brass took a pass on the car, GM did embrace the soft-top sunroof concept and contracted Hurst to install the sliding canvas sunroof on Chevy Novas and Buick Skylarks for 1971.

While Chevrolet had possession of the car, it performed some engine modifications and wind tunnel testing after adding unique front and rear spoilers. Similar spoilers became Chevrolet-installed options late in the model year. The modified car was returned to Dick Jesse, who kept it for a short time before selling it to Alan Jones in January 1971.

The car later ended up with a collector in Michigan who kept it into the 1980s. It was later used as part of a three-car trade for a partially restored 1969 ZL1 Camaro that had been won in a Camaro Club raffle. The car was moved to Southern California where Michael Cruz owned and displayed it for many years.

By 2005, the car had just undergone a professional restoration by Camaro Heaven in Ontario, Canada, using many NOS parts. It was offered for sale at Legendary Motors in Ontario in 2011 and is now a part of Rick Hendrick's personal car collection in Charlotte, North Carolina.

In 1971, Hurst unsuccessfully proposed a Hurst Riviera to Buick. The proposal included a padded top extending along the top of the door from the mirror to the rear bumper. (Photo Courtesy Hurst/Olds Club of America)

Delta 88

Hurst created a Hurst Delta 88 in 1972. The proposal was photographed at Oldsmobile's design studio alongside the first proposal 1972 H/O Cutlass with the fastback-style sail panels. The Delta 88 was a humongous two-door model finished in silver with a black vinyl padded half-top over fastback-style extended sail panels. The lower portion of both side panels was finished in black with large deep-dish mag wheels and white-letter BF Goodrich tires. It also featured lace-design black stripes and a black bucket seat interior with a Hurst Dual Gate floor shifter incorporated into the factory console.

The results of this proposal are unknown, other than the fact Oldsmobile chose not to have Hurst produce any.

Jeep Commando

Hurst was successful in creating a Hurst Jeep Commando in 1971, although it was less than well received.

Shawnee Scout

Hurst built three prototypes of the Shawnee Scout Special for International Harvester in 1981. Based on the Scout II Terra, the convertible-top, the Shawnee Scout came equipped with the largest 345-ci 4-barrel carbureted V-8 with an automatic transmission. Hurst added a special console with dual shifters controlling the Chrysler 727 3-speed automatic transmission and also used a transfer case shift lever for the four-wheel-drive control.

Three prototypes were built, all in black with buckets seats. A built-in oversize rollover bar with a fiberglass bed cover essentially made them two-passenger vehicles. There were no hard doors, just snap-in fabric doors with a bikini-style top.

Linda Vaughn was photographed with one of the prototypes, and it seems the project was slated for the 1981 model year. But the project died along with the continuation of the Scout line by International Harvester in 1981.

The three Hurst preproduction units are alive and accounted for, with one residing at the Auburn-Cord-Duesenberg museum in Auburn, Indiana, while the other two are in the hands of private collectors in California.

Hurst prepared this 1971 Grand Ville Pontiac proposal car. It featured a gold painted roof and sunroof and a heavily padded back-half vinyl top. (Photo Courtesy Hurst/Olds Club of America)

Hurst performed the conversions of the 1975 and 1976 Buick Free Spirit additions. Many received the installation for the Hurst Hatch T-tops as well as the elaborate decal package. This car was most likely the prototype, as it is not sporting the white painted wheels as on the production units. (Photo Courtesy Hurst/Olds Club of America)

Hurst once again tried to work with Pontiac in 1978 with a Hurst GTO proposal. The car featured the traditional black and gold paint with the 15-inch Honeycomb wheels, front and rear spoilers, and dual exhaust splitters. The whereabouts of this car is unknown. (Photo Courtesy Hurst/Olds Club of America)

Hurst prepared the 1975 Buick pace car and support vehicles for the Indianapolis 500. (Photo Courtesy Hurst/Olds Club of America)

Inside the Doors of HQ

Business Changes

Like many businesses, Hurst had constant friction between sales and production. George was responsible for the sales and marketing teams within Hurst, and Bill Campbell supervised production.

The 1972 Pontiac Grand Prix SSJ featured a 455-ci engine that cranked out a pedestrian 300 hp because of its mild 8.4:1 compression ratio and a single 4-barrel carburetor. Unlike earlier Hurst cars, these were dealer-ordered rather than factory-conversion cars. Once the order was placed, Pontiac sent the car to Hurst and then the conversion was performed.

CHAPTER 10

Management Shift

Over 10 years of growth, many talented people held the production manager's position. In 1968, Bill had a great one who was able to increase production to stay ahead of rising demand. This was a first-time occurrence with the growing company, and the production manager went to George complaining that the warehouses were overflowing because the sales department was unable to keep up with projections. As the sales department was one of George's responsibilities he took offense to the criticism, immediately firing the manager.

Bill protested the dismissal, reiterating to George the great improvements that this manager had brought to the production side of the house. George did not reverse his decision, and within weeks he asked Bill to resign his position as well. Under pressure, Bill resigned in January 1969, causing the end of both their partnership and their friendship.

The contrasting personalities of Hurst and Campbell had fueled the growth of the corporation for 11 years. Without Bill Campbell's practical and pragmatic influence, the balance within the company's leadership was lost.

Even without Bill Campbell's presence, 1969 brought a peak in revenues for Hurst. Hurst Performance in Michigan, now managed by Dave Landreth, Don Morton, and Dick Chrysler, was involved in four major OEM programs simultaneously. Besides creating 912 special white-and-gold H/Os, there were two AMC projects of 52 SS AMXs inhouse and 1,512 SC/Ramblers being built in Kenosha, Wisconsin. The fourth was the ongoing Chrysler taxi cab conversion project. In all, more than 25,000 vehicles were built or converted by the Michigan-based Hurst Performance team in 1969.

These programs, along with the sale of stock, brought an influx of operating capital allowing for an expansion of manufacturing capabilities and adding to the company's financial strength. The era of Hurst being undercapitalized was now over, but with this advantage the adequately funded company was recognized. Hurst quickly came to the attention of larger corporations, and stock values had jumped to more than $12 per share.

In 1970, Oldsmobile chose not to continue the H/O product offering due to the lift of the corporate ban on V-8 engines of more than 400 ci in General Motors' intermediate-size cars. Oldsmobile management felt it created a conflict as to which vehicle was the halo vehicle at Oldsmobile, given that it was able to factory-build the W-30 package for the 455-powered 4-4-2. Oldsmobile sold 19,330 of the 4-4-2 units with this monstrous 455 engine as standard equipment without sharing the profit with Hurst.

Sunbeam Buys Hurst Performance

Six months after Bill Campbell's departure from Hurst, he purchased a motor home and traveled the United States with his family. During this time, Sunbeam Corporation, the makers of toasters and can openers, had researched Hurst's financial position in the interest of acquiring it. Sunbeam management approached Bill Campbell and asked to buy his 25.9-percent share of the company.

Eventually, Campbell accepted an offer of $10.50 per share, equating to more than a $6.2 million ownership stake in the company. After Campbell sold his shares in Hurst, Larry Greenwald

George Hurst received this SEMA trophy inducting him into the SEMA Hall of Fame in November of 1978. Hurst supported the organization since the first show in California in 1962. (Photo Courtesy Pete Serio Collection)

soon followed with the sale of his 25.9-percent interest in Hurst to Sunbeam. Almost overnight, George Hurst found himself a minority stakeholder in the business he created.

During his absence from his senior vice president position at Hurst, Bill Campbell and his family purchased a motorhome and traveled the United States. He became enamored with the RV life and was soon working with friend Tom Harbison at his Pennsylvania RV business.

Bill Campbell and Tom Harbison partnered to purchase a stake in Prevost Car, Inc., a bus company in Canada in 1969, joining Prevost's president André Normand. The company and the partnership continue to grow and flourish until they finally sold their ownership stake in 1995, to Volvo Bus Corporation and English-based Henly's Group PLC.

Sunbeam almost immediately reorganized the management structure at Hurst. First, Sunbeam appointed James McNeal as president in July 1970, and George was re-titled as Chairman of the Board. At that time, he focused on completing the Hurst Rescue Tool. George had many conflicts with the new Sunbeam management team running Hurst. Some of the long-term Hurst employees had a deep admiration and respect for George, and many were helping George on development of the Rescue Tool.

The first two production rescue tools were shipped in December 1970. Two days later, George's historic tenure at the company he started in his garage came to an end. He resigned his position as Chairman of the Board.

Interestingly, the Chicago Fire Department was one of the first to purchase the rescue tool. When two commuter trains collided on October 30, 1972, it was put to the test. The high-speed collision compacted two train cars, killing 45 people and injuring 332. The Hurst rescue tool was used to rescue more than 100 of the trapped and injured passengers.

After Hurst's departure from the company he founded, he received a consulting contract from Sunbeam with a $300,000 initial payment. He also received additional incentives of $60,000 per year for three years in consulting fees, with the stipulation that he could not interfere with the management of the company.

George moved to Southern California with his wife Lila, where they settled into a modest Huntington Beach home near the water. He lost the company that bore his name and that he spent a majority of his adult life building. He also lost the right to market products under the Hurst name. Although separated from his company, he was not without ambition or ideas. Unfortunately, alcohol began to play an increasingly large part in his life, to the point that friends and others became openly concerned for his health.

Unhappy with the new management's view of the Detroit operation's value to Hurst, Dave Landreth and Don Morton left Hurst in late 1971 to start their own conversion company. By June 1971, Sunbeam appointed Bob Draper as

Indy was the more affordable line of shifters for Hurst. This was the cover for the 1974 catalog. (Photo Courtesy Mark Fletcher Collection)

the new Hurst president in Pennsylvania. In 1972, Dick Chrysler became the top executive for Hurst in Michigan.

Allegheny Acquires Sunbeam

Allegheny International bought Sunbeam in November 1981 for $532 million. Allegheny immediately sold Hurst for $8 million to Dick Chrysler, former employee and owner of Cars and Concepts in Detroit. The Hurst business in Detroit had been primarily focused on installing T-tops for new GM cars. Dick went on to combine the Michigan-based Hurst Performance with his other company, Cars and Concepts. This allowed him to control more than 70 percent of the T-top installation work being done by third-party contractors.

Once Dick Chrysler settled into the ownership of Hurst, discussions with Oldsmobile began for the successful return of the H/O for 1983 and again in 1984. Early in 1984, Chrysler sold the Hurst Rescue Tool to Shelby, North Carolina–based Hale Products for $5 million.

Hale has retained its ownership of the Hurst rescue tool for more than 27 years and has trademarked the name "Jaws of Life." The product has continued to be successful with more than 35,000 units in use today, with an untold number of lives saved.

Dick Chrysler continued to grow Cars and Concepts, and with the addition of Hurst Performance's vehicle conversion business, the company topped $100 million in sales in 1985. One of the interesting projects that Cars and Concepts worked on with General Motors was to covert the 1986 Monte Carlo and the Pontiac Grand Prix into the Aero Coupe body style so that the cars could be homologated for NASCAR. In all, they produced 200 white Monte Carlos with burgundy interior and 200 silver Pontiac Grand Prix conversions in a 10-week period, starting in late February and finishing in June 1986. They went on to convert an additional 1,118 Pontiac Grand Prixs and 6,800 Monte Carlos into Aero coupes in 1987.

While working on the second year of the GM Aero car conversions, Dick Chrysler decided to sell Hurst. Joe Hrudka of Mr. Gasket bought Hurst Performance on February 27, 1986, for a reported $6 million. Mr. Gasket purchased all of the Hurst Performance products, manufacturing facilities in Warminster and California, in addition to the Hurst name. What wasn't included was the T-top and conversion business that Chrysler had incorporated into Cars and Concepts, which he retained.

During his short ownership, Chrysler reduced his $8 million investment in Hurst to $3 million by selling off the rescue tool for $5 million. Upon selling Hurst to Mr. Gasket, he turned a profit of $3 million, and at the same time eliminated Hurst as a competitor to his Cars and Concept business.

Dick Chrysler chose to sell Hurst to coincide with his first run for political office. He used a portion of the proceeds to self-fund his campaign for Governor of Michigan, in which he fought a highly contested but unsuccessful battle. However, he later successfully won a Michigan seat in Congress in 1995 and held it for a single two-year term.

Joe Hrudka was a racer-turned-businessman, and having competed against Hurst for two decades he was enthused to finally own the company that had surpassed the growth of his own company. Sales of performance products in the 1980s were not expanding at the same pace they had in the mid 1960s. But Joe saw the value that Hurst's products and name continued to command in the smaller performance market. The company acted quickly and continued to market the Hurst name as its own. Hrudka quickly moved all production from Warminster to his Cleveland, Ohio, facilities. Only a small number of Hurst employees stayed with the new ownership and moved to Ohio. Most nonessential documents, awards, and past products were piled into dumpsters at Warminster in preparation for the move to Ohio. As the building was emptied out, some former Hurst employees were able to save some of the historical items.

Hrudka first invited Linda Vaughn back as VP of Public Relations in order to capitalize on her customer connections with Hurst. Linda again became the ambassador of everything Hurst at races and automotive events such as the SEMA Show. Mr. Gasket reinstated the original lifetime warranty on Hurst shifters, although they now charged a $45 handling fee.

During the 1980s, Hrudka had been on an acquisition rampage, buying automotive companies with established names in the industry. Hurst became part of a family of well-known brands such as ACCEL, Cyclone, and Thrush mufflers, Seal-Tite, Cragar, Weld Wheels, and Tru Spoke Wheels, Cal Custom, and Hollywood Accessories.

During those acquisition years, Mr. Gasket grew from $74 million in 1984 to $119.3 million by 1987, but the stock took a slide from a 1985 peak of $18 per share down to $2.25 in 1988, and finally less than $1.75 by early 1991. The value drop was related to a $14.7 million loss in 1988.

Pontiac Grand Prix SSJ Program

Throughout the corporate turmoil, Dave Landreth continued to drive the new-car conversion business of Hurst Performance. Proposals were made to both Chevrolet and Pontiac for a Hurst version of their respective new personal luxury cars. The Hurst Monte Carlo proposal was a 1970 454 SS model with bucket seats, console with "His and Hers" shifter, padded half-vinyl top, and an electric sunroof. Finished in black with gold accent stripes, the proposal to Chevrolet in the fall of 1969 never gained traction and didn't come close to seeing production.

In contrast, Pontiac's sibling to the Monte Carlo was the Grand Prix SSJ and the company readily accepted the proposal for its Grand Prix SSJ, but with a twist. Pontiac did not make a commitment to Hurst based on a certain number of units. Instead, they marketed the conversion as a custom order through the Pontiac system. Dealers placed an order mostly based on a customer presale.

A Cameo White or Starlight Black Pontiac Grand Prix model J was built to the customer's requirements prior to being shipped to Hurst. Ivory, black, or sandalwood interior colors were required. Hurst installed a sunroof and half-landau padded top, masked and painted the hood, roof, and trunk in Hurst Firefrost Gold outlined with black pinstripes, and added SSJ and Hurst emblems to both front fenders.

There were three wheel options: standard Pontiac Rally 2, new Trans Am Honeycomb, and aftermarket American-brand Daisy, all painted in Hurst Gold. Inside, the customer could order either the deluxe bucket seats with a Hurst Dual Gate shifter in the standard console or the standard bench seat interior where a new Hurst Autostick protruded from the floor resembling a Competition Plus 4-speed arm. Only 17 bench seat units were built with this option in the three years of SSJ production. Although the Pontiac Grand Prix was available with the 4-speed manual transmission, no documentation of any 4-speed SSJs have been found.

Interestingly, some Grand Prixs were brought to Hurst by the original owners after they had purchased and taken delivery from their dealers. Hurst accepted these customer drive-ins, and a few of these cars have also surfaced.

Hurst was not concerned with the authenticity of the cars they created, and a few cars have been documented to have been made in colors other than the required white or black. Hurst employees recalled that green, blue, maroon, and sandalwood cars have all received the SSJ treatment.

The first year of production in 1970 was conducted at the Ferndale facility. The two subsequent years saw production at the Southfield, Michigan, location. The conversion cost $1,147 over the roughly $4,500 of a well-equipped Grand Prix J model. The total cost of more than $5,600 did not include shipping charges from Hurst to the final customer. Many new owners picked up the car in person after a 10-day build cycle at the Hurst facility. Interestingly, the Hurst conversion carried a 12-month warranty with the exception of the Hurst Gold paint application that was only warranted for 90 days from delivery.

Additionally, Hurst tried to capitalize on selling extras, from the Hurst Roll Control to a $2,100 mobile phone and a $340 Sony black-and-white portable television, complete with an externally-mounted rabbit-ear antenna attached to the top edge of the side quarter glass.

Hurst introduced the Pontiac SSJ in 1970 when 272 were built. The following year, an additional 157 were converted to the SSJ trim. The final year of 1972 saw only 52 units built, with 481 SSJs built over the three-year run.

Hurst used the Pontiac SSJ program to convert this Monte Carlo into a proposal car for Chevrolet in 1971. (Photo Courtesy Hurst/Olds Club of America)

SSJ HURST

THE ULTIMATE GRAND PRIX

AN EXCLUSIVE CUSTOM CONVERSION BY HURST PERFORMANCE RESEARCH CORPORATION

LINDA VAUGHN, "MISS HURST GOLDEN SHIFTER" AND THE NEW SSJ HURST, SHOWN WITH OPTIONAL WHEELS AND TIRES.

Linda Vaughn stands through the sunroof in the factory Hurst SSJ brochure. (Photo Courtesy Pete Serio Collection)

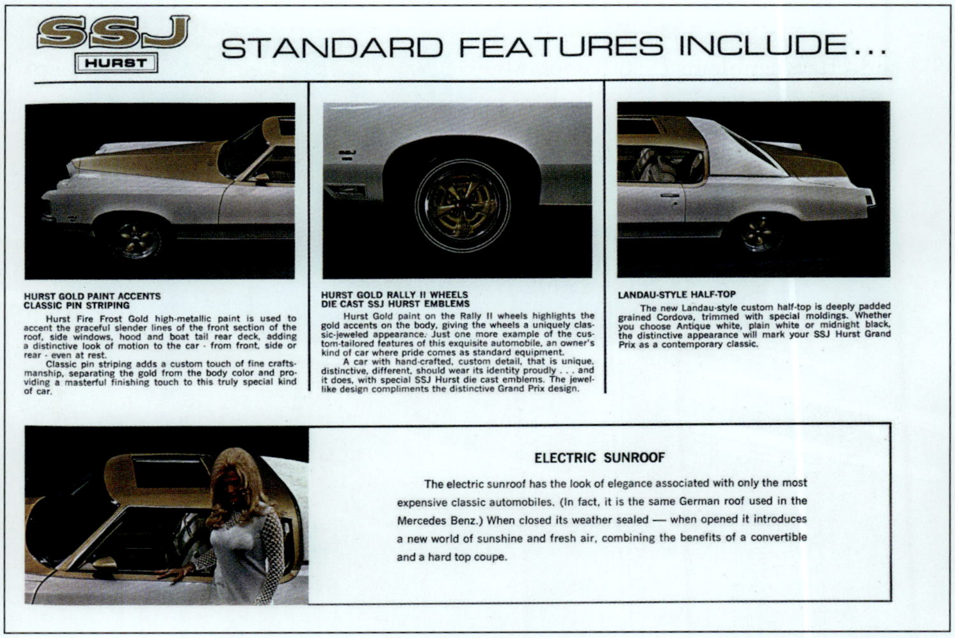

SSJ HURST

STANDARD FEATURES INCLUDE...

HURST GOLD PAINT ACCENTS
CLASSIC PIN STRIPING

Hurst Fire Frost Gold high-metallic paint is used to accent the graceful slender lines of the front section of the roof, side windows, hood and boat tail rear deck, adding a distinctive look of motion to the car - from front, side or rear - even at rest.

Classic pin striping adds a custom touch of fine craftsmanship, separating the gold from the body color and providing a masterful finishing touch to this truly special kind of car.

HURST GOLD RALLY II WHEELS
DIE CAST SSJ HURST EMBLEMS

Hurst Gold paint on the Rally II wheels highlights the gold accents on the body, giving the wheels a uniquely classic-jeweled appearance. Just one more example of the custom-tailored features of this exquisite automobile, an owner's kind of car where pride comes as standard equipment.

A car with hand-crafted, custom detail, that is unique, distinctive, different, should wear its identity proudly . . . and it does, with special SSJ Hurst die cast emblems. The jewel-like design compliments the distinctive Grand Prix design.

LANDAU-STYLE HALF-TOP

The new Landau-style custom half-top is deeply padded grained Cordova, trimmed with special moldings. Whether you choose Antique white, plain white or midnight black, the distinctive appearance will mark your SSJ Hurst Grand Prix as a contemporary classic.

ELECTRIC SUNROOF

The electric sunroof has the look of elegance associated with only the most expensive classic automobiles. (In fact, it is the same German roof used in the Mercedes Benz.) When closed its weather sealed — when opened it introduces a new world of sunshine and fresh air, combining the benefits of a convertible and a hard top coupe.

The Hurst SSJ brochure shows the options. The customer purchased a Pontiac Grand Prix and brought it to Hurst for conversion based on the options and colors chosen. (Photo Courtesy Pete Serio Collection)

Linda Vaughn stands in front of a Hurst Pontiac SSJ with the optional gold American Racing wheels. (Photo Courtesy Pete Serio Collection)

1967 Pontiac Grand Prix Convertible

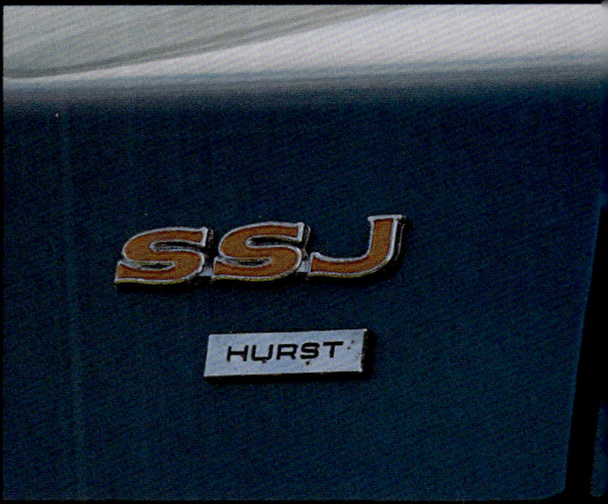

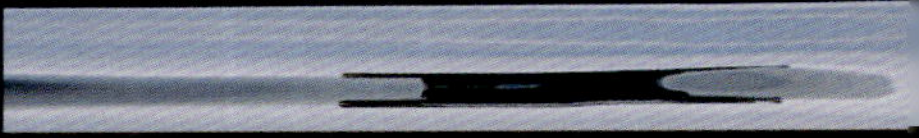

Marketed as the ultimate Grand Prix in the Hurst promotional materials of the era, this 1972 Hurst SSJ is loaded to the hilt. Hurst-installed accessories included a custom moonroof, telephone, cassette deck, and Sony TV, making this SSJ a one-of-a-kind original. (Photos Courtesy Rich Truesdell)

George Hurst's Later Endeavors

After George left Hurst Performance in early 1971, he launched several businesses, but never managed to regain the same success he previously enjoyed.

Customer Support

One of his ventures was a high-performance customer support program. For a $10 annual membership fee, performance-oriented team members could call George during business hours and get advice on aftermarket performance parts. Some members were also asked to test products for manufacturers in order to receive the George Hurst endorsement. Don Garlits interviewed George in an infomercial-style discussion published in the February 1972 issue of *Hot Rod*.

George Hurst Executive System

George also started an auto tune-up shop that picked up cars at the Orange County, California, airport and performed tune-ups in a garage at the Newport Sheraton. It was called the George Hurst Executive System.

George was interviewed in the October 1975 issue of *Bay Window* magazine, a local Southern California publication for the Balboa Bay Club & Resort in Newport Beach, California. George explained his George Hurst Performance Team and his new automotive tune-up shop concept. The one location based out of Orange County airport in Irvine, California, was short-lived, and plans for a franchise never came to fruition. The franchise costs of $10,000, with $5,700 per year in advertising fees, and 5 percent of gross sales surely had an impact.

Tax Evasion

Soon after George left Hurst Performance in the wake of the Sunbeam takeover, he fell under IRS scrutiny, resulting in charges of tax evasion. He was charged and jailed for a short time during 1971. He was released pending the trial, and looked for a settlement with the IRS.

He received a call from his accountant explaining that the IRS agent involved in the investigation may be able to "make the problem go away" for a sizable fee. Unfortunately for George, the offer was a sting, and both he and the accountant were recorded in a phone

Hurst created a catalog for 1976 covering only those items related to automatic transmission products. (Photo Courtesy Mark Fletcher Collection)

conversation and were subsequently convicted of attempting to bribe an IRS agent in 1975. After years of appeals, George spent 18 months in a Memphis, Tennessee, prison in the early 1980s.

Transmission Rebuilds

By 1983, George was once again working alongside General Motors. He attempted to launch an automatic transmission rebuild exchange program. His concept was to create automotive repair shop franchises to purchase Hurst factory-rebuilt transmissions from GM dealers and install them in a customer's vehicle. With the correct transmission rebuild in stock locally, it was possible to complete the exchange in just a single day. The concept included painting the transmissions and attaching a serialized ID plate to identify the units. Although George received publicity and media attention, this project never caught on and failed to move beyond the preliminary stage. He ended up parting ways with General Motors.

Author

Following these setbacks, George wrote a book in 1984 with religious overtones about a soul that returns to Earth as persons until he gets it right. Titled *The Perfect You*, it combines many Christian beliefs, being both esoteric and somewhat confusing to the reader.

New Inventions

In 1985, George was the General Manager at Custom Engineering in Redlands, California, working for his friend Billy Closson (who also owned and operated West Coast Cobra). The business worked primarily with Pacific Bell Telephone by outfitting the company trucks used for construction. He was once again single after his marriage of 17 years to Lila had ended. After his divorce from Lila, George moved into a small apartment close to his workshop in Redlands. Feeling destined to repeat his success from the past, he was upbeat and optimistic, actively working on three new projects simultaneously in his free time.

The first involved devising a swinging chair that relieved the gravitational pressure on the spine without requiring you to hang upside down from a bar with anti-gravity boots, as was popular in the 1980s.

His second invention was an automatic transmission that worked similar to a torque wrench. This invention was reportedly being considered by General Electric, but was never released as a marketable product.

The third was a system that evenly rewound long, heavy-duty cables on large spools without overlap or binding the cable. This was to be used by tow-truck drivers and telephone companies that were stringing and reclaiming above-ground telephone lines.

George was hoping to revolutionize the automatic transmission industry with a new hydraulic transmission he was working on in 1983. But through various circumstances, the business never got off the ground. (Photo Courtesy Mark Fletcher Collection)

Later Endeavors CONTINUED

Untimely Passing

Hurst was a troubled man, and he still owed back taxes to the IRS. He unexpectedly passed away at his home on May 13, 1986, in a suspected suicide. He was found dead in his car that was parked in an enclosed garage from suspected carbon monoxide poisoning. No suicide note was found, but according to Pat Flannery, paperwork from the IRS was on the front passenger seat. Those who knew George had no indication that he was despondent, and many struggle to this day with the tragic death of this dynamic leader.

Hurst Transmission Systems was George's new company that rebuilt and replaced automatic transmissions through GM-authorized dealers. (Photos Courtesy Pete Serio Collection)

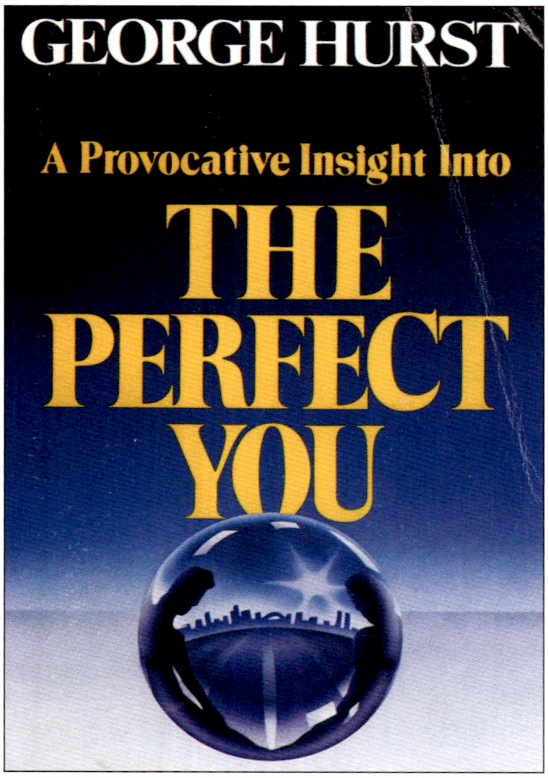

George Hurst was man of many talents and interests. He wrote a religious book in 1984 about a spirit who kept returning to earth until it finally learned the meaning of life. (Photo Courtesy Mark Fletcher Collection)

ABOUT THE AUTHOR

George Hurst was born just in time to spend his childhood during the great depression. He worked in a Defense Plant until he was old enough to join the United States Navy where he spent 10 very memorable years.

Immediately after leaving the Navy he started fixing cars in a two-car garage attached to his home. George took this "two-car garage" to Wall Street via the "HURST SHIFTER" (4 on the floor) and the HURST POWER RESCUE TOOL, the "JAWS OF LIFE," which has been credited with saving thousands of lives all over the free world.

George has the distinct honor of having General Motors produce special cars with his name on them, the HURST/OLDS, a limited production, top of the line Performance Car which has been produced over the past 16 years; and children named after him, by their fathers.

George has been a truly fortunate mechanic who bases his unusual good fortune on the special way that he sees you and me and the World.

In this book he shares his very special World with you.

Printed by Coleman Publishing
99 Milbar Blvd. Farmingdale, N.Y. 11735 ISBN: 0-942494-91-1

This is the back cover of George' Hurst's book, which provides a bio of his life. (Photo Courtesy Mark Fletcher Collection)

George's Final Innovations

During the 10 years Sunbeam owned Hurst Corporation, very few new innovations were successful. Both Don Lane and Marty Danko remained in the product development group in Warminster, introducing new shifters for both street and racing applications. Most of their work centered on automatic transmission shift controls and included the Lightning Rod shifter that was adapted into the 1983 and 1984 H/O vehicles that Hurst Performance had collaborated on with General Motors.

George Hurst remained optimistic and was working on a multitude of ideas into the early 1980s. (Photo Courtesy Mark Fletcher Collection)

Don Lane (left) stands with another Hurst employee in the service bay at the Warminster facility. (Photo Courtesy Don Lane Collection)

Hurst Rescue Vehicle

One other major project was the creation of the Hurst rescue vehicles. These were AMC Gremlins painted white, with bright orange zebra stripes equipped with the Hurst Rescue Tool that had been given the name "Jaws of Life." The small specialized cars were able to maneuver closer to the accident scene than large fire vehicles, allowing for a faster response time in these critical situations.

Long-time Hurst employee Marty Danko recalls that most of the Gremlins were assembled by him at his home garage in Warminster. Each of the 30 vehicles built had a cost of more than $11,000 fully equipped. At least two of these were assembled using 1975 Pacers as the core vehicle.

At least one of these Gremlin-based vehicles remains today, and is still in use by the Murray County Rescue in Chatsworth, Georgia.

George Hurst discusses business with the two Airheart brothers when they visited the Hurst Facility in Warminster, Pennsylvania. (Photo Courtesy Rich Truesdell Collection)

Final Innovations CONTINUED

Talking Car and Auto Scentaire

Some interesting products almost made production during this time as well. Don recalls two in particular. The The "Talking Car" featured a voice that alerted the driver if the oil level was low, the engine temperature was high, if you left your keys in the ignition, or if the door was ajar. Designed as an aftermarket box mounted to the dash, it was obsolete before it was finished as new car manufacturers started delivering cars with very similar functions.

The Auto Scentaire automated air freshener also mounted in the interior of the car.

Both products were considered gimmicks and were typical of the lack of passion held by the management of Hurst at that time.

Murray County Fire in Georgia purchased this Gremlin from Hurst in 1974 and used it for three decades. The side stripes are the original reflective decals. It shows wear to the original paint below the hatch. (Photos Courtesy Derick Dorrah)

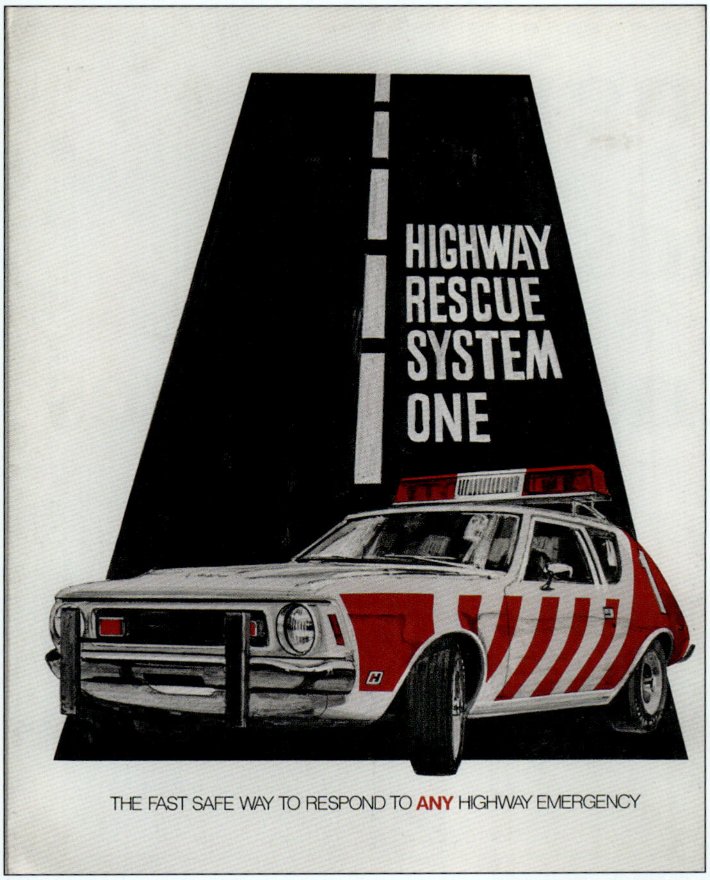

Hurst offered the Gremlin as a complete response vehicle in order to carry the Hurst Rescue Tool close to the accident scene. (Photo Courtesy Pete Serio Collection)

The production rescue tool had a separate power unit attached by a long hydraulic hose to the spreader unit. (Photo Courtesy Pete Serio Collection)

During the Sunbeam ownership years, Hurst introduced many small electronic automotive accessories, such as this Auto Scentaire air freshener. This unit (above) is owned by a past Hurst employee. (Photos Courtesy Pete Serio Collection, left; Marty Danko/Mark Fletcher, right)

Changing Hands and Changing Times

An Era of Transitions for Hurst

After fighting financial turmoil for years, Mr. Gasket's automotive group of companies was no longer a solvent business. In 1993, Mr. Gasket filed for reorganization under bankruptcy protection, and it remained there until the Echlin Corporation bought it in 1995. While the Hurst brand was still well recognized by performance enthusiasts, it became a line-item product in the Mr. Gasket brand portfolio, hidden as a division of Echlin.

Here, the Performance West Group 2005 Chrysler 300C Hurst Edition is shown with its predecessor, an original Hurst-modified 1970 Chrysler 300 two-door hardtop. (Photo Courtesy Richard Truesdell)

CHAPTER 11

Tribute Cars

In almost 20 years of Echlin's stewardship, Hurst mostly languished due to a lack of attention and new product development. It was left to others (mostly private individuals and small companies) to carry on the Hurst tradition of modifying existing production cars and offering something that the original equipment manufacturers did not. When the first edition of this book was written 10 years ago, two cars stood out that shared the white and gold Hurst livery: the Oldsmobile Hurst Hearse and the Chrysler 300C Hurst Edition by Performance West Group.

While many Hurst "tribute" cars have been built, quite possibly one of the best realized is Jim Morris' *Hurst Hearse*. Morris wanted to show the possibilities using the last of GM's full-size rear-wheel-drive station wagons, in this case the Oldsmobile Custom Cruiser, the last of which was built in 1992. (Photo Courtesy Jim Morris)

Oldsmobile Hurst Hearse

Jim and Cheryl Morris of West Allis, Wisconsin, built a 1992 Oldsmobile Custom Cruiser station wagon that was dubbed the *Hurst Hearse*. In 1992, the last rear-wheel-drive Oldsmobile (the station wagon–only Custom Cruiser) shared its platform with the Buick Roadmaster and Chevrolet Caprice Classic, which both offered sedan versions as well.

In its final year of production, only 4,347 Custom Cruisers rolled off of the Arlington, Texas, assembly line. It was modified in much the same way as a Hurst model from the 1960s and 1970s. It featured Oldsmobile Super Stock IV wheels from 1992, hood louvers from a 1973 4-4-2, and the seats and console from a 1975 Cutlass. All of the original exterior emblems were removed, and this lowered station wagon was finished with the traditional Hurst color scheme of white and gold.

Chrysler 300C Hurst Edition

A second Hurst tribute car was introduced 13 years later. It was based on the then-new 2005 Chrysler 300C. Built by the Performance West Group, it was the brainchild of another husband-and-wife team, Larry and Debbie Weiner, the owners of the Performance West Group. As the Chrysler 300C entered production, this car was designed with limited series production potential either with the blessing of Chrysler or through a group of dealers authorized by the Performance West Group.

The Chrysler 300C Hurst Edition by Performance West Group translated many traditional Hurst design cues from the limited production run of the 1970 Hurst-built Chrysler 300. The 300C Hurst Edition's 5.7-liter Hemi was left essentially stock aside from some dress-up items, an engine management system that was optimized by Kenne Bell, and a cat-back exhaust system from MagnaFlow, which combined to bump horsepower to the 400 benchmark.

The interior was enhanced with the addition of Katzkin white leather trim with contrasting accents and a Hurst-style shifter. Externally, the Chrysler 300C Hurst Edition was treated to a set of 10-inch-wide, 22-inch-tall Oasis wheels with 285/35R22 Toyo Proxes tires. Of course, it's the modern interpretation of the classic Hurst white and gold color scheme that sets this 300C apart from its OEM counterparts.

Not long after the 300C Hurst Edition completed its run of auto shows, Chrysler's fate had turned. The success of the 300C was followed by losses. DaimlerChrysler, under pressure from its mostly German shareholders, was forced to divest itself of its American subsidiary in 2007, selling Chrysler to Cerberus Capital Management, a private equity firm. That was followed by a painful bankruptcy in the wake of the 2009 economic recession. Before Chrysler was liquidated, Italy's Fiat (with a healthy push from the Obama Admin-

While the proportions are decidedly different, there's no mistaking the link between the original 1970 Hurst Chrysler 300 two-door hardtop and the four-door 2005 Chrysler 300C that re-launched rear-wheel-drive performance sedans from the Auburn Hills automaker, which at the timed was aligned with Daimler-Benz. (Photo Courtesy Richard Truesdell)

istration) stepped in to assume control of Chrysler's US assets. At the time, the Obama Administration was more concerned with the $25-billion restructuring of General Motors.

B&M Acquires Hurst

In 2007, the Hurst name and product line was purchased by B&M Automotive Group of Chatsworth, California. The Hurst product line was reinvigorated with the guidance of enthusiasts once again and led by longtime industry aftermarket leader Nate Shelton, who was instrumental in the rise of K&N filters. An increased emphasis was placed on marketing the traditional strengths of the Hurst brand, especially in the aftermarket shifter category.

Under B&M ownership, Hurst returned to its roots as a seller of top-quality high-performance shifters, and Hurst hardware was once again found in a comprehensive 38-page catalog.

Currently, Hurst offers a full line of automatic and manual shifters, as well as shifter accessories and service parts. Hurst has applications for every major American automobile manufacturer, and even some less-prominent makes, such as Studebaker.

Hurst Performance Returns

After a 20-year hiatus of building specialty conversion muscle cars, Hurst (through B&M) made a triumphant return, and Shelton relaunched the performance-car operation under the Hurst Performance banner based in Irvine, California. First in that pre-Hellcat era was a Hurst Edition supercharged 2009 Dodge Challenger. It was followed by distinctive, limited-production versions of all three modern muscle cars: the Dodge Challenger, Ford Mustang, and Chevrolet Camaro.

At the same time, Hurst Performance's Irvine facility built a number of cars and trucks with limited series production potential. One was a turbocharged V-6 Camaro that was built in conjunction with BFGoodrich and dubbed the Red Line Series Hurst Camaro, a reference to the throwback-style red-line tires. The rear-mounted turbocharger used a Hurst-modified exhaust system. As gasoline prices moderated, the V-6 Camaro project stalled. However, a project that certainly impressed was the 50th Anniversary Hurst/Viper. Hurst took the already-renowned supercar to a new performance level. Wearing the signature Hurst colors, this radical supercar was fitted with Hurst's Hard-Drive gold anodized pistol-grip shifter, Moton Club Sport adjustable coilover suspension with Eibach springs, a choice of either Hurst 19- or 20-inch aluminum wheels, and Corsa exhaust.

The Hurst Challenger was the most popular of the Hurst Conversion cars to come out of Irvine. Similar to the Viper, the Challenger was equipped with the 9.26-inch-tall Hard-Drive shifter, 20-inch polished aluminum wheels with painted spoke inserts, BFGoodrich

Available in four stages of tune, this car, which was featured on the cover of the January 2009 issue of *Musclecar Enthusiast*, features a Vortech-supercharged version of the SRT8's normally naturally-aspirated 6.1-liter V-8. With 560 hp on tap and a long enough stretch of open road, this Series 4 version of the Hurst Challenger could probably nudge 200 mph (with no Highway Patrolmen around). (Photo Courtesy Richard Truesdell)

Under the hood of the Hurst Edition Series 4 Challenger is a stock SRT8 6.1-liter V-8 massaged through the addition of a Vortech supercharger providing 560 hp. (Photo Courtesy Richard Truesdell)

KDW performance tires, a Magnaflow stainless steel cat-back system, Eibach coilover adjustable suspension, and a heavy-duty anti-roll bar. The appearance package featured the Hurst interior and graphics treatment.

The Hurst Camaro was another impressive conversion. The Series 4 Supercharged Camaro used a Magnuson centrifugal supercharger to produce 600 hp and 550 ft-lbs of torque. As always, exhaust modifications were mandatory; therefore, a Magnaflow cat-back exhaust system was used. The seminal Hurst Hard-Drive shifter was also an integral part of the package. Also included was Eibach coilover suspension, 20-inch wheels, and a Hurst Air Speed rear spoiler. This 600-hp engine pushed the Camaro to a 0–60 (mph) time of just over 4 seconds and a quarter-mile time in the low-12-second range.

Hurst's Mustang received a special blend of performance parts to make it a special tuner car. This 2010 model was equipped with a 4.6-liter V-8. A Roush supercharger forced air into the Modular engine, increasing horsepower from 315 to 435. High-performance parts included the Hard-Drive Pistol Grip shifter, 20-inch wheels, special exterior Hurst graphics, and the Hurst dash emblem. For performance hardware, it had Eibach adjustable coilover suspension, Magnaflow stainless steel exhaust, and a K&N air filter.

But in a challenging economy (unemployment hovered around 10 percent), the performance car business could not sustain itself. On July 19, 2011, B&M Automotive Group announced that it would shut down the Hurst Performance car-building operation. This was due in part because the 2012 Dodge Challenger SRT8 featured an engine management system that was un-hackable at the time. You could not program your own ignition curve. Thus, it was impossible to offer a supercharged version of the 6.4-liter, 392-ci Hemi, which was the same obstacle faced by the rest of the aftermarket.

While Hurst Performance enjoyed some success with the Mustang and Camaro, the Challenger was the heart of the program, and since a supercharger could not be added, the B&M Automotive Group made the painful decision to shut down the Irvine operation. There was a sense of déjà vu in a way because it was similar to how the original Hurst Performance operation closed its doors in Michigan.

Hurst Today

In 2015, four years after B&M ended its run of limited-production supercars, Hurst Heritage by GSS, in conjunction with Norm Kraus, aka Mr. Norm, picked up the torch. Led by the builders of the 2005 Chrysler 300C, industry

The first of the Hurst Heritage by GSS cars debuted at the 2015 edition of Mopars at the Strip. Sporting the iconic Hurst white with gold stripes paint scheme, it was a huge hit among the Hurst and Mopar faithful and relaunched the Hurst brand to modern muscle car fans. (Photo Courtesy Richard Truesdell)

Like the 2015 version, the 2016 version replaced the factory leather with the unique white/black leather trim. (Photo Courtesy Richard Truesdell)

This angle showcases the updated Hurst wheels. In this case, they are 22-inches in diameter. (Photo Courtesy Richard Truesdell)

1969 Hurst AMC SS/AMX, 2017 Hurst by GSS Dodge Challenger Patriot, and 1969 Hurst AMC SC/Rambler

Shown are a 1969 AMC Hurst SS/AMX, the Hurst Heritage by GSS Dodge Challenger Patriot Edition, and a 1969 AMC Hurst SC/Rambler. (Photo Courtesy Richard Truesdell)

This shows the evolution of Hurst car interiors separated by almost five decades: a 1969 AMC Hurst AMX/SS (top), a 1969 AMC Hurst SC/Rambler (middle), and a 2016 Hurst Heritage by GSS Dodge Challenger Patriot Edition (bottom). (Photo Courtesy Richard Truesdell)

Even standing still, the Hurst Heritage by GSS 2016 Dodge Challenger Patriot Edition shows the link to the Hurst SC/Rambler, especially with the huge hood scoop. Its design was inspired by the SC/Rambler's mailbox slot design. (Photo Courtesy Richard Truesdell)

veterans Larry Weiner and GSS Supercars designed and built modern muscle cars that were infused with the same DNA as their legendary Hurst predecessors.

However, while these advances resulted in superior performance compared to their storied ancestors, development of every new Hurst Heritage by GSS vehicle is based on more than five decades of tradition. For example, the Patriot Challenger was inspired by the pocket rocket of the muscle car era: the incredible 1969 Hurst S/C Rambler. The Patriot is authentic right down to the original Hurst S/C Rambler A-Paint scheme with its bold red, white, and blue panels; outrageous mailbox hood scoop; and original Hurst S/C fender emblems.

The same attention to detail is on full display with the 1968 Tribute 50th Anniversary GSS Hellcat Wide Body. Seen here painted Peruvian Silver Metallic, this is the same Toronado-specific color that was applied to every 1968 Hurst Olds, along with contrasting Tuxedo Black panel graphics and Ermine White pinstripes that were inspired by those on the original. The 50th Anniversary Hellcat matches the timeless original down to the spoiler-delete black trunk lid and

With the 2016 introduction of the Dodge Challenger, the Hurst Heritage by GSS team turned its attention to the year's Hellcat-powered version. It was a combination that truly improved on the OEM version. (Photo Courtesy Richard Truesdell)

To celebrate the 50th anniversary of the 1968 Hurst Oldsmobile (since Oldsmobile is no longer with us), the Hurst Heritage by GSS design team applied the same Peruvian Silver Metallic with black accents to the 2018 Hurst Heritage Edition by GSS Dodge Challenger Widebody 50th Anniversary Edition. (Photo Courtesy Larry Weiner)

After the inception of the Hurst Heritage by GSS program, its success spawned an extension of the Hurst brand to Chevrolet's Camaro. Inspired by the great Camaro COPO cars, this is the 2017 Hurst RPO L78 Camaro Custom. (Photo Courtesy Larry Weiner)

The 2018 Hurst Heritage by GSS Chrysler 300H was a reprise of the 2005 Performance West Group (precursor of Hurst Heritage by GSS), which shows how Chrysler's designers kept the rear-wheel-drive 300 fresh over its 15-year run through 2020. (Photo Courtesy Larry Weiner)

Since 2016, the Hurst Heritage by GSS team turned its attention to the Mustang as well. This is the 2018 Hurst Heritage by GSS Kenne Bell R-Code Mustang. The Mustangs were a collaborative effort between Hurst Heritage by GSS and Jim Bell at Kenne Bell superchargers. (Photo Courtesy Larry Weiner)

white pinstripe that frames the backlight. Details abound inside and out, including a Hurst shifter that is topped off with a Consistent T-Handle for 6-speed manual applications, a vintage Hurst *Warning* shifter label, and Hurst lowering springs for a bold stance. Outside, Hellcat Wide Body fender flares are reminiscent of the bold Toronado-style wheel arches on the 1968 Hurst Olds and were introduced prior to the FCA-introduced widebody Challengers and Chargers.

Over the years, in addition to the Olds 442, Hurst packages were offered on a wide range of vehicles that included the Pontiac Grand Prix, the SC/Rambler, the Chrysler 300, and even the Jeepster Commando. Like Hurst, Heritage by GSS carries this tradition forward and offers unique, serial-numbered limited-edition packages for each of the popular domestic performance cars. In addition to the Challenger, included are the Charger, Chrysler 300, Camaro, and Mustang. Some are descendants of the originals that Hurst built, while others fill the gaps left from vehicles like the 442, Grand Prix, and Rambler, which are no longer in production.

While new vehicles have been added to the roster to make up for those that are missing, tradition runs deep in each of the modern Hurst Heritage by GSS vehicles. Regardless of brand, each vehicle has a link to the past. For example, the RPO L78-series Camaros are offered in black-over-silver paint that is split by a thin red stripe in a theme that is reminiscent of the 1983 Hurst Olds, whereas the RPO ZL1-series Camaro retains the classic gold-over-white color combination that was popular on the 1971 Hurst SSJ Grand Prix. Another example of adhering to grand Hurst tradition is the 50th Anniversary Chrysler 300H. Taking its cue from the 1970 Chrysler 300H, the new Chrysler not only proudly wears the customary gold-over-white theme but also sports a custom hood with a center scoop in a salute to the original car. While the 1970 Chrysler 300H was powered by a potent 375-hp 440 TNT V-8, this land yacht would have a hard time keeping up with its modern Hemi-powered counterpart. The modern Hurst paint schemes are inspired by their predecessors from more than four decades ago.

The Hurst Heritage by GSS Kenne Bell R-Code Mustang may not have an equal dating back to the beginning, but it has certainly written a new chapter in the program with its style and sizzling performance. Packing a 750-hp Kenne Bell supercharged V-8 engine, the R-code Mustang is not a muscle car with which to be trifled. It speaks to both the traditional and youthful performance enthusiast in a way that more-pedestrian muscle cars do not.

The Hurst Heritage by GSS 2019 Dodge Challenger widebody is shown on display in Saudi Arabia. (Photo Courtesy Larry Weiner)

When it comes to shows and events, Hurst Heritage by GSS follows the trail blazed by George Hurst. A nationwide show and event schedule enables enthusiasts to see Heritage by GSS vehicles in person. Events such as the Carlisle Chrysler Nationals, Mopars and Muscle Cars at the Strip, Muscle Car and Corvette Nationals, and the GM Nationals allow enthusiasts to see modern Hurst performance cars.

Passion for Hurst vehicles hit an all-time high when the first Hurst Nationals took place in partnership with Carlisle Events and Heritage By GSS. Hurst vehicles of all years and types proudly displayed there, and seminars were hosted by original Hurst employees who dated back to the golden era of Doc Watson. Even Bill Campbell (who passed away recently), George Hurst's business partner and the engineer responsible for developing the incomparable Hurst Competition Plus Shifter, attended the party.

The headliner for the second year of the Hurst Nationals was Linda Vaughn, the legendary Miss Hurst Golden Shifter. Wearing her signature gold outfit, Linda reprised her famous pose with the larger-than-life Hurst Golden Shifter on the platform of the actual Hurst Oldsmobile convertible that she toured with in 1972. When the parade reached its destination, Bob Riggle (famous for standing the *Hurst Hemi Under Glass* on the back bumper at dragstrips all over the country since the mid-60s) climbed onto the platform with her to the amazement those who attended.

Recently, the Hurst Heritage by GSS tour extended around the world, reaching all the way to Riyadh, Saudi Arabia, where the 50th Anniversary Hellcat Wide Body and the Hemi Classic were displayed at the Global Auto Salon. Amazingly, many show attendees had seen the cars in magazines and YouTube videos, demonstrating that interest in Hurst vehicles shows no signs of slowing down regardless of location.

Today, Hurst Heritage by GSS is the standard bearer for the vehicles that George Hurst and the companies that followed his ownership had the vision to create. They may be big shoes to walk in, but as *Hurst Hemi Under Glass* legend Bob Riggle explained when the first modern Hurst cars debuted at Mopars at the Strip in 2015, "Hurst Heritage by GSS is the perfect company to build these cars, and wherever George is, he's smiling."

That's heady praise from one who knows, bringing the Hurst legacy deep into the 21st century.

The Hurst Heritage by GSS Dodge Challenger Hemi Classic is shown on display in Saudi Arabia. (Photo Courtesy Larry Weiner)

Afterword: Hurst Legacy

Under the stewardship of the B&M Automotive Group, the Hurst shifter legacy is in good hands. Hurst continues to be a prominent brand in the B&M Group's performance portfolio, and Hurst products continue to lead the shifter industry that it helped develop. For more than 50 years, Hurst has played a pivotal role in the shifter and aftermarket parts business, as well as the specialty muscle car conversion business, and there's no reason to believe that Hurst will not continue to be a leader in this business in the future.

Only time will tell, but we are left with a legacy of Hurst products and vehicles to cherish. That's the legacy of the visionary George Hurst who, with a talented supporting cast, helped shape the automotive aftermarket as we know it.

To him and people like Bill Campbell, Jack "Doc" Watson, Linda Vaughn, Bob Riggle, Dave Landrith, Dick Chrysler, and so many others, we all owe an immense debt of gratitude.

Index